The Time Is Not Yet Ripe

—Contemporary China's Best
Writers and Their Stories

Edited by Ying Bian

FOREIGN LANGUAGES PRESS   BEIJING

First Edition 1991
Second Printing 1995

ISBN 7-119-00742-4

Published by Foreign Languages Press
24 Baiwanzhuang Road, Beijing 100037, China

Distributed by China International Book Trading Corporation
35 Chegongzhuang Xilu, Beijing 100044, China
P.O.Box 399, Beijing, China

Printed in the People's Republic of China

Editor's Note

China experienced a great flowering of literary creativity in the years from 1976 to 1989. It was a time when writers explored with boldness different themes and experimented with different styles. This book introduces eleven of China's best contemporary writers and their stories—their work being representative of this new literary age.

In compiling this book, the editor has taken into consideration the position of the author in contemporary Chinese literary circles and the representativeness of the story in the author's creative work. Each story is preceded by a biography of the author. Most of the biographies are written by the authors' personal friends and literary critics.

The writers included are all national literature prize winners, and some have gained an international literary reputation. Thus the stories selected to some extent reflect present-day writing standards and inform readers as to social conditions and literary creation in China.

December 1990

CONTENTS

AH CHENG AND HIS
KING OF CHESS

Denis C. Mair

The publication of Ah Cheng's *King of Chess* in the July of 1984 issue of the *Shanghai Literature* made the reading public sit up and take notice. Articles by Wang Meng in the *Literature and Art Gazette* and Wang Zengqi in the *Guangming Daily* set the tone for enthusiastic discussion of Ah Cheng's work in magazines and newspapers. The popularity of Ah Cheng's work was not confined to mainland China. American scholars hailed his work as proof of a new vitality in Chinese literature. Ah Cheng's work was so well received by American lovers of Chinese literature that he was eventually invited to the International Writers Program at Iowa University. The Hong Kong director Xu Ke made plans to film a movie based on *King of Chess*. A collection of Ah Cheng's stories, entitled *King of Chess*, ranked among the top fiction bestsellers in Taiwan in 1985.

This combination of critical acclaim and popular success for a writer's first story may seem surprising, but a look at Ah Cheng's background shows that his success was the result of a long apprenticeship. Ah Cheng gave an encapsulated account of his life in this self-introduction he wrote for the *Writer* magazine in 1984: "My name is Ah Cheng, and my family name is Zhong. I began writing this year. I sign my own name to my stories, so as to take responsibility for what I write. I was born on

1

the Tomb Sweeping Day in 1949. Just when the Chinese people were commemorating the dead, I came willy-nilly into this world. Half a year later the People's Republic of China was founded. In the traditional manner of speaking, that makes me a holdover from the old society. After that came primary school and middle school. Before I was through middle school, along came the Cultural Revolution.[1] I was placed with production brigades in Shanxi and Inner Mongolia, and I later went to Yunnan. This lasted not much longer than ten years. In 1979 I returned to Beijing, got married, and got a job. My wife and I had a child as lovable as other people's children. My experiences are within the bounds of imagination of any Chinese person. I have lived the way everyone else has lived. I still live the way everyone else does. The difference is, I write down words now and then and submit them to places that can print them with lead type. I do it to earn a little extra money for my family. I am a craftsman, like a carpenter who does extra work on the side. That is why I say I am like everyone else: there is not really much difference."

One thing Ah Cheng does not mention is the special education he received in his own family. He is the son of Zhong Dianfei—graduate of the Lu Xun Arts Academy in Yan'an, secretary of the Chinese Film Association, and president of the Chinese Film Critics Association. Zhong Dianfei once remarked to a friend that the two key elements in his thinking were the ideas of Marxism, which he "lived by," and Chuang Tzu's philosophy of that which is "vast and without a particular aim," which for Zhong "made life worth living."[2] As a young boy Ah Cheng, frail with tuberculosis, was moved into his father's office to avoid infecting his two brothers. Thus Ah Cheng grew up very close to his father, learning from him an approach to life that spanned the twin poles of political commitment and Taoist philosophy. In the early 1960's Zhong Dianfei, who had been overseeing films at the Central Propaganda Office, was attacked by Jiang Qing and others for presuming to speak on behalf of workers, peasants and soldiers. He was sent away to do farm work in Hebei, leaving his family in difficult straits. At one point Ah Cheng's mother was forced to sell his father's books to raise money for food. She gave Ah Cheng the task of selling the books to a used-book dealer. But he could not bear to let the books go without gaining something from them, so he stayed up at night and skipped meals to read them, selling the books in batches as he finished them.[3]

In the late sixties Ah Cheng was sent down to the countryside. Though this may have ruined his chances for a university education, it gave him broad experience and an understanding of many walks of life. Rather than surrendering to the monotony of life as a school-leaver, he sharpened his powers of observation by continuing to practice drawing and painting. He served a unique sort of writer's apprenticeship by telling stories to audiences of school-leavers and peasants. In Yunnan groups of peasants took turns inviting him to their houses to tell serialized novels over periods of months. He told them stories he remembered from *A Dream of Red Mansions*, *Outlaws of the Marsh* and Tolstoy's *Anna Karenina*, modified to suit local tastes and customs. The peasants had no way to show appreciation but to hand him cigarettes continually, which may explain his formidable smoking habit.

When Ah Cheng returned to Beijing in 1979 he carried inside himself—like the sheep in his sketch which "carry their own mutton across the mountains to Beijing" —a cornucopia of stories. Ah Cheng soon became a popular figure at gatherings of young painters, writers

3

and filmmakers in Beijing. His storytelling talent was as welcome among them as among the peasants of Yunnan. He continued talking with people from all walks of life, and was as likely to spend an evening eating Mongolian hot pot with a group of laborers as joining in a social gathering of artists.

Ah Cheng was appreciated professionally for his many talents, beginning with his work for the magazine *Shijie Tushu* (*World Books*). He helped to organize book exhibitions in Hong Kong which gave the outside world a look at the new variety of book publishing in China. While moonlighting from his regular job, Ah Cheng drew illustrations and cover designs for numerous publications. He organized art exhibitions and was involved as consultant in newly founded advertising companies run privately by young Beijing artists. He wrote scripts for the films *Da Mingxing* and *Jufeng Xingdong* directed by Teng Wenji. Ah Cheng was also a member of the "stars" school of painters, and as such was tied to the larger circle of young people caught up in the spirit of the Democracy Wall period. Friends wondered why Ah Cheng was content to illustrate other people's stories. The same thought had occurred to him, but he had been reluctant to presume on his father's reputation, and he was waiting for the right moment. Eventually his friends prevailed on him to submit his first story. Encouraged by the success of *King of Chess*, Ah Cheng went on to write two more long stories —*King of Trees* and *King of Children*—plus a number of short stories and sketches. Ah Cheng's three "king" stories are made up of vivid, concrete incidents from the lives of young people sent to the countryside. But the raw incidents fit together in a way that suggests a higher vantage point. There is an esthetic element in these stories reminiscent of classical Chinese poetry. A line in a classical poem is a series of substantive words: the reader gives the line many layers of depth by making connections among the words. There is no finally correct line of connections among the words; the reader finishes the poem with the sense that he has not exhausted its possibilities. In the same way, Ah Cheng's stories present personalities and incidents which encourage the reader to step back for progressively broader views. In attempting to connect the elements of the stories, the reader is led to reflect on why people are as they are. There is a pleasure here of contemplating man's nature as in a mirror or a deep well. There is some of the endless fascination which human beings find in regarding their own image. A philosophical questioning of the human condition is part of the esthetic experience literature offers. Of course many writers prompt us to such questioning, but the elements which Ah Cheng places together invite the reader to seek out unusual levels of connectedness.

King of Chess presents the reader with a contrast in the personalities of two young men. One, Wang Yisheng, is crazy about chess. Chess is what makes life interesting for him: other things in life pale to insignificance. Eating is of intense importance to him, but it is something to be gotten over with quickly. The narrator, on the other hand, thinks that eating is more than just refueling the body—it is something to be relished for its own sake. When the narrator tells stories "about eating," the chess-fiend is entertained by them, but he concludes that people from privileged backgrounds like the narrator are "greedy" and are always wanting to "embroider flowers on brocade." That is, on top of the brocade of the body's basic need for food, they embroider the flowers of cooking fancy dishes and reading books that tell of, among other things, food. There is something strange in the chess-fiend's idea of what is basic and what is embroidery. Chess is an intricate logical exercise. It satisfies what may or may not be one of the basic needs—the need for entertainment. But surely there is a more basic way to satisfy the need for entertainment than a game that requires such highly developed powers of abstract thinking. Eating itself, and telling stories about eating, can be a form of entertainment. When the school-leavers cook and eat the snake they are not just satisfying their hunger—they are entertaining themselves by varying their monotonous diet.

The chess-fiend's passion for chess goes beyond a mere wish for entertainment. He is, as the Chinese phrase puts it, "greedy" to play chess at every opportunity. His love of chess has put him in the habit of thinking abstractly, and this habit seems to eclipse certain other human needs at times. Not just his need for food, but even his need for friendship takes second place. He begins his relationship with the narrator by asking to play a game, seeing the narrator first as a chess partner and secondly as a conversation partner for the long trip. When the cultured young man Ni Bin realizes what an excellent player Wang Yisheng is, he is filled with admiration. He gives up his family's antique chess set, hoping to persuade the cultural secretary to allow Wang Yisheng to compete in a chess tournament. This sacrifice is an act of friendship and an expression of respect for Wang's ability. But Wang does not accept this gesture. He wants to prove his mastery on his own terms; friendship can have no place in helping to bring about his victory. It seems likely that his omission from the tournament name list resulted from his failure to make arrangements in his own district. Instead of playing in preliminary or qualifying matches, he was out wandering about the countryside, seeking partners in his own way. When he finally does get to play against the top players, he proves his mastery by beating them in a simultaneous blindfold match. To perform this amazing feat of concentration, he must remove his thoughts utterly from his surroundings (and his friends). When it is over, he snaps abruptly out of his world of chess combinations and rediscovers his need for closeness. He asserts this need in a jerky, compulsive fashion, grabbing hold of his friends and calling for his mother. Wang Yisheng's ninth opponent—the old chess-player who calls for a tie to save his pride—asks Wang Yisheng to stay the night. Wang Yisheng refuses, saying "No, I have other friends. We came here together, so it's better if we go back together. We're going to the Cultural Center: we have another friend there." The old chess-player is clearly a man who has assimilated chess into a philosophy of self-cultivation. He is a bearer of a tradition that teaches how to balance an extremely abstract form of thinking with more basic human needs. For a chess-fiend like Wang Yisheng, this is obviously a good friend to have. And the old man is ailing, so this may be Wang Yisheng's last chance to know him. But Wang Yisheng refuses, showing again the compulsiveness of his friend-ship in an act of unnecessary exclusivity. Instead of befriending the old man, and then setting off with his friends the next morning, he stays with the friends he already has.

Perhaps it would not be exaggerating to say that Wang Yisheng used his brain like a computer. He played with such absorption that his mind was taken over by an intricate, ever-branching tree of chess combinations. With his mind thus engaged, it was impossible for him to think of human concerns. But yet, the more obsessively he played, the more he embodied certain human qualities.

7

The narrator, on the other hand, was always occupied with human concerns. He thought of food and ways to enjoy it. He read books and liked to tell stories that revealed what he observed about people. The narrator could not generate interest in the abstract realm of chess, but while Wang Yisheng played the final match, the narrator was overwhelmed by the drama of the event. He could feel the vast sweep of something carried down in history, something larger than people which depended on people to exist.

Chess is an art which people continue to explore and which has an inherited tradition. It is an enjoyment beyond mere material comforts. But intrinsically it is a rule-governed system which relies on the minds of human beings to exist. The players get enjoyment through the game, and through the players the game is able to go on unfolding. People come and people go, but this system keeps unfolding, because it does not have human desires or wishes built into its rules. People may manipulate this system because of their desires (a computer can also manipulate it), but that does not make the system human. The player is human, and his human desires cause him to become obsessed with chess. His desire to prove himself and be a hero of the chess-board are quite human. But often people who are good at setting such a highly logical system in motion are influenced, in their expression of the more basic human needs, by the "non-human" qualities of the system. Thus, the influence of the "non-human" on the "human" can be seen not only in social and economic institutions, but also in an individual's thinking and feelings.

The social theories of Max Weber and modern behavioral biology have taught us that man is the only animal which is incomplete at birth. Other animals are born with an instinctual pattern of bahavior already formed. Learning for them is a process of matching their inborn behavioral blueprints with the outside world through trial and error. The instinctual pattern of man is incomplete and open-ended. This incomplete pattern is filled in or completed through assimilation of socially conditioned patterns, or culture (including, of course, language). Thus we find that the boundary between the human and the non-human becomes hard to discriminate. People are never completely human until they assimilate patterns or systems such as language which, taken intrinsically, are not human. A non-human element in an individual's thinking can be almost directly opposed to the human elements (when, for example, a repressive system of morality is set up in opposition to basic desires). The non-human element may be extremely abstract and disconnected from the basic needs, in such a way that the former and the latter are active in alternation, as with Wang Yisheng's chess playing and his need for friendship. It is also possible that a non-human element can be tied closely to human elements, as is the case when language symbols are used to investigate and communicate about human needs. We can see the route Ah Cheng took in grappling with these issues in his article "Culture Controls Mankind."[4]

Ah Cheng is more than just a "back-to-roots" writer. *King of Chess* does deal with the question of inheritance of traditional culture, but the complexity of the question is preserved. Reading the story as a simple affirmation of cultural roots distorts it. At least one reviewer claims that Wang Yisheng represents the continued vitality of traditional spiritual culture and moral values.

Other readers, taking a less approving view, have identified Ah Cheng with the "back-to-roots" movement in literature. One argument claimed that Chinese literature in the period 1976-1986 reached a point of crisis. Critics holding this view argued that in an era of utterly new challenges, literature should help strip away people's pat assumptions, instead of encouraging self-congratulation. They claimed that some authors turned nostalgically to the past to find a uniquely Chinese ethos to rest their hopes on. Ah Cheng is thereby cited as an author who turned his gaze backwards to the philosophy of Zen Buddhism and Chuang Tzu.

Both the positive and negative views of Ah Cheng as a "back-to-roots" writer overlook the fact that Ah Cheng is not advocating traditional art or Taoist philosophy: he is presenting a knot of cultural concerns for the reader to think about. Wang Yisheng is certainly not a paragon of a bygone spiritual civilization. He has a certain stubborn pride, but he is as yet too narrowly obsessed to assimilate his remarkable skill into a balanced philosophy or way of life. His chessplaying skill is not a symbol of tradition. It is, rather, a fragment of tradition which has been taken from its context by a young man who must now find a new place for it. Wang Yisheng won his victory not just because of what he learned from older players, but because of his own determination to gain mastery. At the end of the story he stands aligned with his school-leaver friends. He must find his own way to balance his passion for chess with his other needs. He shows no sign of relying on the philosophy of his mentor to give meaning to his skill. He still throws himself into the game for its own sake. Without the benefit of a philosophy, he manages to limit his appetites and takes pleasure in the activity of his own mind. Drawing lopsidedly on portions of the culture handed down to him, he recreates for himself a morally creditable way of living. But he lacks understanding of those who have picked up different threads than he. Though his first mentor cautioned him that the game of life does not put all its pieces on the table, and that chess is not a substitute for life, Wang Yisheng devotes himself to a game which has all its pieces out in the open.

Ah Cheng's stories lead us to examine how the unraveling threads of traditional culture relate to the present world of our desires. The tracing of these tangled threads is such an imposing task that many prefer to look forward to present challenges, reluctant to hold their attention on past influences for too long when so much waits to be done. Ah Cheng's eyes are not glued to the past either, but he includes it in his view of the present. He shows us people caught in history, acting to assert their own existence. In response to a friend's question on the message of *King of Chess*, Ah Cheng made this statement: "*King of Chess* has my philosophy in it. That is, the life of educated youths, which many people think is pretty tough, is really a whole lot better than the life of educated children of the poorer classes! Another point is that the 'heroic' acts of ordinary people are miniature versions of history. A common person in a situation of stress may exhibit a certain brilliance for a time. Then the common person goes back to being a common person, and he is often amazed at what he himself has done. Thus, from the individual's point of view, he often begins at zero and ends up at zero. But from this history takes a step forward."[5]

Ah Cheng's work shows not a nostalgic longing for a vanished past, but a clear-eyed look at the present. As Su Ding writes in an article on the "tragic consciousness" of Ah Cheng's stories, Ah Cheng does not write of great enterprises undermined by inner flaws or defeated by

11

fate.[6] His tragedy is that of the ordinary man, arriving quietly at an understanding of his limitations, which are imposed not from without but by the problematic nature of human desires.

Ah Cheng's *King of Trees* points to the problematical quality of man's urge to conquer Nature. It is problematical because man's nature is part of Nature, and is therefore nurturant as well as self-serving. *King of Children* examines the individual's problematical awareness of the needs of other individuals within the setting of an impersonal institution (in this case education). *King of Chess* is about the difficulty of balancing abstract systems, including those taken from tradition, with an individual's basic needs. Taken together, these three stories distill a remarkable range of thought. Though they do not harken back to Zen Buddhism and Chuang Tzu's philosophy as solutions to problems, the stories display a breadth of vision that owes something to these philosophies. I have heard that Ah Cheng originally planned to write eight "king" stories. I hope to see the rest of them soon.

Notes:

[1] The Cultural Revolution (1966-1976), also known as the "ten years of turmoil," was initiated by Mao Zedong (1894-1976), former chairman of the CPC Central Committee and forefather of the PRC. In his late years, Mao suspected that the young republic was endangered by a combined ideology of feudalism, capitalism, and revisionism, and believed that a new revolutionary movement would free his people from contamination. During that period the whole country was stormed with various brainwashing practices. Human nature was extensively distorted. The results include setbacks in economic construction, constraint in human relationships, and destruction of a large quantity of cultural heritage.

[2] Zhong Chengxiang, "Ah Cheng Qi Ren" (This Person Ah

Cheng), *Renmin Ribao Haiwaiban* (overseas edition of *People's Daily*), Jan. 7, 1987.

[3] Ibid., Jan 10, 1987.

[4] Discussed in Ji Hongzhen, "Preface," *Qi Wang* (*King of Chess*), Zuojia Chubanshe, Beijing, 1985.

[5] Zhong Chengxiang, "Ah Cheng Qi Ren," *Renmin Ribao Haiwaiban*, Jan. 9, 1987.

[6] Su Ding, "Quedao Tianliang Haoge Qiu" (The Bracing Cold of a Nice Fall Day), *Dushu* (*Books and Reading*), May 1987.

King of Chess (Chapters 3-4)

Ah Cheng

3.

FROM then on we often talked about Wang Yisheng when we were at a loose end, relishing the memory of his bare-shouldered battle with Legballs. When I told them what a hard life Wang Yisheng had had Legballs said, "My father says that 'great scholars come from poor families.' He told me that Ni Yunlin of the Yuan dynasty was our ancestor, and he liked having everything clean. At first the family was rich, so he could have everything just so. After that we were ruined by the wars, so our ancestor sold the family property and wandered all over the place. He often slept in villages and inns in the back of nowhere and met a lot of great scholars. Later on he got to know some people living in the wilds who could play chess, and they taught him to play really well. Nowadays everyone's heard of Ni Yunlin, the great poet, calligrapher and painter who was one of the four masters of the Yuan period. They don't realize he was a chess player too. Later on he became a Zen Buddhist and brought chess into the Zen tradition. He developed his own school of chess that was only handed down in our family. I don't know what school Wang Yisheng belongs to, but he beat me and he's certainly a very good player." None of us knew who Ni Yunlin was, and we only half believed Legballs' boasting. But we accepted that Legballs knew a thing or two about chess, and that as Wang Yisheng had beaten Legballs he must be even greater. All the other educated youngsters there came from the common people of the cities, and most of them were from poor families, which made them appreciate Wang Yisheng even more.

Nearly six months passed, but we saw no more of Wang Yisheng. All we got were reports from here and there that someone called Wang Yisheng whose nickname was Chess Maniac had played chess with someone or other at some place or other and beaten him. We were all delighted, and even when there was news of his being beaten we always refused to believe it: how could Wang Yisheng possibly lose? When there was no answer to the letter I wrote to him at his branch farm, the others all urged me to go and see him. But what with one thing and another, and on top of everything else the frequent feuds between the young school-leavers in the farms, and the shooting at each other with firearms that had been brought in, I did not go in the end.

One day on the mountainside Legballs told me that he had put his name down for the chess tournament and would be going to the farm headquarters in a couple of days' time. He asked me if I'd had any news of Wang Yisheng. I said that I had not. We all said that Wang Yisheng was bound to go to the farm headquarters for the chess tournament and we agreed that we would all ask for leave to go to the headquarters to watch.

A couple of days later the work in the brigade slackened off and the others all asked for leave to go to the headquarters on various pretexts in the hope of seeing Wang Yisheng. I asked for leave too and went with them.

The farm headquarters was in the district capital, and it took us two days to get there. Although the place was an administrative center ranking immediately below provincial level, it simply consisted of two streets that crossed each other with some shops in them. The shelves in the shops were either empty or full of "Display Goods—Not for Sale." But we were still excited, and felt that we had come to somewhere prosperous and splendid. We ate our way from one inn to the next along the street. We called for plain boiled pork and wolfed dish after dish of it, then we patted our bellies and found the sunlight rather dazzling. We were half drunk with meat, so we found some grass on which to stretch out. We smoked then went to sleep. When we woke up, we went back to the shopping streets to eat with deliberate relish some grain-based food, then went to the farm headquarters.

A whole column of us went to the headquarters in the highest of spirits, where we found an official who dealt with education and sport and asked whether someone by the name of Wang Yisheng had reported in. The official spent a long time checking the register then told us that he had not. We did not believe him, so we grabbed the register and all snatched at it as we looked through it, only to find that his name really was not there. We asked the official if Wang Yisheng could have been left out by mistake, and the official said that the register had been compiled from the names the branch farms submitted. Everyone had been given a number and assigned to a group. The games would begin the next day. We all looked at each other in bewilderment. "Let's go and find Legballs," I suggested. He was in the thatched huts where the athletes were staying, and as soon as we saw him, we asked him. "I can't understand it either," he said. "It's chaos here. I've been given a number as a chess player, but they've put me to stay with the ball players. They insist that I've got to take part in this evening's training session for the headquarters team. I argued for ages but it was no use at all. They said they'd be depending on me to get the ball forward." We all burst out laughing and said, "Never mind what kind of competition it is: you'll be eating well enough. But it's a real pity that Wang Yisheng's not here."

Even when the games began there was still no sign of Wang Yisheng. When we asked some people from his branch farm they all said that they had not seen him for ages. We were worried, but there was nothing we could do, so we went to watch Legballs playing basketball. He was having a thoroughly miserable time. He knew none of the rules, could not even hold on to the ball properly, and missed every time he threw. Whenever there was a scramble for the ball that got at all fierce he removed himself and watched wide-eyed while the rest of them struggled. The official in charge of culture and sport was scratching his ears in despair and everyone else was rocking about with laughter. Every time he came off Legballs yelled and complained about how barbaric and filthy it all was.

After two days of trials among all the farm headquarters, teams were chosen for the games. When we saw that there was still no sign of Wang Yisheng, we all agreed that we would go back. Legballs wanted to stay with the district secretary for culture and education for another couple of days, and he saw us off on the beginning of our journey. We had almost reached the crossroads when someone pointed and said, "Isn't that

Wang Yisheng?" We looked that way and saw that it really was him. Wang Yisheng was rushing towards the corner and had not noticed us. When we all called out to him, he came to a violent halt, saw us, and crossed the road towards us. As he came close we all asked at once why he had not come to take part in the tournament. He looked very anxious as he replied, "I've been taking leave to go off and play chess for the last six months, but when I knew it was time to put my name down and come back, the branch farm wouldn't let me come here for the tournament. They didn't even put my name forward. They said I'd been behaving too badly. I've only just found an excuse to come here and watch the tournament. How is it? How's the play been?" Everyone answered at once that the early rounds were over and that what was happening now was the competition between the county teams for the district championship.

Wang Yisheng was silent for a while. Then he said, "All right. The players who are going in for the district championship must be the best from all the counties. It'll be worth watching." "Haven't you eaten yet?" I asked. "Come on, you can grab something in the street as we go." Legballs shook Wang Yisheng by the hand, full of sympathy for his plight. We all crowded into a small restaurant where we bought some food that we ate with many a sigh. "I want to watch the district chess tournament," said Wang Yisheng. "What about you lot? Are you going back?" The others said that they had to be getting back as they had been away for too long. "I'll stay here with you for another day or two," I said. "Legballs will be here too." Two or three of the others then also said that they'd hang around for another day or two.

Legballs led all of us who were staying in town off

to the culture and education secretary's house, saying that he'd see if there was any chance that Wang Yisheng might be able to take part in the tournament. It did not take us long to get there. There was a small iron gate, which was closed. When we went in we were asked who we were looking for, but once they saw Legballs no more questions were asked and we were told to wait. A moment later we were called in, and we all trooped into the large house.

There was a row of well-tended plants on the window-sill. On the big wall was a hanging scroll of one of Chairman Mao's poems mounted on the palest of thin yellow silks. The only furniture in the room was a few cane chairs and a low table on which were several newspapers and some mimeographed reports. It was not long before the secretary came in, a fat man who shook each of us by the hand, called for somebody to take the mimeographed reports away, and invited us all to sit down. None of us had ever before been into the home of a man who ruled several counties, so we all peered around. The secretary was quiet for a moment before he asked, "Are you all fellow-students of Ni Bin's?" We all turned back to look at the secretary, not knowing what to say. "They're all from our brigade," Legballs said, leaning forward. "This is Wang Yisheng," he continued, waving at him. "So you're Wang Yisheng, aren't you?" said the secretary, looking at him. "Good. Ni Bin has been talking about you a lot the last couple of days. Well, have you been selected for the district tournament?"

Wang Yisheng was just going to reply when Ni Bin cut in with, "Wang Yisheng was held up by a number of things he had to do, so he wasn't able to put his name down. He's done what he had to do now. Could he possibly get into the district tournament? What do you think?" The secretary's fat hands lightly patted the arms of his chair a couple of times, slowly and gently scratched the side of his nose. "Oh. So that's the way it is. It's tricky. It's tricky if you haven't qualified at the county level. I hear you're a genius, but people would complain if you were let into the tournament without having qualified." "I don't want to take part," said Wang Yisheng, his head bowed low, "I just want to watch." "That's OK," said the secretary. "You'd be most welcome. Ni Bin, go to the desk, the one on the left, and you'll find a duplicated schedule for the games. Bring it over and we'll see how the board games competitions have been organized."

Ni Bin stepped into the inner room and came straight out again with the papers. "The tournament lasts three days," he said when he had looked at them, then handed them to the secretary. The secretary put them on the table without glancing at them, flicked them with his fingers and said, "Yes, there are several counties involved. Well? Any other problems?" We all stood up and said we had better be going. The secretary was very quick to shake hands with the one of us who was nearest to him and say, "Will you be coming over this evening, Ni Bin?" Ni Bin bowed and accepted, then left with the rest of us. Once out in the street we all breathed a sigh of relief and started talking and joking.

As we wandered aimlessly down the road we wondered whether we had enough money with us to stay here for three days. Wang Yisheng said he could find us somewhere to sleep, and there'd be no problem even though there were so many of us. Not staying in an inn would save us a lot of money. Ni Bin explained with some embarrassment that he would stay with the secretary. The rest of us went off with Wang Yisheng to find somewhere we could put up.

Wang Yisheng had been to the district capital several times before, and he knew a painter who worked in the cultural center. It was here that he led us all. When we reached the cultural center and went inside, we could at once see people singing and playing instruments some distance away. We guessed that they must be the propaganda team rehearsing. Three or four women in blue knitted clothes, their breasts held about as high as they could be, wiggled their way up to us. As they came closer they did not make way for us at all, but went straight on without so much as a sideway glance. We moved aside as quickly as we could, all blushing. "They're the district's star performers," whispered Ni Bin. "It's really something to have people as talented as them in an obscure place like this." We all looked back at the stars.

The painter lived in a tiny corner of the place with ducks and hens wandering in and out of the door. Bits and pieces were piled along the foot of the wall with weeds growing between them. The door was hidden by many clothes and cotton sheets hanging out to air. Wang Yisheng led the way, ducking through the clothes, and called out the painter's name. Someone came clattering out at once, saw that it was Wang Yisheng and said, "It's you. Do all come in." The painter only had one little room with a narrow wooden bed in it. The room was full of books, magazines, paints, paper and brushes, and the walls were covered with pictures. We all trooped in, one after the other, and the painter moved his things about to make just enough room for us all to sit down, though we did not dare move. The painter made his way past all of us to go outside and came back a moment later with a thermos flask from which he poured us all some hot water. We passed each other mugs and bowls of every kind from which we all drank.

The painter sat down too and asked Wang Yisheng, "Are you taking part in the games?" Wang Yisheng gave a sigh and told him the whole story. "It's just as well," said the painter. "Are you going to stay for a few days?" "That's why I've come to see you," said Wang Yisheng. "These are all friends of mine. Could you find us somewhere where we could all squash in and sleep?" The painter thought for a while before replying, "When you come by yourself you can squeeze in here with me and we get by. But this many...Mmm, let me see." Then his eyes lit up and he said, "There's an auditorium in the cultural center with a very big stage. There'll be a show tonight for the people taking part in the games, and you can sleep on the stage afterwards. How about it? I can even take you in to watch the show today. The electrician's a friend of mine. I'll have a word with him and there'll be no problem about going in and sleeping there. The only thing is that it's a bit dirty." We all said at once that it would be perfect. Legballs, evidently relieved, stood up carefully and said, "Fine, gentlemen. I'll be off." We all wanted to stand up to say goodbye to him but none of us was able to. Legballs held us down, repeatedly said that there was no need to get up, and stepped outside with a single stride. "He really is tall," the painter said. "Is he a basketball player?" We all burst out laughing and told him the funny story about Legballs. When the painter had heard it he said, "Yes, you're all filthy. Go and get washed. I'm coming with you." We all filed out in order, but still kept knocking noisily against things.

A river flowed past the district capital at some distance from it. We had to walk a long way before we reached it. It was not very wide, but the water flowed very fast, making little whirlpools near the bank. As there was nobody else anywhere around we all stripped right off and gave ourselves a really good wash, using up the cake of soap that the painter had brought with him. Then we soaked our clothes in the river, pounded them clean on boulders, wrung them out and spread them out on the rocks to dry. Apart from some who swam the rest of us sunbathed on the bank. The painter, who had finished washing long before us, had brought out a sketchbook and was drawing. When I noticed this, I went over and stood behind him to look. He was doing a nude sketch of us. The picture made me realize how remarkably strong we men who worked so hard in the mountains were, and I could not help sighing with admiration. Everyone else crowded round to look as well, their white bottoms flashing around. "Laboring people have something very distinctive about the lines of their muscles. They're very clearly visible. The development of the different parts may not always be very even, but real bodies are often like that, infinitely varied. When I did life studies at art college they were mostly of women, but they tended to be too standardized. The male models were usually static too: you got no feel of moving muscle, and the more you painted them the deader it all was. Today's a rare opportunity." Some of them said that their private parts were not nice to look at, whereupon the painter used his pencil to turn their privates in the picture into a big lump, which made everyone laugh. By now our clothes were dry and we all climbed back into them.

It was almost dusk, and the sun was setting between two mountains, making the river ripple with gold and turning the rocks on the bank as red as hot iron. Birds

23

were darting across the water with cries that could be heard from far away. On the opposite bank someone was singing a long-drawn-out folksong: we could not see him, but we could hear his voice gradually fading away. We all gazed in rapt concentration. After a long time Wang Yisheng sighed but said nothing.

We all went back, and along the way we dragged the painter out to have something to eat with us. He turned out to be quite a drinker. It was now dark, and he took us in through the stage door of the auditorium, where he gave someone a nod, had a word with him, and gestured to us to go in very quietly, hide in the wings and watch from there. The curtains did not open when they were supposed to because, it was said, the secretary had not yet arrived. The performers, all dressed and made up, were walking to and fro backstage, stretching and joking with each other. Suddenly there was a noise in the house. I lifted a corner of the curtain to see the fat secretary make a leisurely entrance and sit in the front row. All around him were empty seats, behind which the auditorium was a densely crowded mass of people. The show now began.

It was a very impassioned performance that raised clouds of dust everywhere. On stage the performers had tears in their eyes, but once they were in the wings they all started giggling and going on about all the things that had gone wrong. But Wang Yisheng was completely carried away by the show. Sometimes his face was overcast and at other times he looked happy, and his mouth was gaping open all the way through. The calmness with which he played chess had vanished completely. When the show ended he started applauding all by himself from the wings. I stopped him at once and looked down from the stage. The front two rows were once again empty. The secretary had left some time earlier.

We all went outside and groped our way through the dark to the painter's room. Legballs was there before us, and as soon as he saw us coming, he came out with the painter to stand outside. "Wang Yisheng," the painter said, "you can take part in the tournament." "How's that?" Wang Yisheng asked. Legballs explained that, when he had been at the secretary's home earlier that evening, the secretary had mentioned in the course of the conversation that a dozen or so years ago he had often visited Legballs' home and seen a lot of paintings and calligraphy there. He wondered if they had been lost since the movement had started. Legballs had replied that they still had some left, after which the secretary had said nothing more. A little later the secretary had added that there should not be any problem about Legballs' transfer: he could find a place for him in a culture or education office in the district capital. He would have a word with his subordinates and it could all be done quickly. He hoped that Legballs would write home about it. The secretary then turned the conversation back to calligraphy, paintings and antiques. People didn't know the value of such things these days, he said, but he often thought about them. Legballs had said that he would write home to see if they could give one or two scrolls to the secretary, who deserved thanks for being so very helpful. He had also said he had a superb Ming chess set in ebony back in his brigade. If the secretary liked the sound of it he could bring it with him next time. This had got the secretary very excited: he had repeatedly urged Legballs to bring it along to let him have a look. Then the secretary had mentioned Legballs' friend Wang Yisheng. He could have a word with his subordinates. It was only a district tournament: there was no need to be too strict. After all, when it came to real talent you did not have to avoid recommending your friends. He had then made a phone call and been told that there would be no problem. The secretary need not worry. Wang Yisheng could take part in the tournament the next day.

We were all very pleased to hear this and said that Legballs was a real operator. Wang Yisheng said nothing. When Legballs had gone the painter took us all off to find the electrician, who opened the stage door of the auditorium and let us go quietly in. He offered to let us take the curtains down to use as blankets as the weather had now turned cool. We all jumped at the chance and climbed up to take the curtains down and spread them out in the stage. One of our group walked to the front of the stage, bowed to the empty seats and declared in the strident tones of an announcer, "The next item, now beginning, will be—sleep." We all had a quiet laugh then crawled under the curtain and lay down.

After I had been lying there for a long time I noticed that Wang Yisheng was still awake. "Go to sleep," I said, "You've got the tournament tomorrow." "I'm not going in for it," he replied in the darkness. "There's no point. It's ever so kind of Ni Bin, but I don't want to go in for it." "What are you worrying about?" I said. "You get into the tournament and he gets transferred here. A chess set's nothing." "But it's his father's chess set," said Wang Yisheng. "It's not the quality of it that counts but what it means. I've always guarded like my life the chess set without any writing on it that my mother left me; and I can't forget what she told me, now that my life's easier. How can Ni Bin give the set away?" "Legballs' people have got loads of money," I replied. "What's a chess set to them? If it means their son can have an easier time, they'll be glad to part with it." "Say what you will, I'm not going for it," answered Wang Yisheng. "It'd look as though I was cashing in on someone else's deal. Whether I win or lose should only depend on me. If I played on those terms there'd be something jabbing at my conscience." One of the others, who was still awake and had probably heard all that we had said, mumbled, "You really are a maniac."

4.

First thing the next morning we all got up, covered in dirt, and found some water to wash in. After that we tried to get the painter to come out for a meal with us. He insisted on refusing, and as we were talking, Legballs turned up looking in very high spirits. "I'm not going in for the tournament," Wang Yisheng told him. Everyone was dumbfounded. "That's just great," said Legballs. "Why won't you? People are coming from the provincial capital to watch." "I won't, and that's that," said Wang Yisheng. When I explained why, Legballs sighed and said, "The secretary's a cultured man who's crazy about that sort of thing. Although the set's a family heirloom, I really can't take life on the farm. All I want is to be able to live somewhere clean where I won't get filthy dirty every day. I can't eat a chess set. If it'll get me over a few obstacles it's worth it. My parents aren't very well off: they won't blame me."

The painter folded his arms, rubbed his cheek with one hand, looked up at the sky and said, "Ideals have all gone: all that's left is ambition. I don't blame you, Ni Bin. Your demands are nothing very much. In the last couple of years I've often done stupid things. My life is too much tied up with trivialities. Luckily I can still paint. What is there to ease melancholy, save ..." He sighed. Wang Yisheng gazed at him in astonishment, then slowly turned towards Legballs and said, "Thank you, Legballs. As soon as it's obvious who the best players in the tournament are I'll challenge them. But I won't take part in the tournament." Legballs cheered up at once, clenched his enormous hand for a moment and said, "I've got it. I'll go and have a word with the secretary and get him to organize a friendly match. If you can beat the champion you'll unquestionably be the real champ. And even if you lose, it won't be too much of a loss of face." Wang Yisheng paused, then said, "Don't say anything to the secretary, whatever you do. I'll get them to play myself. If they'll agree I'll take the top three on together."

None of us knew what to say after that, so we went off to watch the games. It was fun. Wang Yisheng made his way to the hall where the board games were being played and watched the big scoreboards on which all the games were set out for spectators. On the third day the winner and the two runners-up emerged. After that the prizes were awarded, there was another performance, and the place was so noisy and chaotic that you could not hear who had won what.

Legballs told us to wait where the games were being held and came back a little later with two men in blue cadre uniforms. He introduced them as the second and third prize-winners in the chess tournament. "This is Wang Yisheng," he continued. "He's a terrific player and he'd like to have a game with you two distinguished players. It'll be a chance for you all to learn from each other." The two of them looked at Wang Yisheng and asked, "Why didn't you go in for the tournament? We've been hanging around here for ages and we've got to go back." "I won't keep you waiting," said Wang Yisheng. "I'll play you both at the same time." The two of them looked at each other, then the penny dropped. "Playing blind?" they asked. Wang Yisheng nodded. The two of them changed their attitude now. "We've never played blind," they said with apologetic smiles. "Doesn't matter," said Wang Yisheng. "You two can have boards to look at while you play. Come on, let's find somewhere."

Somehow or other the news got out, and it created an immediate stir. The people from all the different counties who had come to the games told each other that some whipper-snapper from a state farm, who hadn't gone in for the tournament, wouldn't accept the result and wanted to play the runner-up and the man in the third place at the same time. A good hundred people crowded round us, pushing and shoving to get a look. We all felt responsible for Wang Yisheng and stood around him. Wang Yisheng bowed his head and said, "Let's go, let's go. We're attracting too much attention here." Someone pushed through and asked, "Which of you wants to play chess? You? Our uncle won this championship. He's heard that you aren't happy about the result and has sent me to invite you over." "That won't be necessary," said Wang Yisheng. "If your uncle would like to play I'll take all three of you on at once."

This caused a sensation among the onlookers, who all headed towards the chess hall with us. There were over a hundred people all marching along the street with us in a crowd, which set the passers-by asking what was up and wondering if the school-leavers were going to have a brawl. When they found out what was happening, they tagged along too. By the time we had gone half way down the street, there were upward of a thousand people milling round. Assistants and customers alike came out of the shops to see what was going on. The long-distance bus had to go this way, but could not get through: the passengers craned their heads out to stare. The street was a sea of heads. Clouds of dust were rising, and amid the general hubbub was the scrunch of waste paper being trodden underfoot. A halfwit stood in the middle of the street singing a wordless howl of a song until someone had the charity to pull him out of the way. The idiot went on with his song beside the wall. Four or five dogs rushed around, barking as if they were leading a wolf hunt.

By the time we reached the chess hall, there were several thousand people around us. The cloud of dust they had raised would take a long time to settle. The slogans and signs at the hall had already been taken down. A man came out and blanched at the sight of so large a crowd. Legballs went over to negotiate with him. He took a quick look at all the people, nodded repeatedly, and took a long time to realize that they wanted to use the hall. He hurriedly opened the door, and kept saying, "Yes, yes," but when he saw that they all wanted to come in, he became anxious. We stood guard at the entrance and only admitted Legballs, Wang Yisheng and the two prize winners.

Just then someone emerged from the crowd and said to us, "If the master is willing to play three people at once, one more won't matter. I can be one of them." There was another commotion in the crowd and someone else volunteered. I did not know what to do and had to go inside to tell Wang Yisheng. He chewed his lips then asked, "What do you two think about it?" The two of them stood up and agreed straight away. I went outside to count, and including the champion there were ten opponents altogether. "Ten's unlucky; it's a round number," said Legballs. "Nine would be better." So the number was kept down to nine. The champion had not arrived, but someone came to tell us that, as it was blind chess that was being played, the champion would stay at home and have messengers pass the moves on. Wang Yisheng thought for a moment, then agreed. The nine of them were then shut inside the hall. As one chess board outside the hall was not enough to show the moves made, eight full sized sheets of paper were fetched and marked out with the chessboard grid. Hundreds of square chessmen were cut out of card, and painted with the names of the different pieces in red or in black, and string tags were attached to the back by which they were hung up at intersections on the grids. When the wind blew they fluttered gently, to roars from the crowds in the street.

More and more people were still arriving. Hard though the latecomers pushed, they could not squeeze through the crowd, so they grabbed hold of others and asked what was going on, imagining that an execution announcement had been posted. Much further back there was another circle, this one made up of women holding children in their arms. Many other people had put their bicycle stands down and were standing on the rear carriers of their machines and craning their necks to look. With all the pushing and shoving a whole lot of people fell over amid many shouts. Older children were squeezing their way through and being pushed out again by adults' legs. The hubbub of the thousands of people made the street seem to rumble with thunder.

Wang Yisheng was sitting in the middle of the enclosure on a chair with a back, his hands on his legs

31

and his eyes staring blankly. His face and hair were utterly filthy, making him look like a criminal brought in for interrogation. I could not help bursting out laughing, and I went across to brush some of the dirt off him. He pressed on my hand, so that I could feel him trembling. "It's getting out of hand," Wang Yisheng said very quietly. "You and your friends keep an eye on things. If there's any trouble we'll make a break for it together." "There won't be," I replied. "As long as you win there'll be no problem. You'll be able to hold your head high. Well? Are you sure you can cope with nine of them? Including the first three in the tournament?" Wang Yisheng was silent for a while before he replied, "What I'm scared of are the players from the wilds, not the men from the emperor's court. I've seen how the people in the tournament play, but there's no way of telling that I won't find my match among the other six. Take my satchel, and whatever happens don't lose it. I've got ..." he gave me a look, "my mother's chessmen in it." His skinny face was both dry and dirty, and even the sides of his nose were black. His hair was standing upright, and as his throat moved his eyes looked alarmingly dark. I realized that he was putting everything he had into these games, and felt very anxious. "Be careful" was all I said as I left him alone in the middle of the enclosure looking at nobody. He was as still as a lump of iron.

The chess began. A hush fell upon the crowd of thousands. The only words came from the volunteers who were calling the moves out, sometimes fast and sometimes slow, for the volunteers outside to move the pieces on the eight big boards. The boards were rustling in the breeze, which set the pieces fluttering. The setting sun shone on everything with a dazzling glare. The front few dozen rows had all sat down and were looking up, while the people behind them were packed close together, all looking filthy dirty and with their hair, long or short, blowing in the wind. Nobody else moved. It was as if they were all fighting for their lives in the chess games.

Something very ancient suddenly welled up in my heart, which rose in my throat. Of all the books I had read, some came close to me, some moved away. Everything was muddled up. Xiang Yu and Liu Bang, those legendary generals of over two thousand years ago I so much admired, were glaring at each other in stupefied fury. But the dark-faced soldiers whose corpses littered the plain were rising from the ground and slowly moving, not making a sound. A woodcutter was holding his axe and singing wildly. Then I seemed to see Chess Maniac's mother folding printed sheets one at a time with her feeble hands.

I found myself feeling inside Wang Yisheng's satchel. My fingers gripped a little cotton bundle that I took out to examine. It was a little bag made of worn blue twill that had been embroidered with a bat. The corners had been sewn into scallops with very fine stitching. I brought out one of the chessmen. It really was very small and in the sunlight half translucent, like the gentle look of an eye. I held it tight in my hand.

The sun finally set, bringing immediate coolness. People were still watching, but they had now started discussing the game. Every time one of Wang Yisheng's moves was called out from inside the hall there was a murmur in the crowd outside. There were several messengers carrying the moves to and from the champion's home by bicycle. We were no longer on our best behavior, and had started joking and talking.

I went back inside to see Legballs looking very

excited, which made me feel a lot less tense. "Well then?" I said. "I can't understand chess." "It's terrific," said Legballs, stroking his hair, "terrific. I've never seen anything like it. Just think: one man against nine; nine games at once. A huge campaign on a 360-degree front. I'm going to write to my father and tell him all the moves in all the games." Just then two men stood up from their boards, bowed to Wang Yisheng, and said, "You're too good for us." They went outside, kneading their hands. Wang Yisheng gave a nod and glanced at their boards.

Wang Yisheng had not changed his position. He still had his hands on his knees and was gazing straight in front of him. He might have been looking into the furthest distance, or staring at something extremely close to him. A large jacket was draped over his skinny shoulders. He was still covered with patches of dirt that had not been brushed off. It was a long time before his Adam's apple moved. For the first time I accepted that chess too was an athletic activity—a marathon, a double marathon. I had done some long-distance running at school. After five hundred meters I had felt exhausted, but after passing a certain limit my brain had no longer been involved in running. I had become like a pilotless aircraft or a glider that had reached a great height and was just gliding down. But chess was an athletic activity in which you had to use your intelligence from beginning to end to fight your opponent and wrestle him into submission. You could never be careless for a moment.

I was struck with anxiety about Wang Yisheng's health. Because we were so hard up, we had not eaten very well during the previous few days and had gone to bed very late, never imagining that anything like this was in store. As I looked at Wang Yisheng sitting so steady there, I felt a surge of sympathy for him: "Hold on!" When we were carrying logs in the mountains, two of us to a log, even if the paths were lousy and the valleys turned out to be dead ends we gritted our teeth and never gave up. If either of you collapsed because you could not take it, you would of course be injured yourself, and your partner would be hit so hard by the log that he vomited blood afterwards. But this time Wang Yisheng had to cross the creeks and gullies by himself: we could not help him at all. I fetched some cold water, which I quietly took to him and held up in front of his face. He shook, looked at me with eyes like swords, and took some time to recognize me and give me a joyless smile. I pointed at the bowl of water, which he took and was about to drink from, when a messenger came to report a move to him. He raised the bowl till it was level with his eyes, making not a ripple and gazed at the rim of the bowl as he announced his own move. Then he moved the bowl slowly to his lips. Just then the next messenger reported another move. His mouth stayed fixed at the rim of the bowl as he said what his move was. Only then did he swallow a mouthful of water with a terrifyingly loud noise. There were tears in his eyes. He passed the bowl back, gazing at me with a look in which there was something bittersweet that could never have been put into words. A trickle of water ran slowly down from the corner of his mouth and washed a channel through the dirt on his chin and his neck. I handed the bowl back to him. He raised his hand to stop me and returned to his world.

When I came out, it was dark. Some of the mountain folk were holding torches of burning pine and other people had electric torches, which all made a mass of bright yellow light. Probably the district offices had just finished work, for there were more people there than ever. Dogs were sitting in front of the people, watching with mournful expressions as the hanging chessmen were moved: it was as if they understood and were worried. Several of the school-leavers in our brigade were surrounded by people asking them questions. Before long the information was being passed on: "Wang Yisheng," "the Chess Maniac," "an educated youngster," "he plays Taoist chess" and so on. I found this laughable and wanted to go into the crowd and explain, but then I stopped myself: let them pass it on, I thought. At this point I started feeling happy. There were only three games still being played out on the wall.

Suddenly a roar went up from the crowd. I looked round and saw that there was only one game now, the game with the champion. There were few pieces left on the board. Wang Yisheng's black pieces were all in his opponent's half of the board apart from his commander, which had an officer to keep him company. They were like an emperor and his courtier talking while waiting for the army at the front to send back the report of victory. You could almost make out servants preparing a banquet and lighting foot-long red candles, while the musical instruments were being tuned, ready to burst out into triumphant music as soon as the messenger fell to his knees to announce the victory. My stomach gave a long rumble and my legs felt weak. I chose somewhere and sat down, gazing up at the final hunt, terrified that something might go wrong.

The red pieces had not moved for a long time, and the crowd was looking out for the arrival of the cyclist with a general buzz of impatience. Suddenly the people in the crowd started moving about and opening a way through. An old man with a bald head slowly walked out of the crowd, helped by those around him. As he examined the boards on which the endings of the other eight games were displayed, his lips moved. Everyone spread the news that this was the man who had just won the district championship, a member of a distinguished local family who had emerged from his seclusion just to play chess for fun, never expecting to take first place. His comment on the tournament had been to sigh for the decline of chess. When he had examined all the games he gave his clothes a gentle tug, stamped, raised his head and was helped into the chess hall. The crowd pushed in after him. I pushed my way anxiously towards the entrance as I followed behind. The old man went inside, stopped and looked in front of him.

Wang Yisheng was sitting alone in the big room, staring towards us, his hands on his knees, a slender pillar of iron who seemed to hear and see nothing. An electric light high above him shone dimly on his face. His eyes were sunken, and very dark. It was as if they were looking up at an infinite number of worlds, at the vastness of the universe. All his life force seemed to be concentrated in his mop of tousled hair. For a long time it did not disperse, then it gradually spread out, burning our faces.

They were all astounded and said nothing. After everything that had been said outside for so long, they were now faced with a black, skinny little soul sitting there in perfect stillness. They all gasped.

After a while the old man gave a very full and deep cough that resonated round the room. Wang Yisheng suddenly shortened the focus of his gaze, saw the crowd and tried to get up, but he could not move. The old man shook off the people who were supporting him and took a few steps forward, stopped, gently stroked his chest with both hands, and said in a loud, clear voice, 'Young man, I am old and infirm, which was why I could not come here to play you. I had no option but to ask messengers to pass on the moves. I can see that despite your youth you really do understand the Way of chess. You combine the Zen and the Taoist schools and you are brilliant at grapsing your opportunities and at making plans. You know how to seize the initiative through a display of strength, and also how to win by letting your opponent attack first. You can get rid of the dragon and bring the waters under control, and combine the positive and the negative. That is all the great players of ancient and modern times have there had at their disposal. I am lucky to have encountered you in my declining years. I've been deeply moved. China's chess is not finished after all. Will you grant me your friendship despite the difference in our ages? I have played this game for fun. Would you be willing to settle for a draw and leave me a little face?"

Wang Yisheng tried and failed again to get up. Legballs and I rushed over to him and helped him to his feet by lifting him under the armpits. His feet hung in mid-air bent in a sitting posture and could not be straightened. I felt as if the weight I was lifting was only a few pounds, so I gave Legballs a sign to put Wang Yisheng down and massage his legs. Everyone crowded round. The old man shook his head and sighed. Legballs rubbed Wang Yisheng's body, face and neck gently and firmly with his big hands. After a while Wang Yisheng's body relaxed and he leant against our hands, his throat rasping. Slowly he opened his mouth, closed it, opened it again and groaned. It was a long time before he gasped out, "Call it a draw."

"Won't you eat at my place tonight?" the old man

asked with great emotion. "Will you stay on for a couple of days so that we can talk about chess?" "No," said Wang Yisheng quietly with a shake of his head. "I'm with friends. We all set out together and we're going to stick together. We're going to the cultural center. I've got a friend there." "Let's go," said the painter from the middle of the crowd. "Let's go to my place. I've bought some food. You can all come. This is a rare occasion." The others were packed all round us as we slowly pushed our way out. We were engulfed in the light from a ring of blazing torches. We were surrounded many times over by mountain folk and people from the district capital, who all struggled to catch a glimpse of the chess master's elegant bearing then nodded and sighed.

Slowly I helped Wang Yisheng along, and the light came with us all the way. It was a bit like what I remembered of Rembrandt's *Night Watch*, which I had seen in my childhood. We went into the cultural center and on to the painter's room, and although people tried to persuade them to go away, the windows were packed with onlookers. This made the painter so anxious that he put some of his pictures away.

Gradually the crowd dispersed, but Wang Yisheng remained rather numb. Suddenly realizing that I was still clutching that chess piece in my left hand, I held it out to show Wang Yisheng. At first he gazed at it stupidly, appearing not to recognize it, but then there was a noise in his throat and he brought up something viscous with a violent retching sound. He started weeping and saying through his sobs, "Mum, I've understood now. You've got to have something before you can really live. Mum ..." We all felt upset. We swept the floor, fetched him some hot water, and tried to calm him. After crying and getting those pent-up emotions off his chest, Wang

Yisheng bucked up again and ate with the rest of us. The painter finally got himself blind drunk, lay down on his wooden bed and went to sleep, ignoring everyone. The electrician took us all, including Legballs, to our bed on the auditorium stage.

The night was so dark you could not see your hand in front of your face. Wang Yisheng was already sound asleep. I still seemed to hear the hubbub of voices and see everything lit up with blazing torches as the stern-faced mountain folk walked through the forests with firewood on their shoulders, singing their songs. I smiled and thought that only by being one of the common people could one enjoy such pleasures. My family had been destroyed, I had lost my privileged status and was now having to do manual work every day, but here there was a remarkable man whom I was very lucky indeed to know. Food and clothing were the basic stuff of life; and ever since the human race had existed they had kept us busy every day. But to limit oneself to these was not to be truly human. I was being gradually overcome by tiredness, so I wrapped myself up in the curtain and fell fast asleep.

Translated by W.J.F. Jenner

DENG YOUMEI AND HIS FICTION

Gladys Yang

Beijing is inevitably being modernized. As its life style alters and tower blocks spring up, changing parts of the city out of all recognition, Deng Youmei by vividly conjuring up scenes and characters from old Beijing has done us a great service.

Deng was born into a poor family in Tianjin in 1931. When his father lost his job, they moved to their ancestral home, Deng Village in Shandong. After the Japanese invasion he delivered messages for the Eighth Route Army, but, being only eleven, he was sent back to Tianjin where he did odd jobs until forced to go to Japan as a laborer. In 1945 he returned to China and joined the New Fourth Army as a correspondent. After the Japanese surrender he took part in the War of Liberation (1946-1949) and wrote about army life and his experiences in Japan.

After Liberation Deng came to Beijing and attended the Literary Institute of the Writers Association. There his tutor was Zhang Tianyi (1906-1985), a writer of stories for children and a good stylist. He also received encouragement from Zhao Shuli (1906-1970), the popular author of *Rhymes of Li Youcai*, who modeled his works on traditional story-telling and used idiomatic turns of phrase enjoyed by peasants. Zhao had a strong influence on him.

His story *On the Precipice*, written in the early 1950s, dealt with a young couple whose marriage was wrecked by an attractive girl, a heartless flirt. It opposed selfish individualism and stressed the need to show concern for others. However, in 1957 it was criticized and he was declared a Rightist. For the next twenty years he worked as a manual laborer in Beijing and the provinces.

During this period Deng made many friends including rickshawmen, musicians, craftsmen and curio-dealers. His hardships had made him sympathize with underdogs in whom he found admirable and lovable qualities. In 1962 he went to the Northeast to work in a clock factory. As it had no dormitory, he bought a shelter which he shared for six years with a Manchu. From this friend and from a Manchu actor he learned a great deal about old Beijing. He did not plan at the time to write about Manchus, but his interest in them had been aroused as a boy when his family shared a courtyard in Tianjin with the widowed concubine of a Manchu noble who, though destitute, still gave herself grand airs.

He returned to Beijing in the Cultural Revolution. In his spare time he went on studying the city and its history, and people of all walks of life and their social customs. He also picked up anecdotes from actors, birdfanciers and old Beijing residents who went each morning with him to Taoran Pavilion Park to practise Chinese boxing. He came to appreciate the wry Beijing humor, a distinctive blend of the capital's long cultural tradition and the cynicism resulting from a series of upheavals in which humble townsfolk were always victimized.

After the fall of the Gang of Four[1] he resumed writing. *Our Army Commander* deals with Marshal Chen Yi (1901-1972), under whom Deng had served in the New Fourth Army. Written in the vein of socialist realism, it won an award in 1978. In 1980 he published a collection of short stories.

Black Cat, White Cat (1980) takes its title from Deng Xiaoping's saying, "Black cat or white cat, a mouse-catcher is a good cat." This challenged the ultra-Left view that class origin was all-important, professional expertise irrelevant. The story presents an able engineer, Kang, who is criticized for pointing out faults in a Soviet expert's building plans. It portrays the alienation caused by the anti-Rightist campaign when he and his colleague Jin, a Manchu, find it safer to ignore each other. But even when describing this abnormal phenomenon, Deng brings out the two men's humanity and mutual trust.

After the engineer is cleared, he urges the authorities to check up on the buildings. Breaks and flaws are found, and Kang is commended for his responsible attitude, which shows that now he is taken seriously. Jin, too, is given a worthwhile job. They drink to celebrate this. "Black cat or white cat, at least they count us as cats, right?" The story ends on this optimistic note, showing the improvement in the treatment of intellectuals.

At this time, Deng recalls, new fiction was appearing like mushrooms after rain, and he wondered how best he could make his contribution. Comparing his qualifications with those of other writers, he concluded that there were many ex-Rightists who could write about their bitter experiences, and that he was less skilled than Wang Meng in highlighting social problems. His forte was his knowledge of Beijing. The Gang of Four had tried to stamp out traditional customs, an intrinsic part of the cultural heritage, but now some were reappearing and Deng believed that young people should learn about them, that a writer's chief task was educating readers. He resolved to write stories with a strong local flavor set in old Beijing.

His Beijing stories *Han the Forger*, *Na Five*, and *Snuff-Bottles* have the best qualities of popular literature, as they are compulsive reading with unforgettable characters and packed with information. They show us the thieves' market, labor market and flower market; the temple fairs, tea-houses, antique shops, restaurants and parks of Beijing. They also describe martial arts, handicrafts, private opera performances, cock-fights and other pastimes of the bankrupt yet colorful old capital. In this respect Deng has been compared to Balzac for his capacity to provide the social history not found in history books. He sets out to fill in a gap in the general knowledge of the younger generation, to show that the Qing dynasty fell because the descendants of the Manchu warriors who carved out the empire had degenerated after centuries of soft living. Na Five, introduced in Deng's story, epitomizes this degeneration.

In 1953 Premier Zhou Enlai (1898-1976) gave a talk at Beijing No. 101 Middle School, a school for the children of high-ranking Party cadres. He warned them to learn a lesson from the effete descendants of Manchu bannermen, and not to exist as parasites living off the achievements of their parents.

Unfortunately, only thirty years later, feudal nepotism re-emerged. There was widespread dissatisfaction over the privileges and abuse of power of the children of some high officials. This gave the story of Na Five a topical significance. It made a strong impression on young readers because it depicted a society completely strange to them, and showed why it was doomed to collapse. It spans the first half of the century. The political upheavals of that period are not explicitly described, but the main trends are evident in Na's adventures, since he is a product of his environment.

Na's grandfather, a wealthy Manchu official, dies leaving a frugal, hard-working concubine, Cloud. She rents her rooms to an old physician, Guo, and looks after him well, calling him Brother Guo. Na's father then dies, having squandered the family fortune. When Na's attempt to sell stolen porcelain fails, he asks Mistress Cloud to take him in, then repays her kindness by treating her like a servant. Dr Guo urges him to study medicine, but, unwilling to study seriously, he plans to be an abortionist to make big money. After that Dr Guo ignores him. This is where our extract starts. We see Na Five swindling others and being swindled, living as a parasite, too proud to take up an honest trade. In the later part of the story he joins a Beijing opera club, then becomes an announcer in a radio station and coaches a spare-time opera troupe. After the peaceful liberation of Beijing he asks a PLA cadre for a job, bragging and lying about his qualifications. Finally he is assigned to the office in charge of popular literature. Deng concludes: "What ridiculous adventures Na Five had in New China will have to be related in another story."

Na Five won a national award.

Chinese readers like Deng's Beijing stories not simply on account of the subject matter but also because of their form. Whereas many other writers are drawing on Western techniques, he has developed traditional story-telling and has mastered the Beijing idiom. He worked hard at this, frequenting the Tianqiao fairground to listen to professional story-tellers who held their audiences spellbound with tales about the capital in the old days. He has their mastery of thumbnail sketches and humorous, dramatic dialogue. His stories are traditionally structured: told chronologically, proceeding from a gripping start to an ambiguous ending and leaving readers to imagine the sequel.

Deng's longer work *Snuff-Bottles* was chosen as one

of the ten best novellas of 1984. Generally considered his masterpiece and likened to genre painting, it is highly recommended reading. It has a lead-in about snuff-bottles before the action starts, a practice dating back to the stories told in market-places in eleventh-century China. The year is 1899 and Beijing has been occupied by the allied army of eight imperialist powers. We see the inter-action in those troubled times of a complex cast of characters: Japanese officers, Manchu princes, banner-men, actors, craftsmen and other members of the lower classes. The central figure Wu Shibao is an affable, timid Manchu. He learns in prison from the potter Nie how to paint the inside of snuff-bottles, and makes a living from this when his pension stops. Then he moves to Nie's house to become his apprentice, becomes engaged to his daughter Willow, and learns to paint eggshell porcelain.

To curry favor with the Japanese, a Manchu prince orders Nie to paint snuff-bottles showing them in their uniforms in scenic spots in Beijing. Rather than do this, he throws himself in front of the prince's carriage to break his right hand. Willow hastily marries Wu, then with Nie they flee Beijing.

This story with no explicit political statements actually presents a clear picture of the social contradictions of that time and the different stances of all its characters. It has been filmed by the Kunlun Studio in Hong Kong as *Descendants of Bannermen*.

Deng decided to write about snuff-bottles after read-ing an account of Wang Xisan, who painted bottles for his farming production brigade to sell to finance their water conservancy project. He was doing well till the Red Guards attacked him for his "decadence." Deng then read up on snuff-bottles and made friends with old craftsmen. While collecting material, he was struck by their patriotic enthusiasm and strong sense of self-respect. In a temple in Foshan he saw a bronze incense-burner cast during the Boxer Uprising (1900), with four legs planted on four foreign agressors. The man who made that did so at the risk of his life. This helped Deng to visualize an honest, high-minded craftsman who would never stoop to flattery or deceit, and so he created the memorable potter Nie.

Predictably, Deng collects antiques and handicrafts. He used to take snuff till his doctor advised against it. Now he smokes cigarettes if he can evade the watchful eyes of his wife and younger daughter.

Since he was elected to the secretariat of the Chinese Writers Association in 1985, he has had little time for writing. He is now working, however, on another book. Meanwhile, as the director of the Foreign Liaison Department of the association, and as one of the directors of China International Cultural Exchange Association, he is also fostering cultural exchanges and dialogues between Chinese and foreign writers.

Note:

[1] The Gang of Four refers to Jiang Qing (1915-), widow of Mao Zedong, and her followers Wang Hongwen (1932-), Zhang Chunqiao (1917-), and Yao Wenyuan (1932-). They formed a clique to carry out counter-revolutionary activities during the Cultural Revolution and planned to take advantage of Mao's death, to usurp the supreme power of the Party and state but were soon overthrown, and put under house arrest. They were tried and imprisoned in January, 1981. This designation was attached to them subsequently.

Na Five (Chapters 5-10)

Deng Youmei

5.

AFTER Na Five had stayed with Mistress Cloud for less than a month, though he was supplied with food and clothing, he couldn't stand being hard up and felt intolerably lonely. As his clothes were out of hock, he begged his friends to find some job for him. It was time for his luck to change, and while in a claque with Suo Seven he met Ma Sen, editor of the *Violet Pictorial*. Since Na Five knew many actors and could take photographs, Ma asked him to join the pictorial as a reporter.

This pictorial published features on actresses, backstage gossip, romances, adventure stories and other sensational items. Its office, in a small shop in Coal Market Street, had a staff of only two: Ma Sen and his assistant editor Tao Zhi. The two men looked very different. Ma wore Western-style suits and leather shoes, Tao a blue cloth gown. Ma shaved twice a day and had a hair-cut every three days; Tao wore his hair down to his ears, and had a stubbly beard. The office contained only two desks and three chairs. Newspapers and magazines were piled on the floor. On the day Na Five started work, the editors invited him out to lunch and explained their rules to him. He would receive neither salary nor traveling expenses, and the pay for each contribution was nominal. But he was given a reporter's card and could start work in the name of the magazine, and make a living on his own.

Na Five felt he had been taken in. But having accepted, he could hardly back out now. He decided to give it a try. After two months associating with other reporters, he realized that he was on to a good thing. When he wrote cracking up an actress, he was paid not only by her but by her backers too. In his wanderings through the town, if he found empty rooms in some lodging-house or a restaurant selling some new delicacy, he would write an item entitled "An Empty Haunted House" or a letter denouncing the restaurant for selling maggoty food. He showed these to the landlord and restaurant owner, claiming that he had suppressed them for several days so that they could read them first and see if they could be hushed up. To keep out of trouble such men invariably paid to have the manuscripts suppressed, while Na Five gloated over each new stroke of luck.

The *Violet Pictorial* was now serializing the romance "A Pretty Young Lady" by the popular writer Master of the Drunkard's Studio. Sixteen instalments had been published, but he had failed to deliver the seventeenth. As Na Five was in the office, Tao Zhi asked him to fetch the manuscript and pay the author.

6.

The Master of the Drunkard's Studio lived in a narrow lane with few houses in it. His was an old-style two-storeyed building of brick. It overlooked a court-yard, in one corner of which was a rickety staircase just wide enough for one person. Several rooms opened off the passages upstairs and downstairs, each with a briquette stove, a water vat and a dustpan by its door. Na Five was looking round when two people came downstairs. One was a woman with permed hair and penciled eyebrows in a fancy, short-sleeved gown and embroidered satin slippers; the other was a middle-aged man in a grey cloth suit, cloth shoes and a felt cap. At the sight of him they exchanged glances and halted.

"Who are you looking for, sir?" the man asked.

"A novelist ..." he said.

"Oh." Looking disappointed the man jerked his chin at the space below the stairway, then nodded to the woman, and they left. Na Five stooped to get under the stairs, and saw a door covered by a bamboo curtain, with a signboard engraved "The Drunkard's Studio."

Inside were two rooms, but it was too dark to see the back one distinctly. In the other room was a hardwood desk inlaid with mother-of-pearl, which looked out of place there. There were two wooden chairs and a deck chair. The desk was crammed with books, papers, stationery, packets of cigarettes, ashtrays, inkstones and brush pots. Hearing footsteps, a man came out from the dark room. He was tall and thin with a pale face and a moustache.

"Who are you looking for?"

"Does the Master of the Drunkard's Studio live here?"

"That's my humble self. Please take a seat. Where are you from?"

"The pictorial. My editor's sent me for your manuscript."

"Well, sit down. The last couple of days I've been so busy, I forgot all about it!"

"Oh, we're waiting for your manuscript to go to

press."

"Never mind, if you'll wait a bit I'll write it for you now. How far did I get last time?"

"Eh?" Na Five flushed, not having read this work. His host laughed. "Never mind if you've forgotten. I have a record here."

He sat down at his desk and pulled out from a stack of papers a blue ledger. Leafing through it he asked, "Are you publishing my 'Two Swallows'? "

"No," said Na Five. "We're the *Violet Pictorial*. We're printing your 'A Pretty Young Lady.' "

" 'A Pretty Young Lady.' " The other riffled through his ledger, then shoved it aside and pulled out another. Leafing through this he exclaimed, "Where's my record of 'A Pretty Young Lady'? Oh, I know!" He pushed aside the second ledger and pulled out from a drawer a thick stapled manuscript of rice-paper. Inserted in this was an empty cigarette packet, and opening it here he said with a smile, "You're in luck, I don't have to write a new instalment. I'll just copy this out." With that he spread out a sheet of manuscript paper, picked up a brush and set to work copying.

Na Five was holding the dollar note he had brought. As soon as the novelist had finished copying and put the manuscript in an envelope, he laid the note on the table. The other glanced at it but didn't touch it. He turned to call towards the back room, "We've a visitor, brew some tea, quick!"

A round-faced woman in her fifties emerged and curtseyed to Na Five. "Please sit down, sir! Don't laugh at our shabby abode." Picking up a kettle she reached out for the dollar note on the table. "I'll go and fetch water."

Na Five said, "All the tabloids outside are printing

your novels, sir. How many do you write at once?"

"Eight or nine."

"Do you finish them all and keep them here?"

"No, I write an instalment at a time, and get paid for each instalment."

"But surely that manuscript of 'A Pretty Young Lady' which I just saw is finished?"

"Well, that's second-hand."

"Second-hand? What do you mean?"

The novelist explained that writers who hadn't made a name were unable to get their work published. Others wrote for fun, not to make a reputation. Yet others were so desperate for money that they couldn't wait to be paid in instalments. So they sold their novels to him, and he made a profit by having them serialized.

Na Five exclaimed, "So if you can afford to buy a manuscript, you can win fame without even lifting a finger!"

"That's how it has always been," was the reply. "A prince once published a number of operas, not a word written by himself."

Na Five's face lit up. He said as if jokingly, "I must buy a couple of manuscripts myself so that I can enjoy being famous."

The other answered seriously, "In your profession, unless you have a name people will look down on you and you'll get nowhere. You need to make your mark. Besides, when you buy a manuscript you have to read it, then copy it out. You soon get the knack of it and can write yourself. There's nothing difficult about writing novels."

He had just bought an adventure story entitled "The Carp Dart," and he offered this to Na Five for a hundred dollars. As Na Five happened to have with him a fake painting which he meant to pawn, this offer tempted him. As soon as he had raised three hundred dollars at the pawnshop he went straight back to the Drunkard's Studio and announced, "I've brought the money. Can I have a look first at the manuscript?"

"Don't be so naive!" said the other. "Buying a manuscript isn't like buying cucumbers that you can pick over and taste. Suppose you read it then refused to buy it, and went off to plagiarize it, what could I do? You'll just have to take it on trust."

As he fingered his money uncertainly, the other pounded his desk. "All right, we're friends!" He went into the inner room, rummaged in an old shoe box kept under the bed and took from it a manuscript on red-lined paper. He carried this outside to brush off the dust, then handed it to Na Five. "Have a look at the contents first."

Na Five read a few pages—it seemed really exciting. Then he weighed it in his hand and sized up its thickness. "This surely isn't enough for a hundred instalments," he said. "If I spend a hundred dollars on it, and it's only thirty instalments ..."

"How green you are! You can't expect to win fame and profit together. Don't you first want to make a name? This manuscript is well written. I guarantee it will create a sensation! Once you're famous you can make money."

Na Five paid over the money and left with the manuscript under his arm. Without reading it through he asked the editors to serialize it. Ma Sen accepted it, then sat on it for a month. Each time he was asked about it he replied, "I haven't finished it yet, but it seems not bad." He said nothing, however, about publishing it. When Na Five asked Tao Zhi about it, the latter laughed.

"Didn't the fellow who sold you this tell you the rule for getting a manuscript published?"

"We don't seem to have any rules for the Master of the Drunkard's Studio. We pay him a dollar for each instalment, don't we?"

The assistant editor laughed. "He's like a famous actor—as soon as he takes the stage people start applauding. But you're like an amateur. They don't make money acting, instead they have to pay for the privilege. Have to rent the theater themselves, hire costumes and other actors; then throw a feast and hand out tickets —otherwise who'd come to applaud? Professionals perform in order to eat, amateurs to make a name or just for fun. Of course the popular ones can turn professional, but only after they've paid to establish themselves."

Then Na Five forked out another hundred dollars and asked Tao Zhi to draw up for him a list of guests to invite to a restaurant. Only then did "The Carp Dart" begin to be serialized under the pen-name the Master of the Windy Pavilion. After that some friends referred to him as a "writer" and congratulated him on "creating a sensation," predicting that he would go far. He answered modestly, though inwardly bursting with pride. His way of talking changed too and he walked with a lighter step, feeling that his two hundred dollars had been well spent. Though his painting had been exposed as a fake, and he had had to sell a Western-style suit to square the pawnshop, still, confident that he would soon be famous, he did not lose heart.

When seven or eight instalments had come out, things started to go wrong. Either Tao Zhi's list had been incomplete and he had offended someone, or people were out to make trouble. Some other tabloids printed reviews ridiculing and attacking "The Carp Dart." Some accused him of plagiarism or writing nonsense. Someone wrote, "The Master of the Windy Pavilion is the grandson of a former official in the Ministry of Internal Affairs. As his grandfather was indebted to a boxer of the Bagua School, he has written this novel to extol that school and run down the Xingyi School."

In his indignation he called on the Master of the Drunkard's Studio.

"What taboos did that manuscript of yours break?" he demanded. "Why has it given rise to all this talk?"

In fact the Master of the Drunkard's Studio had bought the manuscript from an opium addict for ten dollars without reading it. So raising clasped hands he replied, "Didn't I tell you it would cause a sensation? Congratulations! When people find fault, that's good publicity. I used to commission articles running me down. Just think, if you simply publish a novel, your name only appears in the paper every three days. But when it gets reviewed, whether unfavorably or favorably, your name keeps appearing and readers remember it. Besides, success and failure go together. When some people curse you, others are bound to praise you. Leave them to fight it out while you cash in without lifting a finger yourself. You're in luck."

Na Five thought this made sense and cheered up. But a few days later when he went to the office, Ma Sen handed him a letter and said sternly, "This is your letter, Fifth Master. Up till now, we have always co-operated well, so don't involve my partners and me in any trouble. Leave us the *Violet Pictorial* to eke out a living."

At first Na Five thought he was joking. But the letter, when he read it, gave him a sinking feeling as if he had fallen into a deep well.

Written in thick black ink on a sheet of rice-paper

with eight red lines it read:

"To the Master of the Windy Pavilion. On the sixth of this month, at three in the afternoon, I expect you in the Happy Longevity Opium Den in Dazhalan. If you don't show up, look out! Don't say you haven't been warned!" The signature was "Wu Cunzhong."

He asked Ma, "Who's Wu Cunzhong? The name sounds familiar."

Without a word Ma tossed a tabloid at him. An article in it was outlined in red ink. The caption was, "Old age and ill health make Wu Cunzhong decline the post of bodyguard." There followed an account of Wu. He had been a boxer of the Xingyi School at the end of the Qing dynasty and had performed in Tianqiao in the early years of the Republic, but after the Japanese invasion had switched to making straw ropes. Recently a county head had offered him big money to be his bodyguard, but he had refused.

When Na Five had read this, Ma added, "Did you hear about that Russian strong man who used to challenge people in Sun Yat-sen Park? He promised ten gold medals to anyone who could throw him."

"He was thrown by Li Cunyi, wasn't he?" said Na Five. "I heard he broke a leg."

"Right. Wu Cunzhong and Li Cunyi were sworn brothers taught by the same teacher!"

He broke out in a cold sweat, saying wretchedly, "He'll break me in two when he sees me!"

"Why, in your novel, did you have to drag in that rivalry between the Bagua and Xingyi Schools?" Ma demanded.

"Heavens I didn't know a thing about it! I bought that manuscript."

Tao Zhi took pity on him then and said, "Don't get

het up. With men like that you can usually appeal ↴
their better nature. Just kowtow to him and don't defend yourself. Seeing you've knuckled under he'll probably let you off."

"You've got to go and meet him," declared Ma Sen.
"Or I would not put it past him to wreck this office, and
that would finish us off."

For the next three days Na Five didn't eat a square
meal, didn't have a night's sound sleep.

7.

On the sixth a fiery sun shriveled the leaves of the
trees and melted tarmac roads as Na Five dragged himself to Dazhalan. Turning into a lane he saw a big white
porcelain lampshade bearing the name "Happy Longevity Opium Den." He went in. Opposite him was a stairway, dank and dark. He went up and found white
curtains over the doors on both sides. Drawing one of
these he poked his head in. A fat middle-aged man
sitting in the doorway was fanning himself with a rush
fan. "Want to buy opium?" he asked.

"I'm looking for Wu Cunzhong ..."

"In the second private room over there."

He drew back the curtain and entered the room. It
was long with a wooden partition down the middle. On
each side were four small doors, all with short cotton curtains on which a number was printed. He approached No. 2 and asked softly, "Is Mr Wu there?"

There was no sound inside. At this point a waitress
came in carrying a brightly polished smoking-set. She
indicated that he should go in. Nodding gratefully he
raised the curtain and entered. This tiny room contained

only a couch and a chair, but it was spotlessly clean. On the couch were a mat and a pillow, and paintings and calligraphy hung on the walls. An old man in a white cotton jacket, with a long beard, lay there on his back, his eyes closed. There was no knowing whether he was asleep or awake.

Na Five said softly, "Mr Wu, I've come as you instructed!"

The old man's eyelids didn't even twitch. After a brief hesitation he withdrew to stand helplessly outside. The waitress happened to come back just then. He stuffed a one-dollar note into her apron pocket. "Mr Wu is asleep," he said. "Will you find me somewhere to rest and call me when he wakes?" With a smile she pointed at No. 2, shook her hand to hush him, pushed him towards the door, and left.

He went in again and stood silently waiting for Wu Cunzhong to open his eyes. After his long walk he was hot. But the rule of this house was not to open windows or install an electric fan. Sweat poured down his face like creepy-crawly insects, but he had to hide his frantic anxiety. When five minutes had passed and still the old man did not stir, Na Five fell on his knees in desperation.

"Mr Wu, Grand Master Wu! I've come to apologize. I'm a scoundrel, an utter idiot. I was talking through my hat. Please make allowances for me, I'm really beneath contempt...."

The stern-faced old man burst into laughing. Hitching himself up he said, "Stop kneeling. Get up."

"I humbly beg your pardon!" Na Five kowtowed, then stood up.

"You had everything so well figured out, I thought you must be a boxer yourself." Wu said smiling.

"I'm nothing," answered he. "A fly licking a ladle."

"Well then you should have asked around before writing, instead of running people down right and left!"

"I'll come clean with you, sir. I didn't write that novel, I bought it from someone. I wanted to make a name for myself, little thinking it was going to make you so angry."

The old man roared with laughter, mollified by Na Five's submissiveness. "Sit down," he said more mildly. "Have a smoke?"

Na Five sat down. Wu asked his family background and sighed on hearing that his grandfather had served in the Ministry of Internal Affairs.

"It seems we were fated to meet," he said. "Once I went to Mongolia on business, and brought back a gift from a Mongolian prince to your grandfather. When I delivered it he invited me to stay to a feast. Of course I didn't see the inner apartments, but I was fairly dazzled by the outer courtyard! It struck me at the time as going too far—as if he thought his office would last for ever. The way he was pouring money out like water, he'd have finished off even a gold mine. And what would happen to his sons and grandsons, who'd no idea how hard it is to make a living? So you get by, do you, by writing rubbish?"

Na Five flushed and nodded.

"You're still young," said Wu, "and you've enough education to learn a profession. A skill is worth more than ten thousand strings of cash. Why not get off your high horse and settle down to a job? If you earn your keep you can hold up your head no matter where you are."

"You're right! My father died early and I've had no one to teach me. Thank you for putting me straight."

Though he was so glib, he struck the other as genuinely grateful. So Wu said, "I live by the Temple of Agriculture. I've bought a machine to plait straw ropes. If you can't make a go of it anywhere else, come and join me. I need someone who can read and write right away."

Na Five thought: You rate me too low. Even if I'm down and out, how can the descendant of nobles work like a coolie! Not daring to show that he despised the job, he hastily said, "Just now I can manage all right, but I shall certainly ask for your help in future."

Seeing his reluctance, Wu did not insist. He said they could forget about that novel. Some of his sworn brothers had threatened in their rage to wreck the office of the *Violet Pictorial*, but he had persuaded them to wait till after he'd met the Master of the Windy Pavilion. Now that he'd settled the dispute, they'd have to let it drop. Na Five bowed and thanked him profusely, then took his leave.

"Wait a bit," said Wu. "I can't have you coming all this way for nothing. China's martial arts are going to the dogs and the country's in a bad way. Still we do have a few good boxers in various schools. Go out and write us up to boost our morale. I'm no good any more, but I'll put on a little show for you. Number Three!"

"Here!" answered a booming voice behind the partition.

"Go and light the lamps."

Wu got up, put on his shoes and tightening his girdle, went out. Four or five men were waiting in the passage. The two youngest had brought a table, and the waitress made haste to light three opium lamps for them.

At sight of Na Five these tough customers at once exchanged glances and grinned, making him rather nervous.

"Don't worry," said Wu. "These are all my apprentices. We thought you might know a trick or two, so they were ready to take you on. Now we've made things up, fine! We can all be friends."

By now more people had gathered round, crowding the passage.

The opium lamps, known as the Taigu Lamp from Shanxi, were about the size of a tea bowl, with brass oil-cups below their thick, tapering glass shades. You could only extinguish them by blowing straight into the aperture at the top. When the waitress had lit them and an apprentice had set them out in a row, Wu inspected them and adjusted their position. He then fell back five paces, took the "horse-stance" and breathed in so deeply that his belly underneath his girdle bulged. After slightly swinging his arms he stood stock-still and blew hard. The flames in the three lamps flickered, and one by one they went out, while the onlookers shouted "Bravo!"

Wu raised clasped hands. "I've made an exhibition of myself. Now I'm old, all I can do is raise a laugh."

Na Five's legs were trembling, he was in a cold sweat. He staggered out to hire a pedicab to the editorial office. When he told the editors of his narrow escape they congratulated him and invited him out to Fengzeyuan Restaurant, where they ordered wine and food to help him get over his shock. Ma Sen returned him the manuscript of "The Carp Dart," as they could no longer serialize it. They also said he was now too well-known to work for their pictorial and took away his treasured reporter's card.

8.

Since becoming a reporter Na Five had rented a small room in the south city and cut himself off from Purple Cloud. But now that he had no money for rent or food, he bought some cakes and went to call on her. The few months of his absence had seen big changes: the old doctor had died of a sudden illness, and the courtyard looked neglected. Mistress Cloud was taking in laundry. When Na Five reappeared, she broke down.

"I didn't take proper care of you," she sobbed. "Fed you so badly that you left in a huff. But you shouldn't be so intolerant. After all we still belong to one family, don't we? Who else is left of the Na family? When we were rich, carriages and sedan-chairs thronged our gate; but after we lost our money who would own to knowing us? We've only each other now."

His nose tingled when he heard this. He exclaimed gruffly, "Granny!"

That reduced Purple Cloud to tears again. "You'll be the death of me," she protested. "If you've any pity for a poor lone widow, don't leave me again. With my washing and sewing I can make enough to keep the two of us. When you marry I'll look after you and your wife. And when you have a son I'll nurse him, if you don't think me too far beneath you. What you call me doesn't matter!"

When he agreed to this she gave thanks to Buddha. "Just stay here reading or amusing yourself. So long as you don't leave I'll feel secure. Sit down now while I clear out your rooms for you."

Purple Cloud made ready the doctors' rooms for him, then called him over to inspect them. The inner room was simply furnished with a bed, a table and a chair. In the outer room were two hardwood bookcases stacked with thread-bound books on medicine as well as a few works of literature.

"I sold everything else to pay for the old man's funeral," she told him. "His students wouldn't let me sell these books unless it were to them, for fear I'd be swindled. I thought maybe some were worth money, so I waited for you to decide which of them to keep. You can take your pick. Those you don't want we'll give to his students. When the old man was dying they helped me out, and I've no other way of thanking them."

"Tell them to take the lot," said he handsomely. "Just leave me the bookcases."

From that day on Purple Cloud wore a smile again. She got out all his clothes to wash, starch and mend. When she had money to spare, she gave him a few cents to hire a novel from the stall at their gate. The adventure stories he read reminded him of the manuscript he had bought from the Master of the Drunkard's Studio. He felt he shouldn't have let the man off so lightly. So one day he asked Mistress Cloud for some rickshaw money in order to call on a friend. She gave him two dollars she had just been paid, saying, "That's right, go out and have a good time before you fall ill of boredom. But don't go mixing with rowdies; remember we're a respectable family."

After the plain fare he'd been having, his stomach was crying out for something richer. So first he went to Dongsi for a bowl of boiled offal. Then at Longfusi he had a plate of chitterling broth. When he reached the Drunkard's Studio and raised the curtain, its master hurried out in his slippers to greet him. Taking his hand he exclaimed, "So you made a pile! Where did you disappear to?"

"Made a pile, did I? On that book of yours 'The Carp Dart'? I nearly had my back broken by Wu Cunzhong!"

"You'd only yourself to blame," was the retort. "Who would think of publishing a manuscript he's bought without changing a single word? If you'd altered the names Bagua and Xingyi, you wouldn't have had any trouble. But that's past and done with. Today I have a good proposal for you."

"Don't think you can fool me again."

"Whether you believe me or not, sit down while I see to some business. I'll be straight back." He poured Na Five some tea then went out and could be heard going upstairs.

After the time it takes to eat a meal, the Drunkard led in a stranger, telling him, "Didn't you want to meet this young gentleman? He happens to have dropped into my humble home. Let me introduce you: Manager Jia Fenglou."

Na Five recognized the middle-aged man who had told him the way the first time he came. He stood up and nodded. "We've met."

"That's right. I saw at a glance that day that you were someone special. Someone exceptional! Don't take offence, but you impressed me so much that I'm overjoyed at this chance to talk to you...."

"You're too polite, too polite, sir."

"It's the honest truth. When I heard later that you were the grandson of a high official, I was tempted to slap my own face. How could a nobody like myself presume to call on someone so distinguished?"

The Drunkard put in, "Young Master Na's most obliging, he never gives himself airs."

"Yes, he's told me several times that you never put on side, you're so magnanimous. Now that you're here again, sir, you must do me the favor of coming to my home so that we can get acquainted."

"You do me too much honor," replied Na Five. "I've simply cashed in a bit on my ancestors; apart from that I'm good for nothing. Please sit down."

Jia Fenglou suggested with a smile to the Drunkard, "Why don't you both come to my place?"

The Drunkard told Na Five, "As soon as Manager Jia heard of your arrival he sent out to order a meal. It would be ungracious to decline. Let's go up."

"This is the first time we've met," protested Na Five. "Why not let me invite you to a restaurant?"

"Won't you give me this pleasure?" retorted Jia. "My younger sister wants to meet you too. Shall I ask her to come and persuade you?"

The Drunkard took Na Five's arm and he and Jia between them propelled him upstairs.

Jia had four rooms, one for himself, one for his sister, and two reception rooms. He ushered Na Five into the northern room. On the wall hung enlarged photographs of his sister Fengkui in ordinary costume and on the stage. Stuck in the frames were cuttings from newspapers, all fulsome reviews of her performances. On a stand stood an octagonal drum with red tassels. By this hung a three-stringed fiddle. On the red-check varnished cloth on the red-lacquered desk lay some magazines and pictorials alongside musical scores and a list of performances. On one teapoy was a gramophone with a big loudspeaker atop it. Na Five realized that Jia and his sister were artistes.

When they were seated the Drunkard said, "You're a Beijing opera and *pingju* fan, Master Na, you seldom go to hear ballad singers. When you've time you should go and hear Miss Jia—she's brilliant."

Na Five bowed. "I will certainly give myself that pleasure as soon as I can."

"You must be too busy, sir, to do us that honor. And my sister's singing would grate on your ears."

"Now you're being polite!" the Drunkard said emphatically. "Fengkui is a first-rate artiste, very kind and warm-hearted too. Her fans are in luck, that's what I always say."

Na Five thought: It's no use your trying to trap me. My father was the one to play patron to ballad-singers. Even if I wanted to I haven't the money.

Just then the door curtain swished and in came Fengkui.

Today her lips were lightly rouged but otherwise she wore no make-up, which made her look much younger than the first time he saw her, seventeen or eighteen at most. She was wearing a short-sleeved gown and embroidered white satin slippers. Her hair, loosely swept back behind her ears, was fastened with a pearly clasp. Above one temple she wore a white orchid. With a cool smile she laid both hands on one hip and curtseyed to Na Five.

"Excuse me, sir, for not being here to greet you. Please come into the next room for a snack."

Manager Jia led Na Five into the next room where the table was laid with some dishes, a bottle of liquor and another bottle of high-grade Shaoxing wine.

As they drank Jia went on flattering Na Five, who after a few cups of liquor relaxed and started joking with Fengkui. She neither responded nor cold-shouldered him but seemed completely detached, sometimes smiling at what they said, sometimes looking pensive.

After the meal Jia took his guests back to the other room. The Drunkard excused himself on the pretext of business, while Fengkui cleared the table. When Na Five began to take his leave his host stopped him. "I've a favor to ask you," he said. "You mustn't go yet."

He had to sit down again.

Having poured him some tea Jia told him, "There's some easy money to be made if someone will lend us a hand. I was hoping to take advantage of your good fortune."

"What does it involve?"

"Recently a newly-rich upstart has been making a bid for my sister. We sell our art, not ourselves!"

"That's the spirit!" approved Na Five.

"The fact remains, though, that artistes need patrons. We can't let him have her, but we want his money. Those people are stinking rich—all ill-gotten gains—so why not make him fork out?"

"Well, how can you get him to part with his money for nothing?"

"We need another money-bags who admires my sister too, who will outbid him. Since he's infatuated and can't bear to lose face, you may be sure he'll spend every cent he's brought. When he finds himself outmatched he'll slink away."

"I understand. You want me to bid against him."

"Exactly."

Na Five laughed. "That's a fine idea, and I have the highest regard for your sister. The trouble is, I have no money."

"What are you thinking of? This is between friends. If we ask you to help we won't let you be out of pocket. And when we've pulled it off I shall express my thanks."

Na Five perked up then. He asked, "Tell me your plan in detail. I don't want any thanks. I shall be only too glad to help a friend."

"You're so kind. The thing's as good as done then. Starting tomorrow I want you to go every evening to hear the ballad-singing in Qingyin Teahouse at Tianqiao. Someone will offer you a towel and some refreshment. Just take them. When my sister comes on and one of the audience calls for an encore, you follow suit. Do that each time he calls for an encore. But when he gives a ten-dollar tip, you must give at least fifteen or twenty dollars."

"Paid on the spot?" asked Na Five.

"Of course. But don't worry. When the time comes I'll get a waiter to slip you the money. Give as much as he hands you, not keeping any back. At the end of the performance I'll be waiting upstairs to treat you to a midnight snack and settle accounts with you."

"Can do!" cried he eagerly. "Fine!"

"Only ..." Jia looked grave and lowered his voice. "This must be a secret between the two of us. And you'll need a different leaf."

"What is 'leaf'?"

"Outfit that is. You're dressed like a young gentleman. Young gentlemen are open-handed, but they're in no position to outbid a rival, as their fathers hold the purse-strings. For you to spend too much would look suspicious. So get yourself up like a rich businessman."

"Can do!" Na Five chuckled. "It's hard for me to pass myself off as a poor man. A rich merchant's more in my line."

"That's why I singled you out from the start."

As Na Five left Jia thrust a red paper package into his hands. "You'll need some loose change in the teahouse. Take this to pay for tips."

When he declined politely, Jia retorted, "Friendship is one thing, business is business. I can't put you to any expense."

9.

On his return home he told Mistress Cloud that a friend of his wanted him to help out for a few days with his wedding.

"At home you count on your parents, outside on friends," she approved. "To put yourself out for friends is all to the good."

"But my clothes are so shabby, I was thinking of asking you for a little money to rent some second-hand ones."

"You won't find any second-hand clothes to fit you. And if you burn or tear them they'll make you pay a big fine. I've some of your grandfather's clothes here, all first-class material. When I've altered them for you, I promise you you'll cut a fine figure." With that she measured him, then got out from her camphorwood chest some gowns and waistcoats of gambiered Guangdong gauze, Hangzhou silk and other rich fabrics. He chose those he fancied, and she sat up sewing all night by a paraffin lamp while he enjoyed a sound sleep. When he opened his eyes the next morning the neatly ironed clothes were folded on his chair. He leapt up to try them on. Not only did they fit, they were in fashion, for Mistress Cloud knew the latest styles, having recently been living on tailoring. Once dressed he went over to thank her, but she had gone out to do the marketing. He examined himself in the mirror. He looked for all the world like a wealthy young merchant, except that he couldn't afford a suitable cap. To make up for this he went straight to have a haircut and set, and anointed himself with pomade.

Qingyin Teahouse was off the beaten track in the southwest of Triangle Market, a bowshot from the center of Tianqiao. To reach it he had to pass amusement stalls and refreshment booths with low stools and canvas awnings. Then he skirted round a wrestling ground both sides of which were packed with more stalls run by chiropodists, professional letter-writers, fortune-tellers, dentists and oculists. There you could also find cures for acne, watch performing monkeys, or have your photograph taken in opera costume. In front of one shop was a cauldron in which an apprentice was pounding the ingredients for a plaster, calling out, "A guaranteed cure-all!"

At the west end he finally spotted the wooden sign of Qingyin Teahouse which had walls of sorghum stalks plastered with lime. A short curtain hung over the door, and a man in a straw hat, his white cotton shirt unbuttoned, was rattling some coins in a basket-tray and yelling, "Who has a sweet tooth? Who has a sweet tooth?"

Na Five wondered if they had switched to selling cakes.

But the fellow went on, "Jia Fengkui has the sweetest voice ever heard. Just come and try—it's sweeter than honey or crystal sugar...."

A red notice on the wall listed such performers as Pearl and White Jasmine. Some names, including that of Jia Fengkui, had been cut out of gold paper and pasted up.

As he reached out to draw aside the curtain, the man with the tray barred his way. "Your honorable name?"

"My name's Na. What of it? Do we have to register to come to your teahouse?"

Ignoring his sarcasm, the man pulled back the curtain and yelled:

"Fifth Master Na is here!"

Shouts went up inside: "Fifth Master Na!" "A seat for Fifth Master Na!" Waiters hurried over to greet him and show him to a place slightly left of center. The table was heaped with melon seeds and slices of water-melon. One waiter brought him a bowl of tea, another a hot scented wet towel. As he took the towel, a roll of bank-notes was stuffed into his palm. After wiping his face he looked down and saw twenty dollars folded round a slip of paper on which was written "Returning in Wind and Rain."

He settled down to size up his surroundings.

The teahouse was not too big, with seven or eight tables, most of which had plates of fruit on them. The few at the back were empty. Several customers were seated at the front tables. The man seated alone at the table next to his looked a few years younger than Na Five. He was wearing a Western-style suit, leather shoes and a crimson tie embroidered with a gold dragon. On both sides of the room and at the back were benches which were packed; but just before each item ended the customers rushed out, tearing in again as soon as the collection had been taken.

There was no backstage area. Some auspicious couplets hung on the wall behind the platform, with below them a dozen seats in a semi-circle for the women artistes in their colorful costumes. While one performed, the others nodded, smiled or called out to friends of theirs in the audience.

A plump woman was performing a drum-ballad. When she finished she put down her castanets and bowed, her head on one side. As applause broke out

71

below, waiters holding basket-trays darted down both sides of the room and to the back, calling, "All contributions gratefully received!" To the left of the stage were notices of the different performers' names, and during this confusion someone went over and picked out the one with the big characters Jia Fengkui. At once the young man in the Western suit cried, "Bravo!" He beckoned to a waiter who hurried over and stooped to hear his instructions and take his money, then shoved his way to the stage holding up a square tray. "Master Yan gives ten dollars to hear *Golden Lotus*," he cried. At once the actresses on the stage and the waiters scurrying below it chorused:

"Thanks!"

Jia Fengkui stood up and glided gracefully forward to bow with a smile to the young man.

Today she was wearing a loose-sleeved tunic and wide trousers of pale green with embroidered borders. Her wig, plaited in a thick glossy braid, was tied with a red ribbon and decorated with red tassels. She also wore long earrings of pearl and jade. Na Five thought, "No wonder I didn't recognize her."

He was staring raptly when somebody nudged him. It was the waiter who had brought him a towel.

"Fifth Master!" The waiter pursed his lips silently at the twenty-dollar notes.

Na Five nodded and promptly returned the notes to the waiter, who strode straight to the stage with his tray. "Manager Na has given twenty dollars to hear *Returning in Wind and Rain*."

A roar of approval went up. Fengkui stepped forward to bow to him and said with a sweet smile, "We all thank you, Manager Na."

A buzz of speculation broke out as all eyes turned to

him. The young man in the Western suit stood up to glare at him, not sitting down till the music started up. Na Five felt transported back to the heyday of his family. In his pride and elation he no longer seemed to be acting a part—this behavior came naturally to him.

The waiter came back several times with that twenty dollars, on the pretext of offering him a towel, then delivered the money on his tray to the stage. After six repetitions of this merry-go-round, Master Yan was cleaned out. Huffing and puffing he pounded his table and left, escorted out by the waiters. At the door he looked back at Na Five and declared loudly, "Reserve the three front tables for me tomorrow. I'm bringing a few friends to enjoy Miss Jia's performance."

Na Five felt as invigorated as after a drink of iced sweet-sour plum juice in a heatwave. For months other people had cocked a snook at him; today he had cocked a snook at someone else—what a treat! But after his rival left, before he'd had enough of parading his wealth, the waiter stopped bringing him money. He listened listlessly to some more singing, then was told that Jia Fenglou was waiting for him at Two-Friend Tavern. Leaving a tip on the table he made off while the waiters announced his departure.

Jia was waiting in Two-Friend Tavern. As they went upstairs he said, "You're a born aristocrat—it comes natural to you. You've done us a very good turn."

Though there were only the two of them the meal was a lavish one. On parting Jia thrust a red package into his hands. When he opened it on the rickshaw he found it was the twenty dollars he had handed in so many times that evening. Since he reckoned that his rival had spent at least 150 dollars, this seemed to him a niggardly payment. However, it was disgusting, he reflected, for a gentleman to haggle with those low people. After all he had made a profit too, he gloated. When they reached a confectioners' he got off and bought two packets of plum-juice powder. He gave these to Mistress Cloud, who was waiting up for him, and urged, "You must try this." Mistress Cloud wrinkled up her eyes in a smile.

"Where did you get the money?"

"Won it at cards."

"Well don't play any more. We can't afford to lose. Gambling debts are no laughing matter. I've driven out the mosquitoes and put down your net. Have a good wash and turn in now. This hot weather is so tiring."

10.

In a dozen consecutive visits to Qingyin Teahouse Na Five made Yan spend over a thousand dollars. Today the young man arrived with a bulging briefcase and called for song after song until it was late. A curfew had been imposed and everyone had to be indoors by midnight. The manager and Jia Fenglou came down to explain this and invite both gentlemen back the next day. Na Five nodded his agreement. But Mr Yan said, "I thought you were out for money. I've money to burn and haven't spent it yet."

In the confusion as the artistes were leaving, Fengkui stepped up behind to warn him softly, "There's going to be trouble. Go back, quick!" He woke up then and hastily squeezed his way out.

Outside he realized how late it was. The stalls on either side had long since closed. The trams had stopped running. The place was so dark and deserted that he took fright. He cleared his throat and sang a few bars to give himself some courage.

"Anyone want a ride?" A pedicab for two had come alongside. Its fare, a man in a grey suit, was nodding and snoring. The driver asked him, "Want to go to the east city? I'll charge less, I'm packing it in."

He was tempted. "How much?"

"A dollar to Dongdan."

"Too much."

"Use your eyes. You can't hire a cab now for two dollars. This is no place to knock about on your own. If you don't run into robbers, the night patrol will nab you and fine you more than a dollar."

The pedicabman had kept going off-handedly and now had passed him. "All right then, stop!" he called.

The driver stopped and nudged his passenger. "Move over, will you? I've another fare."

"Another fare?" mumbled the man. "How many fares can you take?"

"Can't you see this is a two-seater?" The driver shoved him over to one side, then helped Na Five on and pedaled quickly off. But when the time came to head north, he turned abruptly south.

"Hey!" called Na Five. "Where are you going? This isn't the way to the east city."

"Don't move!" The man who had seemed to be asleep grabbed hold of him and in a flash leveled a knife at his middle. "One more squawk out of you and I'll knife you!"

"Ahh ...you ..."

"Shut up!"

He kept his mouth shut but shook so convulsively that the pedicab creaked loudly. The man with the knife pounded his thigh and jeered, "Look at you! Not worth your salt, are you!"

The pedicab turned this way and that till it reached the foot of a high wall. There was a wood here with nobody in sight. As the driver drew up, the other man dragged him off. "Now, mate, do the handsome thing. Your money and your watch, quick!"

He faltered, "I've a watch, but it doesn't work. You can have it if you like. All the money I have is two dollars for my rickshaw fare."

The pedicab driver demanded, "Can a gentleman with no money play the patron? I've been watching you for days now."

"Cut the cackle and search him," snapped the man with the knife.

They searched him from top to toe but sure enough all he had was two dollars and an old watch which nobody would want, not even for spare parts. In a rage the man with the knife slapped Na Five's face. "Take off your clothes!" he ordered.

Na Five stripped down to his underpants, then stood there meekly, shivering. He was no longer afraid, but so cold that his teeth were chattering.

"Your shoes!" ordered the pedicabman.

"Won't you leave me my shoes to walk in?"

"Where are you walking to?" demanded the other. "To the police station to report us? Take 'em off!"

As he stooped to take off his shoes, a blow on the back of his head knocked him unconscious. When he came to he still had his shoes on. But it was pitch dark and where could he go stark-naked? He stood up and did some exercises to warm up—he was frozen.

After a while he heard footsteps, and the sounds of opera singers exercising their voices. When some women walked towards him talking, he ducked behind a tree. In half an hour or so the sky was light. A stooped figure approached him slowly from behind. Na Five called to him, "Sir ..."

The man stopped, looked his way and came over. Six or seven paces away Na Five recognized him as Big Head Hu the fiddler.

"Master Hu!" he burst into tears.

"What's up, Master Na? Why haven't you been to see us for so long? Where have you been practising? Why are you carrying on like that? Is Mistress Cloud ill?"

"No, I've had all my clothes stolen."

"How on earth?" Master Hu took off his gown and passed it over. Underneath he was wearing nothing but a patched vest. Looking from Na Five to himself he said, "This won't do. You can't go about like that, and neither can I. Why don't you wait here while I borrow some clothes from someone living nearby. Don't stir from this spot. If the police see you and charge you with indecent exposure, you'll have to pay a fine."

"What is this place? Is it policed?"

"Your wits must be wandering, this is the Temple of Agriculture."

As Big Head Hu took back his gown, put it on again and left, Na Five looked round to see where he was. Confound it, this was just one street away from the Qingyin Teahouse and at the east end, he recalled, was a police station with a red electric light. Now that the day was bright, more singers and strollers had gathered there. He skulked beneath a tree, not daring to move, less like someone who had been mugged than a thief himself.

Translated by Gladys Yang

FENG JICAI, A GIANT OF
A WRITER IN MORE
WAYS THAN ONE

Li Jun

A towering figure at over six feet two inches, Feng Jicai is the "giant" among contemporary Chinese writers.

Born in 1942 in Tianjin, he has led a life that has been nothing short of a tri-athelon: he is an athlete turned painter, and a painter turned writer. In a piece entitled "My Triple Jump," he vividly describes his childhood and his changes of profession.

At primary school he was mischievous. Keen on all after class activities, he devoted little time or energy to his lessons, managing well nevertheless thanks to a prodigious memory and a fair degree of craftiness. Popular games among his classmates were cracking almonds and catching crickets, but young Feng's talent lay in drawing and sports, especially football. As soon as the final bell of the day rang, he and his classmates would rush out into the playground. They improvised goal-posts with their schoolbags and caps and played until either dusk fell or they had kicked the ball into some dark corner and lost it. During class he best loved to draw. Usually he would open a book and prop it up on his desk so that it screened him from the teacher's gaze. Then, tearing a sheet of blank paper from his excercise book, he would begin drawing. He began by half listening to the teacher, while he drew planes, guns, ships or whatever else came to mind, but gradually he became increasingly immersed in his drawing, until he began thinking aloud, imitating the sounds of gun shots and battle cries. He was then usually caught red-handed by the teacher, who berated him and confiscated his work. His passion for drawing resulted in his scrawling over almost all his textbooks—covers, flaps and blank pages. At middle school, he played center in the school's basketball team and was active in an amateur painters' group. During the winter and summer holidays, he studied traditional Chinese painting with a tutor. As he matured, he rapidly progressed as a painter. In his first year of senior middle school, one of his works was selected for a middle school students' art exhibition sponsored by Tianjin Municipality, and it subsequently won an award.

Young men generally like to dream fancifully about their future lives, being passionate and curious about the things around them. This was true of young Feng. He discovered he had a deep love for poetry. He kept a diary in which he recorded his innermost feelings, and the few textbooks on his classroom desk were buried beneath anthologies of Tang and Song poets and foreign poets such as Pushkin, Lermontov, Heine, Byron and Whitman. He so enjoyed reciting these poems that he would be transported for hours. Imitating his favorite writers, he began to write poems which he later edited into several volumes to which he gave high-sounding and abstruse titles, as well as designing the covers and even illustrating them. It gave him great pleasure to place his "works" alongside those of the masters he so admired. With so many distractions he could not concentrate on his class-work. His grades were merely about average. Weak in science, he often had to sit for posts to "pass."

After graduating from middle school, he one day chanced to meet on the street the coach of the Tianjin Men's Basketball Team, who discerned his promise and recruited him on the spot. That was the "first event" in his "tri-athelon." In the years that followed he became a fine player, but somehow could not part with the books and paintings he cherished. Every weekend he rushed home to engross himself in painting, or to indulge in reading novels, a pastime he found fascinating. He came to realize that playing basketball would not be his ultimate profession. He felt like a bird that had alighted on a blossoming branch. Though fragrant and beautiful, the branch could only serve as a transient resting place. The time came for him to change his life. An injury during a match meant that he had to quit the team, and provided the stimulus for him to devote himself in earnest to painting, which became his second profession.

At first he engaged himself in executing reproductions of ancient Chinese paintings. His great interest in genre painting resulted in his reproducing the famous work by the Song dynasty painter Zhang Zeduan, *Tomb Sweeping Festival by the Riverside*. At this time he also made a copy of this painting for Bettie Lord Bao, the Chinese-American writer. With the passage of time his artistic interests shifted from Chinese to Western works, from the classical to the modern, and from academic to folk art. For a time he extensively studied folk arts: kite making, clay sculpture, tile engraving, New Year pictures, folk tales, and folk customs. Without giving it much thought, he documented his findings in short pieces which he contributed to the *Tianjin Evening News*. When these were published, he was excited and felt encouraged to try to write more. As he grew older, he came to know more about people, life, society and history. He felt painting was too restricted to express his feelings, and his views on man and the world. He became a writer, in order to express himself more fully; and this was his final performance in the "tri-athelon."

He commenced by working on a long historical novel, in collaboration with Li Dingxing, *The Boxers*, which was completed in 1977. This related events surrounding the Boxer Movement of the late nineteenth century and it chronicled the Boxers' struggle to protect the city of Tianjin against the Eight-Power Allied Forces.

He then turned his attention to the recently ended Cultural Revolution, and from his experiences of those eventful and chaotic years he drew materials for many of his later novels and short stories. The best known of these are novellas: *Wrong Road Strewn with Flowers* and *Ah!*, both written in 1979. The first relates the story of a group of young Red Guards who blindly follow the crazy revolution only to find themselves finally betrayed. *Ah!*, a prize-winner in the 1977-78 national novella competition, is a heart-felt cry against the brutalities of that "revolution." His short story, *Figure-Carved Pipe*, a prize-winner in the 1979 national short story competition, is a moving story contrasting a famous painter and an ordinary gardener.

The title story in the anthology, *The Tall Woman and Her Short Husband*, is a touching tale of a couple who despite a 6.7 inches difference in height stay together for life and remain fond of each other, indifferent to the jeers of their neighbors. Come rain or shine, they can be seen walking together, the tall woman carrying her baby, while her short husband strains to hold up an umbrella to shield her from the sun or the rain. During the Cultural Revolution the woman's persecution results in her death. Now a widower, the husband continues to promenade, still holding high out of habit the umbrella with nothing beneath it. This painful void will never be filled for all his remaining years.

As befits a basketball player turned writer, many of his works deal with the lives of athletes. The most popular ones are *Above Love*, *A Hungarian Bike*, and *A Bunch of Flowers for You*.

Feng Jicai writes with great care and craftsmanship. He once said, "I never write from instinct. Before I start writing a novel I always turn the characters round in my mind until clear images appear before my eyes."

Between 1980 and 1983 Feng turned out one novel a year: *Against Cold*, *Magical Light*, *Man Amidst Mist*, and *Into the Rainstorm*, as well as a great many short stories. *Magical Light* portrays ten women who fought in 1900 side by side with the Boxers against the invading forces.

Feng Jicai is a great historical writer. In 1985 he started writing *Voices from the Cultural Revolution*, with the intention of chronicling the years from 1966 to 1976 through the vivid oral accounts of one hundred different persons.

Commencing in 1984 he also began writing another major series of culturally-oriented novels, entitled "Absurdities in an Absurd Age." The series has resulted from his assiduous studies of traditional Chinese culture. His style is now a blend of realism, semi-realism and legend, a mixture of the serious and popular. Like genre paintings, his cultural novels reflect late Qing and early Republican life and society. He uses Tianjin dialect in the narrative and dialogue, bringing bygone social customs to life in these works.

The author takes the view that while traditional Chinese culture is rich and profound, it is also insular. For the past century or more, China's door has been frequently opened only to be slammed shut shortly afterwards, then reopened and closed again. This has been one of the causes of constant social upheaval. With the door to the rest of the world closed, the Chinese took an overweening pride in their culture, but when exposed to other cultures, they were overwhelmed by feelings of inferiority. These extreme reactions resulted in an inability to arrive at a correct understanding of Chinese culture and its Western counterparts, and this unbalanced national mentality hindered the progress of Chinese society. This message is expressed through the actions of the characters in all of these cultural novels.

The first in this series, *The Miraculous Pigtail*, was written in 1984 and has since proved to be a sensation. It won the Third National Best Novella Prize. The protagonist has a miraculous pigtail that he uses as a lethal weapon to defeat his rivals—hooligans, pretentious boxers and even Japanese swash bucklers, who challenge him to duels. He is the author's ideal character—neither arrogant nor self-abasing when dealing with other people, including foreigners. This novel has been adapted into an extremely interesting film that has also been a great hit.

The second, *Small Bound Feet*, was finished in 1986. It portrays a group of young ladies who, as victims of feudal convention, compete with each other in binding their feet, an inhuman practice which the author attacks as a symbol of feudal culture.

The third novel *Yin-Yang and the Eight Trigrams*, finished in early 1988, turns to Taoism for its inspiration.

Feng is sanguine and loquacious, unlike some Chinese writers who tend to be reserved and taciturn. A social activist, Feng is now a member of the Chinese People's Political Consultative Conference, director of the Chinese Writers Association, and vice-chairman of the Tianjin

Artists' Federation. At the Fifth National Conference of the China Federation of Literary and Art Circles held in November 1988, he was elected one of the Federation's executive vice-chairpersons. To promote free debate in literature and art and to voice his own views, he edits two magazines—*Free Speech in Literature* and *Artists*.

Feng Jicai is now a world renowned figure. He has traveled extensively in North America and Europe. The American *Marquise Who's Who* included him in its 1985 edition. An anthology of his stories entitled *Chrysanthemum and Other Stories* has been published in the United States, and his novels have also been published in the Federal Republic of Germany and the Soviet Union.

May 1989

The Tall Woman and Her Short Husband

Feng Jicai

1.

SUPPOSE you have a small tree in your yard and are used to its smooth trunk. If one day it were to become twisted and gnarled it would strike you as awkward. As time goes by, however, you will grow to like it, as if that was how this tree should always have been. Were it suddenly to straighten out again you would feel indescribably put out. A trunk as dull and boring as a stick! In fact it would simply have reverted to its original form, so why should you worry?

Is this force of habit? Well, don't underestimate "habit." It runs through everything done under the sun. It is not a law to be strictly observed, yet flouting it is simply asking for trouble. Don't complain though if it proves so binding that sometimes you conform to it unconsciously. For instance, do you presume to throw your weight about before your superiors? Do you air your views recklessly in front of your seniors? When a group photograph is taken, can you shove celebrities aside to stand swaggering and smirking in the middle? You can't, of course you can't. Or again, would you choose a wife ten years older than you, heftier than you or a head taller than you? Don't be in a rush to answer.

85

Here's an instance of such a couple.

2.

She was six point seven inches taller than he.

Five feet nine inches in height, she towered above most of her sex like a crane over chickens. Her husband, a little over five feet two inches, had been nicknamed Shorty at college. He came up to her ear-lobes but actually looked two heads shorter.

And take their appearances. She looked dried up and scrawny with a face like an unvarnished pingpong bat. Her features would pass, but they were small and insignificant as if carved in shallow relief. She was flat-chested, had a ramrod back and buttocks as scraggy as a scrubbing-board. Her husband on the other hand seemed a rubber rolypoly: well-fleshed, solid and radiant. Everything about him—his calves, insteps, lips, nose and fingers—was like pudgy little meatballs. He had a soft skin and a fine complexion shining with excess fat and ruddy with all the red blood in his veins. His eyes were like two little high-voltage light bulbs, while his wife's were like glazed marbles. The two of them just did not match, they formed a marked contrast. But they were inseparable.

One day some of their neighbors were having a family reunion. After drinking his fill the grandfather put a tall, thin empty wine bottle on the table next to a squat tin of pork.

"Who do these remind you of?" he asked. Before anyone could guess he gave the answer, "That tall woman downstairs and that short husband of hers."

Everyone burst out laughing. Went on laughing all through the meal.

What had brought such a pair together?

This was a mystery to the dozens of households livng in Unity Mansions. Ever since this couple moved in, the old residents had eyed them curiously. Some registered a question-mark in their minds, others put their curiosity into words. Tongues started wagging. Especially in wet weather, when the two of them went out and it was always Mrs Tall who held the umbrella. If anything dropped to the ground, though, it was simpler for Mr Short to pick it up. Some old ladies at a loose end would gesticulate, finding this comic, or splutter with laughter. This set a bad example for the children who would burst out laughing at sight of the pair and hoot, "Long carrying-pole; big, low stool!" Husband and wife pretended not to hear and kept their tempers, paying no attention. But maybe for this reason, their relations with their neighbors remained rather cool. The few less officious ones simply nodded a greeting when they met. This made it hard for those really intrigued by them to find out more about them. For instance, how did they hit it off? Why had they married? Which gave way to the other? They could only speculate.

This was an old-fashioned block of flats with large sunny rooms and wide, dark corridors. It stood in a big courtyard with a small gatehouse. The man who lived there was a tailor, a decent fellow. His wife, who brimmed over with energy, liked to call on her neighbors and gossip. Most of all she liked to ferret out their secrets. She knew exactly how husbands and wives got on, why sisters-in-law quarreled, who was lazy, who hard-working, and how much everyone earned. If she was unclear about anything she would leave no stone unturned to get at the truth. The thirst for knowledge makes even the ignorant wise. And in this respect she was outstanding. She analyzed conversations, watched expressions, and could even tell what people were secretly thinking. Simply by using her nose, she knew which household was eating meat or fish, and from that could deduce their income. For some reason or other, ever since the 1960s each housing estate had chosen someone like this as a "neighborhood activist," giving legal status to these nosey-parkers so that their officiousness could have full play. It seems the Creator will never waste any talent.

Though the tailor's wife was indefatigable, she failed to discover how this incongruous couple who passed daily before her eyes had come to marry. She found this most frustrating; it posed a formidable challenge. However, by racking her brains she finally came up with a plausible explanation, on the basis of her experience: either husband or wife must have some physiological deficiency. Otherwise no one would marry someone a whole head taller or shorter. Her grounds for this reasoning were that after three years of marriage they still had no children. The inmates of Unity Mansions were all convinced by this brilliant hypothesis.

But facts are merciless. The tailor's wife was debunked and lost face when Mrs Tall appeared to all and sundry to be in the family way. Her womb could be seen swelling from day to day, for being relatively far from the ground it was all too evident. Regardless of their amazement, misgivings or embarrassment, she gave birth to a fine baby. When the sun was hot or it rained and the couple went out, Mrs Tall would carry the baby while the holding of the umbrella devolved on Mr Short. He plodded along comically on his plump legs, the umbrella held high, keeping just behind his wife. And the neighbors remained as intrigued as at the start by this ill-assorted, inseparable couple. They went on making plausible conjectures, but could find no confirmation for any of them.

The tailor's wife said, "They must have something to hide, those two. Why else should they keep to themselves? Well, it's bound to come to light some day, just wait and see."

One evening, sure enough, she heard the sound of smashing crockery emanating from their flat. On the pretext of collecting the money for sweeping the yard she rushed to knock on their door, sure that their long hidden feud had come to a head and avid to watch the confrontation between them. The door opened. Mrs Tall asked her in with a smile. Mr Short was smiling too at a smashed plate on the floor—that was all the tailor's wife saw. She hastily collected the money and left to puzzle over what had happened. A plate smashed, yet instead of quarreling they had treated it as a joke. How very strange!

Later the tailor's wife became the residents' representative for Unity Mansions. When she helped the police check up on residence permits, she at last found the answer to this puzzle. A reliable and irrefutable answer. The tall woman and her short husband both worked in the Research Institute of the Ministry of Chemical Industry. He as chief engineer, with a salary of over one hundred and eighty *yuan*! She as an ordinary laboratory technician earning less than sixty *yuan*; and her father was a hard-working low-paid postman. So that explained why she had married a man so much shorter. For status, money and an easy life. Right! The tailor's wife lost no time in passing on this priceless information to all the bored old ladies in Unity Mansions. Judging others by themselves, they believed her.

At last this riddle was solved. They saw the light. Rich Mr Short was congenitally deficient; poor Mrs Tall, a money-grabber on the make. When they discussed the good luck of this tall woman who looked so like a horse, they often voiced resentment—especially the tailor's wife.

3.

Sometimes good luck turns into bad.

In 1966, disaster struck China. Great changes came into the lives of all the residents in Unity Mansions, which was like a microcosm of the whole country. Mr Short as chief engineer was the first to suffer. His flat was raided, his furniture moved out, he was struggled against and confined in his institute. And worse was to come. He was accused of smuggling out the results of his research to write them up at home in the evenings, with a view to fleeing the country to join a wealthy relative abroad. This preposterous charge of passing on scientific secrets to foreign capitalists was widely believed. For in that period of lunacy people took leave of their senses and cruelly made up groundless accusations in order to find some Hitler in their midst. The institute kept a stranglehold on its chief engineer. He was threatened, beaten up, put under all kinds of pressure; and his wife was ordered to hand over that manuscript which no one had ever seen. But to no effect. Then someone proposed holding a struggle meeting against them both in the courtyard of Unity Mansions. As everyone dreads losing face in front of relatives and friends, this would put more pressure on them. Since all else had failed, it was at least worth trying.

Never before had Unity Mansions been the scene of

such excitement.

In the afternoon the institute sent people to fix up ropes between two trees in the yard, on which to hang a poster with the name of Mr Short on it—crossed out. Inside and outside the yard they pasted up threatening slogans, and on the wall put up eighteen more posters listing the engineer's "crimes." As the meeting was to be held after supper, an electrician was sent to fix up four big 500-watt bulbs. By now the tailor's wife, promoted to be the chairperson of the Neighborhood's Public Security Committee, was a powerful personage, full of self-importance, and much fatter than before. She had been busy all day bossing the other women about, helping to put up slogans and make tea for the revolutionaries from the institute. The wiring for the lights had been fixed up from her gatehouse. Really as if she were celebrating a wedding!

After supper the tailor's wife assembled all the residents in the yard, lit up as brilliantly as a sportsground at night. Their shadows, magnified ten-fold, were thrown on the wall of the building. These shadows stayed stock-still, not even the children daring to play about. The tailor's wife led to the gate a group wearing red armbands, in those days most awe-inspiring, who were to stand guard in order to keep outsiders out. Presently a crowd from the institute, wearing armbands and shouting slogans, marched in the tall woman and her short husband. He had a placard hung round his neck, she had none. The two of them were marched in front of the platform, and stood there side by side with lowered heads.

The tailor's wife darted forward. "This wretch is too short for the revolutionary masses at the back to see," she cried. "I'll soon fix that." She dashed into the gatehouse, her fat shoulders heaving, to fetch a soapbox which she turned upside down. Mr Short standing on this was the same height as his wife. But at this point little attention was paid to the relative heights of this couple facing disaster.

The meeting followed the customary procedure. After slogans had been shouted, passionate accusations were made, punctuated by more slogans. The pressure built up. First Mrs Tall was ordered to come clean, to produce that "manuscript." Questions and denunciations were fired at her, hysterical screams, angry shouts and threatening growls. But she simply shook her head gravely and sincerely. What use was sincerity? To believe in her would have made the whole business a farce.

No matter what bullies sprang forward to shake their fists at her, or what tricky questions were asked to try to trap her, she simply shook her head. The members of the institute were at a loss, afraid that if this went on the struggle meeting would fizzle out and end up as a fiasco.

The tailor's wife had listened with mounting exasperation. Being illiterate she took no interest in the "manuscript" they wanted, and felt these research workers were too soft-spoken. All of a sudden she ran to the platform. Raising her right arm with its red armband she pointed accusingly at Mrs Tall.

"Say!" she screeched. "Why did you marry him?"

The members of the institute were staggered by this unexpected question. What connection had it with their investigation?

Mrs Tall was staggered too. This wasn't the sort of question asked these days. She looked up with surprise on her thin face which showed the ravages of the last few months.

"So you don't dare answer, eh?" The tailor's wife

raised her voice. "I'll answer for you! You married this scoundrel, didn't you, for his money? If he didn't have money who'd want such a short fellow!" She sounded rather smug, as if she alone had seen through Mrs Tall.

Mrs Tall neither nodded nor shook her head. She had seen through the tailor's wife too. Her eyes glinted with derision and contempt.

"All right, you won't admit it. This wretch is done for now, he's a broken reed. Oh, I know what you're thinking." The tailor's wife slapped her chest and brandished one hand gloatingly. Some other women chimed in.

The members of the institute were flummoxed. A question like this was best ignored. But though these women had strayed so far from the subject, they had livened up the meeting. So the institute members let them take the field. The women yelled:

"How much has he paid you? What has he bought you? Own up!"

"Two hundred a month isn't enough for you, is it? You have to go abroad!"

"Is Deng Tuo[1] behind you?"

"That day you made a long-distance call to Beijing, were you ringing up the Three Family Village?"[2]

The success of a meeting depends on the enthusiasm worked up. The institute members who had convened this meeting saw that the time was ripe now to shout a few more slogans and conclude it. They then searched Mrs Tall's flat, prising up floorboards and stripping off wallpaper. When they discovered nothing, they marched her husband away, leaving her behind.

Mrs Tall stayed in all the next day but went out alone after dark, unaware that, though the light in the gatehouse was out, the tailor's wife was watching her from the window. She trailed her out of the gate and past two crossroads till Mrs Tall stopped to knock softly on a gate. The tailor's wife ducked behind a telegraph pole and waited, holding her breath, as if to pounce on a rabbit when it popped out of its burrow.

The gate creaked open. An old woman led out a child.

"All over, is it?" she asked.

Mrs Tall's answer was inaudible.

"He's had his supper and a sleep," the old woman said. "Take him home quickly now."

The tailor's wife realized that this was the woman who minded their little boy. Her excitement died down as Mrs Tall turned back to take her son home. All was silence apart from the sound of their footsteps. The tailor's wife stood motionless behind the telegraph pole till they had gone, then scurried home herself.

The next morning when Mrs Tall led her son out, her eyes were red. No one would speak to her, but they all saw her red, swollen eyes. Those who had denounced her the previous day had a strange feeling of guilt. They turned away so as not to meet those eyes. After the struggle meeting Mr Short was not allowed home again. The tailor's wife, who was in the know, said he had been imprisoned as an active counter-revolutionary. That made Mrs Tall the lowest of the low, naturally unfit to live in a roomy flat. She was forced to change places with the tailor's wife and move into the little gatehouse. This didn't worry her, as it meant she could avoid the other residents who snubbed her. But they could look through her window and see her all alone there. Where she had sent her son, they didn't know; he only came home for a few days at a time. Ostracized by all, she looked older than a woman in her thirties.

"Mark my words," the tailor's wife said, "she can only

keep this up for at most a year. Then if Shorty doesn't get out she'll have to remarry. If I were her I'd get a divorce and remarry. Even if he's let out his name will be mud, and he won't have any money."

A year went by, still Mr Short didn't come back and Mrs Tall kept to herself. In silence she went to work, came back, lit her stove and went out with a big shabby shopping basket. Day after day she did this, the whole year round.... But one day in autumn Mr Short reappeared—thinly clad, his head shaven, his whole appearance changed. He seemed to have shrunk and his skin no longer gleamed with health. He went straight to his old flat. Its new master, the honest tailor, directed him to the gatehouse. Mrs Tall was squatting in the doorway chopping firewood. At the sound of his voice she sprang up to stare at him. After two year's separation both were appalled by the change in the other. One was wrinkled, the other haggard; one looked taller than before, the other shorter. After gazing at each other they hastily turned away, and Mrs Tall ran inside. When finally she came out again, he had picked up the axe and squatted down to chop firewood, until two big boxes of wood had been chopped into kindling, as if he feared some new disaster might befall them at any moment. After that they were inseparable again, going to work together and coming back together just as before. The neighbors, finding them unchanged, gradually lost interest in them and ignored them.

One morning Mrs Tall had an accident. Her husband rushed frantically out and came back with an ambulance to fetch her. For days the gatehouse was empty and dark at night. After three weeks Mr Short and a stranger appeared, carrying Mrs Tall on a stretcher. She was confined to her room. He went to work as usual, hurrying back at dusk to light the stove and go out with the shopping basket. This was the same basket she had used every day. In his hand it looked even bigger and nearly reached the ground.

When the weather turned warmer, Mrs Tall came out. After so long in bed her face was deathly white, and she swayed from side to side. She held a cane in her right hand and kept her left elbow bent in front of her. Her half-paralysed left leg made walking difficult. She had obviously had a stroke. Every morning and every evening Mr Short helped her twice round the yard, painfully and slowly. By hunching up his shoulders he was able to grip her crooked arm in both hands. It was hard for him, but he smiled to encourage her. As she couldn't raise her left foot, he tied a rope round it and pulled this up when she wanted to take a step forward. This was a pathetic yet impressive sight, and the neighbors were touched by it. Now when they met the couple, they nodded cordially to them.

4.

Mrs Tall's luck had run out: she was not to linger long by the side of the short husband who loved her so dearly. Death and life were equally cruel to her. Life had struck her down and now death carried her off. Mr Short was left all alone.

But after her death fortune smiled on him again. He was rehabilitated, his confiscated possessions were returned, and he received all his back pay. Only his flat, occupied by the tailor's wife, was not given back to him. The neighbors watched to see what he would do. It was said that some of his colleagues had offered to find him another wife, but he had declined their propositions.

"I know the kind of woman he wants," said the tailor's wife. "Just leave it to me!"

Having passed her zenith she had become more subdued. Stripped of her power, she had to wear a smile. With a photograph of a pretty girl in her pocket, she went to the gatehouse to find Mr Short. The girl in the picture was her niece.

She sat in the gatehouse sizing up its furnishings as she proposed this match to rich Mr Short. Smiling all over her face, she held forth with gusto until suddenly she realized that he had said not a word, his face was black, and behind him hung a picture of him and Mrs Tall on their wedding day. Then she beat a retreat without venturing to produce the photograph of her niece.

Since then several years have passed. Mr Short is still a widower, but on Sundays he fetches his son home to keep him company. At the sight of his squat lonely figure, his neighbors recall all that he has been through and have come to understand why he goes on living alone. When it rains and he takes an umbrella to go to work, out of force of habit perhaps, he still holds it high. Then they have the strange sensation that there is a big empty space under that umbrella, a vacuum that nothing on earth can fill.

May 1982
Translated by Gladys Yang

Notes:

[1] Deng Tuo (1912-66), Chinese historian, poet and essayist, was

the Party secretary of Beijing in charge of cultural and educational work. He was considered a counter-revolutionary in the years of the Cultural Revolution.

[2] In 1961 Deng Tuo, Wu Han (1909-69, historian) and Liao Mosha (1907-, writer) started a magazine column "Notes from the Three Family Village" and published many essays which were well received. During the Cultural Revolution the three scholars were falsely charged as the "Three Family Village."

JIA PINGWA AND HIS FICTION

Sun Jianxi

Jia Pingwa was born in 1952, on the twenty-first day of the second month of the lunar calendar. His birthplace is Lihua Township, Danfeng County in Shaanxi Province. This is the Qinling Mountain area, and a tributary of the Yangtze, named the Danjiang, flows alongside the township. Jia Pingwa's father, Jia Yanchun, teaches Chinese at a local middle school, and his mother is an ordinary village woman. At the time of Jia Pingwa's birth, the whole family of twenty-two souls ate from the same pot. Because his grandmother was still alive and well, and the four male siblings of his father's generation did not divide the property, they all lived with their wives and children in a small courtyard. Each small family was allotted a living space of only ten square meters. In Jia Yanchun's family Jia Pingwa was the oldest son, but in the extended family he was number eight. In such a large family there are lots of mouths to feed, so of course life was tough, but under the strict authority of the oldest uncle, the four brothers and their wives got along fairly well. The children had to take their own seats to school, but there were not enough stools at home for all of them, so the oldest uncle made a rule: only the children who passed the test for advanced primary school could take stools from home, and the ones who went to basic primary school would only get two split logs. Jia Pingwa spent four years of primary school sitting on two split logs, laid between the stools of two of his schoolmates. The old temple that served as his schoolroom is full of associations for him. Seeing the aged murals on its walls, and the verses inscribed there long ago, Jia Pingwa would ask his teachers many questions. His curiosity left such an impression that even now his former teachers, now retired, are unanimous in saying: "That boy was a history buff from an early age." He was studious and obedient in primary school. He served as leader of a Young Pioneers detachment and acted in local variety programs.

But unfortunately just as he entered the second year of junior middle school, the Cultural Revolution broke out in China. Unable to continue his studies, he shouldered his bedroll and returned home to do farm work. This was in 1967, when he was fifteen years old. What was still more unfortunate, his ailing father was labeled a "historical counter-revolutionary" and dismissed from his post.

Thus the family lost its only source of support—his father could not obtain other work, and his brothers and sisters were still too young—so at fifteen Jia Pingwa shouldered the heavy burden of providing for them. At the time water reclamation projects were underway nationwide. Jia signed up to work at a reservoir site. He was small and not very strong, but he was an excellent calligrapher. This came to the notice of his superiors, who gave him the task of publishing a small newsletter that would publicize and spur on their project. Given this chance, Jia showed what he was made of: he concurrently handled editing, type carving, printing, distribution, and the commissioning of articles. The newsletter was a resounding success. Thus in May 1972, when Chinese universities began to accept students for the first time since the outset of the Cultural Revolution, he stepped into his rightful place as a student of Chinese literature at Northwest China University.

While on campus, he put all his energy into his studies and his writing. In August 1973 a Shaanxi magazine *Art for the Masses* published his maiden work, entitled "A Pair of Socks." This was the first time he used his pen name *Jia Pingwa*, which is written differently from his given name but pronounced the same. Years later in an autobiographical sketch he wrote that his mother had given him the name Pingwa (meaning "placid child") in the hope that life would go smoothly for him, but he changed it to mean "plains and lowlands" in acceptance of the tortuousness of life. In his three years at college, he published dozens of pieces and began to win a literary reputation nationwide.

Upon graduating in 1975 he was assigned to work as an editor at the Shaanxi People's Publishing House. Now that he was able for the first time to lead a somewhat settled life, his achievements in literature increased by leaps and bounds. At this stage he focused on writing short stories, taking his material from the villages of the Shangzhou countryside. These stories were marked by a pastoral quality, luminous and lingering like a shepherd's song. Most of his pieces from this period are collected in *Sketches of Mountain Country*, published in Shanghai; and *New Works of Jia Pingwa*, published by the China Youth Press. In 1978 when China's beleaguered realm of fiction held its first selection, Jia's *Full Moon* won a top award. He was twenty-six at the time. One assessment of him at the time was that he had the capacity to be strongly affected by life, that he had remarkable story ideas, and that he used language in a highly individual way. This is a good description of the state of his writing at the period of *Full Moon*.

In the following years he made extensive contacts at

the underbelly of Chinese society and witnessed many abuses. In agonized deliberation, the edge of his thought cut through to things that are deeply embedded in the Chinese national character. With unusual boldness and a sober artistic conscience, he touched on weighty and disturbing subjects in stories like *Apricots in February*, *City of Ghosts*, *Pilgrimage*, and *Late Cry*. These stories led to sharp differences of opinion on the Chinese literary scene. Some said that Jia Pingwa should be given serious attention, while others claimed he was traveling a dangerous path. Jia himself remained untroubled: his stories might have social implications, but in the end they were literature. He extended his field of creative vision over the territory of great Chinese and foreign authors, both ancient and modern. At this stage he delved into the works of great ancient Chinese writers and thinkers: *Lao Tzu: the Way and Its Power*, *Records of the Historian*, *The Master Who Embraces Simplicity*, *New Anecdotes of Social Talk*, *Strange Tales of Liaozhai*, *The Book of Mountains and Seas*, etc. He studied philosophy and probed into religion. He looked into the conditions of people's lives and devoted attention to changes in folkways. At the same time he turned his gaze on certain respected novelists: Yasunari Kawabata of Japan, Tolstoy of Russia, and Gabriel Garcia Marquez of Latin America. He digested them and "read them to get them under his feet." In doing this he discovered himself: he was convinced that "the more rooted a work is in the character of one people, the more universal it is." But he also felt that dogged adherence to ancestral ways is no way to forge ahead in the world. He saw the necessity of drawing on techniques from many sources. He also felt that on a certain level great works may be technically flawed. We do not expect the Himalayas to have tiny, exquisite details. This was the direction of his efforts. He sought to write something with sweep and depth: he sought for a rough but solid grandeur. With this in mind he wrote a series of stories beginning with the *First Shangzhou Records*. The ten novellas he published in 1985 are representative of this series.

The stories of this series that have been best received by readers include the *Tale of Xiao Yue*, *First Month of the Year*, *Dog of Heaven*, *The Wildness of Far Mountains*, and *Old Fortress*. In reading these we clearly sense the broad scope of the author's thinking. His perspectives as a writer give all-embracing illumination to history and reality. His materials and subjects are rich and dense with many-layered meaning. It would not be wrong to say that his artistic framework is dispersed in form but not in spirit. In a grand, uninhibited manner he expresses the points of excitation that bring things alive. Just as a suite of variations has a muted theme running through it, his theme is concern for the Chinese people's personal qualities and their possibilities. It is his pained awareness of the current state of the spiritual culture of ordinary people, and his quest for the superior cultural force of the Han and the Tang dynasties. One critic commented that this series owes its richness of content partly to the strength of the author's feelings, partly to his intelligence, and to a lesser extent to his magic with words. These stories of Shangzhou, positioned in an extensive historical framework, are suffused with a penetrating but soft light that seems to emanate from a heatless source in the upper atmosphere, at once rational and capable of esthetic judgement. It is able to carry its overarching theme into particularized views of the tiniest things. These stories overflow with idealistic flashes of wisdom, and they bristle with a pointed critical impulse. At the same time they are pleasingly faithful word pictures, the savoring of which yields underlying truths of life.

In short, the ambitious structure of these novellas, their profound ideas and artistic mastery place him in a position of eminence and establish him as one of the foremost writers on the Chinese mainland. Thus the noted literary critic Ji Hongzhen, writing in the *Wenyi Qingkuang* (*Literary and Art Scene*), says, "Jia Pingwa has created his own richly significant, resonant style, and his accomplishments with it have scarcely been rivaled in the past thirty years of Chinese literature." His *First Month of the Year* won the national prize for novellas. In the ten years up to 1987, his works won twenty literary prizes. Five of his stories have been made into movies, and many others have been turned into television series. These adaptations have had extensive influence, both in China and abroad.

What is Jia Pingwa searching for in his art? In an afterword written for *A Jia Pingwa Anthology*—part of the New Novellas Series put out by The Strait Press—Jia wrote: "The highest goal of literary art is to express the writer's responses to man and his world. Through it he brings to light moving angles on life; on top of existence he builds the realm of his own impressions. I am searching for a thing that is elusive but vast, a demanding harmony, and my own maturity."

Beginning in 1985 Jia focused his main energies on writing novels. For this purpose he journeyed through more than seventy counties. He weathered unimaginable hardships and risked attacks by wild animals to survey customs and folkways deep in the mountains and remote regions. At the same time he collected unusual prescriptions for folk medicines and learned beautiful folk songs. This undoubtedly enriched and strengthened his creative thinking. He has published four novels, of which the best known in China and abroad is *Flightiness*, which first appeared in the Shanghai magazine *Harvest* in 1987. At the end of that year the Writers' Publishing House in Beijing published it in book form and invited over twenty well-known critics to discuss it at a special colloquium.

Flightiness is a book ambitious in structure and vast in content. It is a work that assesses China's realities from a high cultural vantage point. Taking the whole Shangzhou watershed within its purview, it describes the tortuous economic, political, and personal struggles to throw off poverty, feudalistic authority and mental obstacles as China's rural society confronts the 1980s. The work shows the abundance of the popular traditions the sons and daughters of Shangzhou have inherited, and the weight of grief which these have brought them. This combination makes them at once excitable, quick to anger, crude, bewildered, generous, loyal, narrow, ignorant, shallow, cunning, and flighty. The book captures the shallow, narrow quality of their pathological outcries and their manner of expression, arising from the impatient hunger and the desperate wish for human ideals and a good life of these men who have not clearly figured out where they stand. Deeply rooted in tradition, China's clan-oriented agrarian culture is decidedly unable to move to the rhythm of the far-reaching changes in modern life. It is solidly precipitated in the culture's psychic structures. Its influence is felt in every area of social consciousness. That is, people can destroy old cultural structures by violent revolution and erect new social structures. But people have a difficult time—perhaps it is impossible —doing away with a deep-seated cultural tradition and establishing a new culture according to individual understanding. In this work Jia Pingwa puts across what he

105

learned from his surveys in rounded form. This book is an integration of diverse achievements.

Nevertheless, Jia preserves a shy, retiring disposition which is at marked variance with his impressive career successes. He does not have the ready talkativeness of Tianjin and Beijing writers, nor the expressive face of writers from the South. Strictly speaking he will always be the son of an ordinary peasant, since he is unfailingly humble and kind, industrious and unassuming. Perhaps he has read too many books or gotten to the bottom of too many of life's mysteries: for whatever reason he leads a life of detachment. He eschews controversy and stays clear of frenetic activity. He is fond of visiting scenic spots, but he often avoids the literary meetings that are held at such places. He even begs to be excused from the many prize ceremonies in which he is one of the recipients. He is a tranquil person with few desires. His thoughts are often absorbed in pondering history and current reality.

Besides his fiction writing, he has written a great deal of poetry. he can extemporize new poems on the spot, showing a nimbleness of thought reminiscent of the Han dynasty's Cao Zhi, who composed a poem while walking seven steps. An example is this "Walking Staff Poem" improvised at a meeting:

> Place a walking staff in the ground,
> And hope it will bloom with red flowers;
> Throw pebbles into a pond,
> And watch the little tails of water;
> Press a sheet of paper under a pillow,
> And let dream paints a picture there.
> Paste a stamp over my heart,
> And send it to her, far away....

The Chinese literary scene is abuzz with stories of his poetic talent. Those who are not convinced find ways to put him on the spot, and the results leave them dumb with amazement. In November 1987 a friend of mine, Xiao Ersa, was asked by a magazine to verify Jia's poetic talent. Jia said, "All right, give me a subject!" Seeing that he was smoking a cigarette at the time, Mr Xiao said, "Make the subject cigarette smoking." Through the up-curling cigarette smoke, Jia's gaunt face seemed abstracted and detached, and finally the outlines of his face seemed to grow obscure. Mr Xiao was trying to make sense of these impressions, when out of the smoke came a philosopher's aged and faraway voice:

> Tobacco is a woman,
> A woman is a cigarette,
> Laying claim to men's lips,
> Knocking us off our feet.
> Or else this world would have been too hard and edged;
> It would explode with the restlessness of life.
> Yet women are against our smoking:
> This is the mystery of jealousy....

In 1986 the Huacheng Press in Guangdong published *Blankness*, a collection of Jia's poems. This collection brought a breath of fresh wind to China's somber, mist-obscured poetry scene. Jia says that poetry should abound everywhere. Whichever career a person chooses, success is due to many things, but one of the most important is a poetic spirit. Writing novels, he says, is a toil that keeps him up at night. When he comes to the point of exhaustion, and he wants to extract some pleasure out of his troubles, poetry is just the thing. Poetry is relaxing and pleasing, but it can also stir wild passions, making his heart surge with a plenitude of things to write about. Poetry gives him inexhaustible energy: it helps him keep in mind the beauty of work.

Chinese calligraphy occupies a unique place in the history of world art. It has been called soundless music and painting without color. Jia Pingwa has been a devotee of the brush from an early age. This is why his talent was spotted by his leaders at the reservoir worksite. Once he went out into society, calligraphy became his method of unloading pent-up feelings. Wherever he travels to attend meetings, do field studies or give classes, there is always a crowd of admirers with brush and ink ready asking him to write characters—a doorway hanging, a scroll, a couplet, or a centerpiece painting. The works of his pen are in great demand among his readers. His calligraphy has made its way to every corner of the country, from Guangzhou in the South to Beijing in the North.

Jia remarks, "Poetry can emerge through symbols arranged in lines. But you can also use lines themselves to express it. That is what painting and calligraphy do. There are times like this: I am on a shaded mountain road, seeing flowers bloom and wither, watching clouds drift apart, or gazing at a footbridge over a stream beside somebody's house; there is a silhouetted mountain or a moonrise or sleepy ducks—these things get my poetic juices flowing. They have a significance for me which I can't put into words, so I paint them. When I'm sitting in a room reading a letter from home, I run my fingers over a paperweight: my recollections go back to my childhood and the country people I knew. Poetic feeling wells up inside me, but I cannot write it down, and a painting would not convey everything, so I write a scroll of large characters. Poetry, calligraphy and painting fit together as a whole, but each has its own function. They help me get rid of my moroseness and bring me peace. When I am excited they put me in a ferment: I let myself go and feel an almost drunken intoxication."

His painting is mainly imagistic, and he throws away his work when he finishes it. Though his painting has not found a place in the refined setting of an exhibition, it has been carved on printing blocks and published as a folk collection in Shaanxi. Years later collectors offered high prices for these works but could not buy them. In short, calligraphy, poetry and painting have become part of his creative work. Some say he possesses artistic genius, but he claims to be an honest-to-goodness farm boy. Whichever he is, his inspiration and sensitivity are amazing. As the famed critic Yan Gang remarked, he is "that gifted young man from Shangzhou." And indeed there is something of the prodigy about him.

As of 1988, at the age of 36, he had published a total of thirty books: in ten years he wrote nearly five million Chinese characters, though he only became a full-time writer in 1982. Before that he was an editor and could write only in his spare time. His most famous works have earned him a place at the forefront of young Chinese writers.

Touch Paper, originally published in the monthly *Shanghai Literature* in 1986, is one of the later novellas in his Shangzhou series. It tells the love story of a man who chops bamboo and a woman who makes touch paper in a remote mountain village. In the primitive production relationship of their household workshop, their difficult love is finally smothered by society's feudal ideas.

It is an age-old theme, but under the talented pen of Jia Pingwa, it yields, as if by magic, philosophical meaning. The young couple living in the remote mountains becomes the subject of the conflict described by the ancient Chinese philosophical notion that bamboo as water and paper as fire promote and restrain each other (the unity of opposites); the means of this transformation is the old-fashioned workshop production. Everything there is old and ossified: ancient philosophical notions, the ignorance of the age-old mountain village, old and backward production methods, old and backward thought; only the youth and love of the young couple are fresh and alive. The author uses the old ossified "hard crust" to stifle vitality and he uses the touch paper, made using old methods by those once brimming with love and life, to burn as if in sacrifice their youth, their love and their lives. This artistic notion is truly a return of Lao Tzu's philosophical concept of the fusion of dualities.

The artistic value of *Touch Paper*, as far as Jia Pingwa is concerned, lies in the movement from the "Elegy" of the "Ghost Town" to Shangzhou's dawn light, from writing of the events of change to writing of the transformation of people in times of reform, from description of particulars to significant generalization, from implication to symbolism.

The significance of *Touch Paper* in the development of contemporary Chinese fiction lies in the author's starting with the esthetics of Chinese philosophy and using a contemporary awareness of social and economic reform to temper primitivism and create a new realist literature. The critic Chang Zhiqi writes in a piece in the *Xiaoshuo Pinglun* (*Fiction Criticism*), "A fiction that truly unites an appreciation of Chinese philosophy and the cultural consciousness of the Chinese people to reflect contemporary Chinese society could be beginning with *Touch Paper*."

Now he has many roles. He is a director of the Chinese Writers Association, vice-chairman of the Shaanxi Writers Association, vice-chairman of the Federation of

Literary and Art Circles of Xi'an, and a delegate to the People's Congresses of Shaanxi Province and Xi'an Municipality.

One of his favorite comments is "I will always be a writer for the common man."

Translated by Denis C. Mair
and Cathy Silber

TOUCH PAPER

Jia Pingwa

1.

SLENDER green bamboo clung steadfastly to the gaps in the cliff face. A youth threw bundles of bamboo down onto the rocks below, then tossed his cutting knife down too. It fell silently, and shone with a cold brightness, like a lost crescent moon.

It was dusk over the Han River, time to rest at last after a hard day's work, when the young man took three syrup cakes out from under a rock and sat gazing dreamily over the river where it flowed past the cliff. Syrup cake is wrapped in the leaves of the Mongolian oak, then steamed, so it looks like a glutinous rice cake, and when you open it, the veins of the oak leaves are clearly printed on the cake. Just as he was about to eat them, a crow began circling overhead. Although it had not discovered the cakes when they were hidden under the stone, now it came down and snapped up all the crumbs that fell to the ground as the young man ate, and even snatched a piece from the youth's hand before swiftly flying away. At that moment a shuttle boat sped by, so fast that it would soon disappear behind the cliff where it jutted out into the river. At the bow of the boat stood the boatman holding a punt-pole. He sang in a wolf-like voice:

When you take my hand,
I want to kiss your lips,
Take my hand,
Kiss your lips,
Deep into the mountains the two of us stroll....

This boat carried men along the river to the dense forests in the mountains in the north where they cut laquer. It set out from Twin River Pass, and moored for the night at Gourd Town.

At Gourd Town was Sun Erniang's teahouse. It was said that men from the river would arrive there worn out from their work, flop into the bamboo chairs, sip tea, have a smoke, and listen to Sun Erniang play her *pipa*[1] and softly sing mountain songs. After one had heard a number of her songs one began daydreaming about being out on the river in one's boat, wearing a raincoat made of woven rushes, singing those scandalous ditties and savoring the joys of one's imagination.

The young man thought, Dad had taken this boat up to the forests in the mountains to cut lacquer. He had gone miles to cut and cut for a bit of lacquer, only to have his clothes ripped to shreds cutting incisions into the rough lacquer trees and inserting shells into the incisions. The fate of the lacquer tree was a bitter one indeed. Every spring and summer they would be lacerated by knives. When the bark of the thicker parts had been cut until it could be cut no more, then it was the turn of the thinner parts, until all the good bark had been cut and the sap dried up. Then the tree died, and so did Dad. Dad had been poisoned by lacquer. He was not at all scared of it. However when lacquer got spattered on your clothes you could not wash it off, nor could you wash it off your face and hands, so your face and hands festered. They festered until, like the tree, you had no good skin left, then you died.

Below the cliff somebody yelled in a piercing voice, then shouted abuse, "Dog Ah Ji, what on earth are you doing up there?" Ah Ji was the youth's nickname. His real surname was Liu and his given name Ji. Dog referred to the dog that belonged to Pockmarks Wang who ran the touch paper mill at Seven Mile Flat. Dog often followed Pockmarks Wang's daughter Chouchou around, so when the other youths wanted to make fun of Ah Ji they said he had never seen a girl in his life and thus had even less luck than Dog.

Ah Ji wandered down to the base of the cliff, watching as he went the evening sun shine up the Han River. The cliff face glowed with the dim red of the fading sunlight, while he himself still cast a clear shadow in the bamboo grove and his skin and hair were tinged with the green of the foliage around him. Down on the river bank, the others had already made wooden rafts and piled the bundles of cut bamboo onto them, so they helped Ah Ji make his raft. They blew up two tyre tubes and tied them to the bottom of the wooden platform, then piled the bamboo onto it.

"Ah Ji, have you seen Wang Qi?"

"No."

"He was sitting on the shuttle boat. He cut thirty *jin*[2] of lacquer—made even more money!"

"And he's swollen all over. I'm not going to cut lacquer!"

"Do you think you can get anywhere near a woman with your bamboo cutting? If you don't produce a son for your Dad, you're not a good son!"

"Let's go back. It's getting late."

Ah Ji jumped onto the raft and pushed off with his

puntpole. His raft shot out into the middle of the river and he followed the current downstream. The others soon caught up and formed a straight line behind. By the time they reached Seven Mile Flat it was already dark. The window of the touch paper mill, which was at the entrance to the village, was a blood red color, and the water wheel made a deep splashing noise as it slowly turned and plunged heavily into the water. Ah Ji shivered involuntarily, as every time he heard the sound of that water wheel he became agitated, and dawdled around behind the others.

"Ah Ji, are you handing in your bamboo?"

"You go first, I'll be there in a minute."

The others hauled the wet bamboo to the open ground in front of the workshop, and looked toward the door of the bamboo crushing room. An oil lamp hung from the main beam of the room and cast an even, reddish light, like a sun. The water wheel stood vertically and turned, driving a large square wooden crusher, while Chouchou sat beside it pulling out the crushed bamboo. When the crusher rose, you could see the outline of Chouchou's body and her pale face. When it dropped, her body and pale face disappeared from view. Ah Ji really worried that one day Chouchou would forget what she was doing, or doze off, and the wooden crusher would make minced meat out of her. Of course Ah Ji's concern was unwarranted, for Chouchou had been pulling bamboo out from the crusher for two years and had not lost a hair.

Just then Dog came rushing out from the workshop, barked loudly, and launched an attack on Ah Ji. The sight of Ah Ji being attacked by Dog who could not speak the language of humans gave great amusement to the other bamboo cutters.

115

"Chouchou, your dog is going to bite Ah Ji to death. Aren't you going to do anything about it?"

The water wheel inside the crushing room was very noisy, so Chouchou did not hear them. Instead Pockmarks Wang came out from the paper pressing room and yelled viciously, "What are you saying? If you don't get over here and weigh the bamboo, I won't take any in today!"

Ah Ji cursed Pockmarks to himself. "Nine Pockmarks out of ten are demons; if just one doesn't die it's a calamity!"

2.

The greatest cause of concern to Pockmarks was those youths who cut the bamboo, but he dared not offend them because the touch paper mill was privately run and the raw material for touch paper was the green bamboo which the bamboo cutters sold to him. He could not bear to look at them, but nor could he do without them. As he was not able to get along with them, life became very tiring.

Actually Pockmarks Wang could not be considered a bad man. During communization he had held a post as chairman of the Poor Peasants' Association. Because of his honest nature and his low position, he lived a life of strict frugality. While other people took every chance to grab whatever they could for themselves, he remained in his three roomed stone house with a stone table, stone mortar and pestle, and a gnarled pomegranate tree outside the door. People often said, "If someone has a big family, they never have money; if they have money, they never have a big family." He lacked nothing except money. He had nothing except his wife, who was ill and would die three years later. When his wife died, his daughter was only two, yet he never remarried nor got involved with other women, instead putting all his effort into bringing up Chouchou. Chouchou was his meticulously created work of art. He would carry her on his back to meetings, where he told her not to cry or make a fuss, and cry and make a fuss she did not. When a family in the village was dividing up their household to go and live in separate homes, he would go and oversee. Chouchou would be told not to eat other people's food, which she would not do even if it made her mouth water. By the time Chouchou was sixteen she was completely mature.

Then the communes were done away with and replaced by the township government, and the land was divided up and allocated to families to work themselves. Once father and daughter were up on the hillside digging together in their field, to the side of which grew a peach tree that had blossomed magnificently. Chouchou broke off one of the flowers and put it in her hair. Her father said, "Take that off now! It's as ugly as a goblin!" Another time, some youths in the village had gone down the Han River to Gourd Town, Baihe County and on to the city of Xiangyang, and come back with trousers that were tight at the waist and wide at the bottom, which made them seem instantly taller. Chouchou too sewed the waist of her trousers a little tighter, but when her father saw it he grew angry, saying, "You've turned into a demon," and demanded she loosen them back to their original style. Father Pockmarks enthusiastically welcomed the contract system of farming, but day after day complained about the decline in people's morals, saying people were no longer as pure and honest as they once were. At home he said to Chouchou, "See, people are really selfish. During communization they all loafed about and didn't work hard, but when each person got his own land to work, he worked like crazy! Crazy they might have been, but at least they were still honest peasants. Now they've all started going out and getting involved in trade, and there's never been a crook who wasn't a trader! In the old days if a family was building a house, there wasn't a family in the village that did not go and help. If there was a toilet to be dug, six or seven people would turn out to give a hand. Now they only care about money. If there's not a quid in it, nobody will do any work—they've all become so stuck-up and self-seeking. This policy has to be changed!"

However the countryside no longer had a poor peasants' organization, so Pockmarks' words were in vain. The policy had not changed. The differences were that Pockmarks' prestige had declined, his relations with others had taken a turn for the worse, and he was in dire financial straits. He had no choice but to set up the touch paper mill, because without money one could not do anything, so he converted his three roomed home into a mill. Pockmarks could make paper pulp, and Chouchou's uncle, an old man who could eat but not speak, was called in to scoop out the paper. Chouchou's job was to dig three big pits in the open ground in front of the workshop, put in one layer of bamboo, spread a layer of lime over it, cover the lime with a layer of straw, pour water over that, then bury it all with soil. Two or three months later, when the bamboo had rotted, she would dig it up and dry it in the sun, then sit by that thick square crusher day after day tending it as it crushed the bamboo into fine fibers.

When the water wheel was turning, it seemed nothing else existed outside the bamboo crushing room. Splash, splash. Thump, thump. At first Chouchou's insides had turned at every thump, but by now she did not even hear the noise. All she heard was a heart beating in her chest and a pulse beating in her wrist.

She often thought how strange things were in this world. Touch paper is fire, green bamboo is water, so water can become fire. Was it she, the papermaker, who was working this process of fusion and change between fire and water? Chouchou had not had much schooling, and there were many things she never thought of, or if she did, she could never explain them.

She had to grease the axle of the waterwheel, so she went outside the bamboo crushing room and breathed in the fresh air, looked at the solitary tree on the hill opposite and at the single cloud that floated above it. As she was watching the mist and waves on the river, she saw the rafts carrying bamboo drifting down towards her.

The bamboo cutters were sitting on the rafts, their heads shining and ears sticking out. When they got near the mill and saw Chouchou, they all shouted, "Chouchou, come and weigh the bundles of bamboo for us!"

At first Chouchou laughed, but the sun got in her eyes causing her to blink. "Chouchou, do you like mushrooms? These mushrooms aren't those dog piss ones. They're fleshy and really moist!"

Chouchou ran over. Her waist was very good, but her clothes were too long, so she hitched them up as she ran. When the bamboo cutters said that Chouchou had worn her clothes out, she blushed.

Pockmarks saw all this, so naturally he told Chouchou to go off and crush bamboo, and was as impatient as ever while doing the weighing. He divided the bamboo up into different varieties, then further divided them into grades according to size. He haggled with the youths over the price and grew extremely angry.

"Aren't you being too hard on us?" said one of the youths.

"Who's being hard on you? I've learnt to treat people as they deserve to be treated."

"You're not as good as Chouchou."

"Get off with you!"

When Chouchou saw that her father and the youths were arguing she came over and said, "Dad!" Pockmarks' face went all shades of red, and he yelled at her, "Go back and crush your bamboo!" The youths quickly took their money and left, while Chouchou did not go to the crushing room, but instead sat by the channel and sobbed, taking no notice when her father called her.

When Pockmarks saw Chouchou was crying, he calmed down, and taking his tobacco he went over and crouched down beside her, and lit up a cigarette. After exhaling a few times he said, "Chouchou, are you still angry with your dad? Dad's not blaming you for causing trouble, but he's worried that the sophisticated minds of people today will spoil you. We're decent folk, so although we work this mill, we're not doing anything disreputable; we live cleanly, so when the government changes its policy, nobody will be able to say anything against us."

As Chouchou listened to her father, her thoughts somehow turned to her mother. Her memories of her mother were very vague, and ten years of memories of her father rushed up in their place. Much of what her father said was correct, and who else in this world loved her so much? But what had she done wrong? Where had she lacked circumspection? Chouchou's mind was in a turmoil. She sat completely still watching the water in the channel babble and flow past her. After a while the water wheel started making its noises and the wooden crusher began its thumping. Chouchou could take it no more. She went into the factory and stood behind her father who was pulling crushed bamboo out of the crusher. Her father stood up and she stepped down into his place and began putting bamboo under the crusher. She heard her father say, "So my Chouchou does have some sense after all!"

From then on Dog lay across the entrance to the bamboo crushing room. He was snow-white except for two black eyes. For some reason, every time Chouchou saw the dog she thought of those young men who cut bamboo, but every time they came to hand in bamboo, Dog stood barking loudly by the door of the mill.

One day, Ah Ji bravely made his way towards the crushing room, and Dog went for him. Ah Ji had guts and bared his teeth even more fiercely than Dog. Chouchou stood up and said, "Ah Ji, that dog can really bite! What do you want?"

Ah Ji said, "Chouchou, can't you get out and go for a look around?"

"I have to crush bamboo," she answered.

Ah Ji said, "Your dad never gives up. He really makes life tough for you!"

Although Chouchou did not return Ah Ji's abuse of her father, she was not happy. Dog took a strong hold of Ah Ji's heel, but Ah Ji called Chouchou and threw her a yellow mountain apricot, while Dog pulled off one of Ah Ji's shoes. Chouchou caught the apricot and was throwing the shoe back, when her father came over. Chouchou stuffed the apricot in her mouth and went back to crushing bamboo. The apricot was really ripe, in fact so ripe that it melted into delicious sweet and sour juices as soon as she tried to chew it.

Ah Ji walked down to the bank of the Han River, abusing Pockmarks for being such an old fogey, and vowed to marry Chouchou whenever he got enough money. The other youths laughed at Ah Ji's wishful talk, but after teasing him a while they sighed, got on their rafts and made their way back to their respective villages. On the river they passed a shuttle boat headed for Gourd Town, upon which the boatman was singing boastfully:

> That's her opening her 'brella over there,
> Taking a cold kettle to boil herself some tea.
> Cold kettle boiling tea, tea doesn't boil,
> Made me laugh all the way to the south mountains,
>   north mountains, west mountains.
> Upon the ivory bed, on the lovers' pillows,
> Under the bedclothes I go looking for that flower,
> All of her white flesh soft like tender tea.

3.

Ah Ji's house, which was also built of stone, did not leak when it rained but was filled with spots of light when the sun came out. Ah Ji lay on the *kang*[3] and stared at a shaft of sunlight that shone down through the roof and at the myriad things that flew about in it, and thought about how to make money. If he could make money everything would be all right. He could fill his pockets with cash, go to the touch paper mill and say, "Pockmarks, I'll buy all your touch paper!" Pockmarks would be thrilled for sure, and would not treat him with his usual bad temper. Then he would raise the matter of marrying Chouchou, and next thing you know he'd be calling Pockmarks "Father-in-law"! But how to make money? Cutting bamboo he got a cent per *jin*, and if he worked hard he might make three dollars, which was just enough to feed himself on. There was no way he was going to cut lacquer, so if he wanted to earn money he just had to keep cutting bamboo, but there was not much money in that. Ah Ji said to himself, "Pockmarks, Pockmarks, you stubborn fogey. You've been inflexible all your life and want Chouchou to be the same. You'll see! I'll marry Chouchou and take her to wander the world. When you kick the bucket we'll take no notice and there will be nobody to act the dutiful son at your funeral. And although now you make touch paper, when you meet your end nobody will come and burn paper on your grave!"

Ah Ji had thought it all out, but as soon as he arrived at the touch paper mill he grew scared of Pockmarks and of the dog. So he went back to the cliff to cut bamboo, which he did until he was worn out and fed up, whereupon he made a *xiao*.[4] The people who lived by the Han River knew nothing of musical notation, but the art of playing the *xiao* had been passed down from generation to generation. He played a song of mourning, with such long doleful tones that the others in the bamboo grove felt a chill run down their spines. His mates said, "Ah Ji, Ah Ji, stop playing like that!" But Ah Ji kept playing, so the others could only sigh, "Chouchou's really stolen his heart!" When they called Ah Ji "Dog" before, it was just a joke, but now that he had really fallen in love with her, his mates tried hard to help him find a way to get her.

"Ah Ji, do you really want to marry Chouchou, or are you just doing it out of spite?"

"For real, and for spite!"

"OK then, you little lovebird, here's what you do. Go to Chouchou and put a bun in her oven. Pockmarks will of course hate you for it, but he'll want to save face, so he'll just have to take it on the chin and let you have your way, and there you are. Are you game?"

Ah Ji shook his head.

However, the other bamboo cutters really wanted to help, so when they went to hand in the bamboo some of them crowded around Pockmarks and led him into the paper pulp room, some of them took a bone and led Dog away from the mill, while Ah Ji slipped into the bamboo crushing room from behind the waterwheel to see Chouchou.

Chouchou went into a panic and said "You're brave! As soon as the dog barks, Dad will be in here screaming at me."

Ah Ji said, "Are you that scared of your old man? Your dad's seventy, and you're only eighteen!"

Chouchou said, "My dad doesn't trust you. Always wandering about—you're not straight."

"Your father's talking nonsense. I'm as straight as a die!"

The two of them stood beside the crusher. When it rose, it came up to their shoulders. When it dropped, the ground upon which they were standing shook with the thump. There was no bamboo under the crusher, so it fell with a hollow sound, and whenever Chouchou spoke, Ah Ji had trouble hearing her clearly. For a while Ah Ji said nothing, then he took the *xiao* out from his belt and gave it to Chouchou. She laughed and said, "I can't play it."

Ah Ji replied, "I'll teach you. It's really easy to learn!" Whereupon he put it to his lips and began to play. The tune he played sounded like water, only softer, and was in time with the splash, splash of the waterwheel and the thump, thump of the crusher. Ah Ji looked up at the rainhat shaped spider web in the rafters, at the green moss growing on the axle of the water wheel, then looked at Chouchou's pale face and at where her breasts pushed out against the loose coarse fabric shirt she was wearing. Chouchou became engrossed in Ah Ji's playing. Her eyes would grow bright, then go dim. She wondered how Ah Ji's lips could produce sounds even more ingenious than those of the nightingale.

But then Pockmarks appeared at the door and howled, "Blow your mother's foot!" A bamboo rod came down on Ah Ji's legs with a whack, and the *xiao* fell under the crusher and in a moment was pounded to smithereens. Ah Ji ran out of the bamboo crushing room, but when he heard Pockmarks beating Chouchou he yelled, "If you're going to hit someone, hit me! What do you prove by beating Chouchou!" When Dog heard the noise, he rushed up and bit Ah Ji on the leg, and Ah Ji ran off.

Pockmarks stood on the open ground in front of the mill and pointing at the distant Ah Ji, yelled, "Ah Ji, you scoundrel, if this mill ever buys bamboo from you again, it'll be over my dead body!"

So with this Ah Ji's avenue for earning money was shut off. He lay at home for three days completely dispirited and with nothing to do. Without Ah Ji the other bamboo cutters felt listless, so they took some wine and went across to Ah Ji's house to comfort him with a drink. Wine is supposed to relieve one of one's cares, but on this occasion it only made things worse, and Ah Ji got drunk for the first time. In his cups he repeated Chouchou's name over and over again. When he sobered up he was so ashamed that two days later he caught the shuttle boat to Gourd Town.

When Ah Ji arrived at Gourd Town, there were people coming and going everywhere, but Ah Ji did not know any of them, nor did he have a place to stay. All the boats going up and down the Han River stopped here, and while in port the boatmen would go to Sun Erniang's tea house, so Ah Ji went there too. The teahouse had three rooms, but the dividing walls had been removed leaving four posts. On both the left and right was a row of cane deck chairs, where people sipped tea and listened to Erniang play the *pipa* and sing. Nobody really knew for sure if Sun Erniang was her real name or just what everybody called her. In any case, she wasn't old, somewhere between thirty and forty. She had a pale face, and shining hair, and two large breasts bobbed around under her clothes. She also had a good voice.

> *The man takes the boat down the Han River,*
> *The girl burns incense there in her room.*
> *The incense she places in the incense burner.*
> *One look, two looks, seventy-two looks.*
> *The lands about Nanjing, the walls of Beijing;*
> *Old Goddess of Mercy, and Goddess of Generation,*
> *Please protect my man—may he come home soon.*
> *So as my heart does not break in two.*

Ah Ji listened and thought of Chouchou back there in the touch paper mill, and tears came to his eyes. He lapsed into a daydream and finally fell asleep in the deck chair, only to wake to the voice of Erniang yelling, "Young man, is this your *kang*?" When he opened his eyes he found he was the only one left in the teahouse, so he got out as fast as he could and began wandering about the streets looking for somewhere to stay.

4.

Gourd Town had been in existence for about three hundred years, and was one of the most thriving and lively towns along the Han River. Just to the north, mountains rose and fell like a sleeping dragon, ignoring the narrow town that stood like a patch of reeds on the hill below. The Xun River flowed down from the Qinling Mountains, winding and carving its way around three sides of the town before entering the Han River. Between the rivers stood a jumble of buildings large and small. When Ah Ji was little, he had once come to the town with his father, but now his memories of it were very vague. This time the thing that struck him most strongly was the streets. It was said there were five streets, but in fact there was really only one. It began by the steps that led up from the crossing, went through bustling River Street, wound its way around to the right bank at the back of the town, zigzagged up the slope and over to the left bank, then twisted its way all the way up the hill to the top. On the top was a tall building, the seat of the local people's government. Off this last section of winding street branched four consecutive lanes that went straight up, stone steps all the way. Ah Ji did not know the name of this lane, so he called it "Real Man's Lane." In this area of criss-crossing, winding streets, all the houses were built in strange designs, so that no two houses were the same, and the small houses were wedged in amongst the large ones. Before Liberation, Gourd Town had been a large port. There had been many warehouses, shops, inns and stalls, and wealthy people had the means to construct large and richly ornamented homes. Because they were built according to the lie of the land, these homes spread in all directions, twisting with the land on which they stood. Now these old homes had been divided up and given to the people, and had fallen into disrepair. However, at the same time, new concrete buildings of all different shapes and sizes had been constructed wherever a place for them could be found. There was not a single bicycle in the whole town, but everybody carried a torch in their pockets. Ah Ji had nothing to do, so he roamed every nook and cranny in the town. He saw some people wearing clothing made of straw and felt hats, and others wearing sunglasses and long hair—new and old jumbled together, handsome and ugly side by side. Ah Ji could not help heaving a sigh, regretting that he had not come here more often, and feeling sorry for Chouchou who had never been here in her life. "If Chouchou could come here once, then she'd stop listening to her father!" While thinking this, his stomach began to rumble, and as he looked around at the shops selling little cakes and things, his mouth began to salivate profusely. People are always thinking of ways to make a living, and Ah Ji had a quick mind, so soon he thought of a good way. He went down to the crossing and asked the people who had come up from the towns sightseeing if they wanted to stay in the state-run guest house upon the hill. As the streets in the town were winding and steep, he would be their porter and carry their bags up the hill. City people had money but no strength, so Ah Ji always had an income. On a few occasions, delicate girls would get off the boat, take one look at the hill and not know how they were ever going to get up it. Ah Ji would then set the girls on his shoulders and carry them up the "Real

Man's Lane." From his shoulders the girls would look at the scenes of the town—the labyrinthine old buildings and the taller new structures—with great delight. There was in particular a small courtyard house that had a well in the center surrounded by square buildings with traditional sloping roofs that often caught their attention. Upon seeing all these sights, the girls would start singing with joy. Although Ah Ji was used to climbing mountains and carrying bamboo, he found carrying live people extremely tiring, and eighty *jin* soon felt like a hundred and twenty. What comforted him and made him more or less forget his weariness were the girls' songs and the fragrance of a perfume of some kind that emanated from their bodies.

Now Ah Ji had money. After he had eaten his fill he went and sat by the gate of the Temple of the River God. By the gate was a strangely shaped rock many feet high, and on it grew lichen and a gnarled old tree with red autumn leaves. At the foot of the rock was a spring with ice-cold water, into which had been tossed many, many silver coins. The boatmen threw these in and wished for good luck, then went into the temple and burnt a whole bunch of touch paper to the River God. As soon as he saw the touch paper catch light and the black smoke fly up into the air like a vulture, Ah Ji thought of Chouchou and became melancholy. He gazed at the Han River as it wound its way through the mountains, mists and sandbars towards him, with its rugged banks and swirling eddies.

With that, Ah Ji made his way down to Sun Erniang's teahouse on River Street. There he mixed in with the boatmen. If they said the tea was good, he said the tea was good, if they cheered Erniang's singing, so did he. These visits to the teahouse became a habit, and Erniang came to know Ah Ji, asking his age, where he came from and whether he was married or not. Upon asking the last question, Erniang laughed, and pinching Ah Ji on the cheek, exclaimed, "So you're a bachelor, eh!" Ah Ji did not really understand exactly what she meant, and played dumb anyway to give the others a bit of fun. Although he laughed foolishly, he had sharp eyes and nimble hands, and began helping Erniang stoke the boiler and fill the boatmen's teapots. Erniang liked him and let him sleep by the boiler at night, but warned, "If you're a thief, I'll skin you alive. No matter where you hide, the boatmen can find you anywhere along the length and breadth of the Han River, and they'll bring you back to me! At night, sleep quietly, and if you hear any movements upstairs, don't call out!"

Now Ah Ji had his own nest, he slept like a log. However several nights later he could not get to sleep, and in the middle of the night he heard footsteps upstairs, then a chair move, followed by talking and laughing. Ah Ji thought: Erniang lives upstairs, so could she be talking to her husband? But he had never seen her husband, nor any children! Puzzled, he waited until a time when there was nobody in the teahouse and asked, "Erniang, does uncle do business in another town?"

"He's dead."

"Dead? So you haven't got any children?"

"I've got you for a son!"

Ah Ji choked on his words, and could not say anything. Then Erniang asked, "Ah Ji, what have you heard in the night?"

"I heard you talking to someone."

"Stuff your ears with donkey hair!"

Ah Ji thought, "Erniang is a widow. Could it be that

she has a lover come in the night?" He didn't dare ask. He observed every boatman who came into the tea-house, but none of them seemed likely to be her lover. All of them seemed close to her. When they came in they would give her *mu'er*,[5] or walnuts, or headscarves, and make cheeky comments that exceeded the limits of propriety, or were just outright crude. She greeted them in a hundred different ways, the worst of which was to scowl and abuse the boatmen as if she were scolding her son. Ah Ji did not think Erniang was at all wrong, but rather looked upon her as an elder sister, or mother, or Goddess of Mercy, and at night when he was in bed he would also think of that pair of large breasts moving about under her clothes.

One day, Ah Ji was doing his porter's job on the "Real Man's Lane." On the way up his legs felt weak, and on the way back they ached. He finally arrived back at the teahouse, and while he was taking off his hat and socks and brushing them, Erniang said to him, "Are you going to be a porter all your life?"

"I don't know how to do anything else," Ah Ji replied.

Erniang said, "If you had some capital I could intro-duce you to a boatman and you could go into trade. But you haven't got any capital, so no boatman will take you. Why don't you go up into the mountains and cut lacquer?"

"I'll do anyting else, but no way will I go and cut lacquer," Ah Ji answered.

"Then go back to the fields, and get a wife to accompany you."

"I want to marry Chouchou," Ah Ji blurted out.

Erniang asked, "Who's Chouchou, with such an ugly sounding name?"[6]

131

As he could not fool Erniang, he told her the whole story of his relationship with Chouchou. Erniang listened in silence, then sighed, "Poor Chouchou. If you are a real man, you should go and marry her!" Ah Ji pondered ruefully the fact that he had no special skills nor any money, and could not think what to do. Erniang said, "I've heard there's a hunchback at the Temple of the River God who can tell fortunes by analyzing written characters. Go and have your fortune told and find out what is best for you to do. You can't believe all these superstitions, but you shouldn't ignore them."

Ah Ji went to the temple and found the hunchback by an ancient stele to the right of the large rock and spring. He could tell fortunes and cure illnesses by massage. An old man who had angina was carried to the hunchback, who immediately set to kneading the old man's abdomen, but still the old man could not stand up straight. The hunchback said, "That's OK, that's OK." Whereupon he put his finger on an acupuncture point on the old man's abdomen. When he started rubbing it, the old man died. But the hunchback continued to massage the man's abdomen until the clot dissolved, then he gave the same acupuncture point another knead and the old man revived, his illness cured. People watching exclaimed, "What a miraculous doctor!" Somebody said, "Not only can he bring the dead back to life, he can also tell fortunes by analyzing characters!"

Ah Ji immediately went forward and asked to have his fortune told. The hunchback asked him which character he wanted analysed. Ah Ji said, "My name is Ji so analyse 'ji'!" The hunchback muttered to himself for a moment, then putting his hands together said, "You have a good future. At present you have financial problems, but all the signs are propitious and good things

132

will come to you!" Ah Ji only half believed him, so quickly asked where he should go and what he should do. The hunchback replied, "The character 'ji'(季) has a leftward sloping stroke at the top, which is a black dragon raising its head. In the middle is wood and at the bottom is the character 'zi'(子). 'Zi' belongs to the water element, and if water is below wood, then the wood grows profusely on account of the water. This is a really good character. You should do things in the north, east or west, but avoid the south, as south belongs to the fire element and burns wood." Ah Ji did not understand '*yin*' and '*yang*' and the "five elements," but he understood that if he met water he would thrive, and if he met fire he would suffer. He found himself thinking about cutting bamboo. Then he thought, "Pockmarks loathes me, and if he won't take my bamboo, what can I do about it?" He became despondent. Raising his head again, he saw groups of boatmen going into the temple, and all of them bought touch paper from the stall at the gate. He got a sudden inspiration and rushed back to the teahouse to tell Erniang. "I've found something I can do!" She asked him what it was. He explained that he would go back to Seven Mile Flat and buy Pockmarks' touch paper, then come back and sell it outside the temple. The profits should be considerable. Erniang was happy for Ah Ji and encouraged him to go and do it.

From that time on Ah Ji spent much of his time traveling between Seven Mile Flat and Gourd Town. When Pockmarks saw Ah Ji had come to buy his touch paper, he did not mention their previous quarrel. At first Ah Ji only bought a few bundles of paper. Later he bought a dozen, then more and more as his business increased and his capital multiplied. Pockmarks had always had trouble selling his product, but Ah Ji contracted to buy a third of it. Pockmarks also let him stay for a while in the mill and tell him about the people and ways of Gourd Town, with all its complexities and wonderful happenings. And now he was able to go and see Chouchou on the sly.

Once Chouchou said, "You're less and less like you used to be, Ah Ji. Now you really have a way with words!"

"That's nothing," replied Ah Ji. "The people in Gourd Town are full of news and they really know how to talk!"

Chouchou said, "Gourd Town sounds really good!"

"Then will you go? I'll take you," Ah Ji asked.

But Chouchou replied, "No, I'm not going." Ah Ji took out a bottle of Snowflake Lotion and gave it to Chouchou, who smelt it and exclaimed, "What a beautiful fragrance!" but then returned the bottle to Ah Ji.

"Why don't you want it?" Ah Ji asked. "I bought it specially for you!" Then he pressed it into her hands and left.

Chouchou sat down and started pulling the bamboo out from the crusher again, but her heart was all in a flurry. She rubbed a little of the Snowflake Lotion on her face, but worried she wouldn't rub it in properly and her father would see it. When she went to look at herself in the channel water, she heard Ah Ji singing from out on the river.

> From this mountain I look at how high that mountain is,
> And see a tree bearing the luscious peaches of love.
> Can't reach them with a long stick or short stick,
> So taking off my shoes, I climb the tree to shake.
> To the left I shake, to the right I shake,

Shake until the peaches roll all over the hill.
The young men who pass by take one to taste,
If they don't get lovesick they're bound to get T.B.!
A lovesick man is no matter for concern,
But a lovesick girl has put her life at risk.

5.

Ah Ji's touch paper stall became famous, and soon he moved it to the teahouse. If someone came to buy touch paper, he would go to the stall and sell it. If there were no customers, Ah Ji would help Erniang serve the boatmen. He never tired, always knew what to say, and could deal with anyone or anything, never overlooking the slightest detail. When Erniang played the *pipa*, he would accompany her on the *xiao*. The boatman would say, "Erniang, this disciple of yours is a really quick one!" She would reply, "He's my foster son!" Ah Ji was perfectly willing to accept his position as foster son, never hiding the fact from anyone. With time, he became even more astute and alert. At night Ah Ji still slept by the boiler. One night Erniang came down from upstairs and boiled a pot of tea. While she was drinking it she asked Ah Ji, "Three days ago when you went to the touch paper mill, did you reveal your heart to Chouchou?"

"Yes."

"What did she say?"

"She blushed and left in embarrassment."

"Did you look at her eyes? Eyes can speak."

"I couldn't tell. She walked to the door of the room and just said one sentence, 'aren't you afraid of my father?'"

"Then she's just about agreed! Tell me, Ah Ji, did you

135

hold her hand?"

"Why do you say that?"

"Ah Ji's still shy! You have to take her hand, so by the time you're about to get married you won't be shy at all. I asked you that because I wanted to know what stage this matter has got to."

Ah Ji took note of what Erniang said, as he really wanted to find out exactly what Chouchou's feelings were towards him. The next time he went to the touch paper mill, he was presented with a wonderful opportunity, as Pockmarks was out and Chouchou's deaf-mute uncle was working in the paper pulp room. Ah Ji was able to slip in from behind the waterwheel without Dog, who was busy chewing on a bone. Chouchou was both surprised and happy, and took Ah Ji over to the corner of the room to chat. There the bamboo crusher, now going up and down empty, hid the two of them from view and prevented them from being heard outside. Ah Ji asked Chouchou if she had thought about going with him to Gourd Town. She said her father didn't approve. "How could he not approve?" asked Ah Ji, since by now he bought almost all of Pockmarks' product. Chouchou said, "My father says you've not to be trusted. The more you run about the countryside, the less honest and decent you become. He said once this type of person gets money, you can never rely on them, and in the end you'll be left with nothing!"

Ah Ji said, "Your old man's such a stick-in-the-mud. Is he always going to look upon people like that?" Then he asked, "What do you think?" Chouchou did not answer. Ah Ji looked at Chouchou's pale face and a rush of blood went through him. He took Chouchou by the hand. She struggled to get her hand free, but Ah Ji had it held tight. Ah Ji became confused, Chouchou became confused, and almost unconsciously the two of them pressed together and became one.

When they regained their senses, both were perspiring profusely and frightened out of their wits. Chouchou began to cry loudly. Ah Ji went into a panic, and had not a clue what to do, until in the end he slapped himself on the face and begged Chouchou to forgive him. Chouchou stopped crying and said to him, "Dad said you were bad news, and he was damned right! Get out of here!"

When Ah Ji heard Chouchou speak to him like this, his heart started pounding, and he stayed where he was and asked, "Chouchou, do you really think I'm bad news?"

"Get out!"

"Won't you forgive me? Won't you promise to marry me?"

"Now I have ...I can't do anything but marry you, can I? I told you to go, so go!"

A stone dropped to the ground, and Ah Ji left.

Back in Gourd Town, Ah Ji recalled what happened in the bamboo crushing room with alarm and fear, but after a while he turned it into a matter for joy, and when Erniang asked how things went, he told her that Chouchou had agreed, and said nothing more.

Time slipped by and soon half a month had passed. A boatman from Ziyang came into the teahouse and said that thirty miles up the river at Ziyang a new kind of mountain tea had gone into production. This tea cleaned one's blood, made one's eyes bright, prevented cancer and reduced blood pressure, and what's more it was cheap. Erniang liked the sound of it, and wanted to take the boat up to Ziyang to buy some. Ah Ji said, "You're not so strong, and a few days out there on the river, with its wind and waves, is bound to wear you out. It would be better if I went and bought it for you."

"So I know now that when I die I can close eyes in peace. And when I do meet my end, I can leave the teahouse to you without any qualms! But you haven't been around much, and you don't know anything about tea, so it's still best if I go. For the four or five days I'll be gone, you look after the teahouse properly. The life of a boatman is a tough one, and the fact that they come here shows they like us. So serve them well, and don't look down on these poor men, or our reputation will be ruined!"

Ah Ji reassured her, "Of course, You just put your mind at rest!" At dawn the next day Erniang boarded the boat. The river was enveloped in mist, but one could still see the ancient trees reaching for the skies, the vines hanging from them, the beautiful rocks and the clear springs along the banks. Somewhere a crow cawed noisily, then after Erniang gave a few parting instructions to Ah Ji, the boat departed up the river.

Ah Ji ran the teahouse with great diligence, receiving the customers warmly, and doing all he could to please them. After five days Erniang still had not returned. Every morning before dawn he opened up the teahouse, swept it clean, then looked out over the Han River, only to find a wide empty expanse of water lined with mountains on both sides. Its green-blue waters stretched out below the deep blue skies, in which hung a crescent moon that threw a wan light around Ah Ji. Suddenly he felt a chill run through him. He sneezed several times, then went back into the teahouse to start up the boiler and prepare tea. Soon customers began to arrive in twos and threes. The boatmen who got up early habitually had a cup of tea to start the day. That morning they asked, "Ah Ji, make it a bit stronger. If you drink a pot like this as soon as you get up, you won't get a headache all day! And hasn't Erniang come back yet?"

Ah Ji replied, "She's not back yet, but you never know, she could be back before you finish that cup of tea!" Just as he was saying that, Sun Erniang came back. However the Sun Erniang that came back wasn't a living person but a dead body wrapped up in a mat! She had bought three hundred *jin* of tea and caught the same boat back. After a day and a night on the river, the wind suddenly picked up, the waves became rough, and the boatman lost control of his vessel. The boat was dragged onto some rocks as large as a room and capsized. The boatman knew the waters, but his head was smashed in half. Erniang could not swim, and after flailing about among the waves, she was dragged by a large wave to the river bed. When other boats in the distance saw the boat go over, and they knew that Erniang was on it, they cried out and raced over to the scene, but no trace could be found of her. All the boats moored by the river bank took to the water, and the boatmen dived in to look for her. They found her, but by the time they got to her and pulled her out of the water, she was dead.

All of Gourd Town was shocked at the news of her death. The boatmen came to the teahouse to mourn her passing. They all chipped in to buy a top quality coffin and woolen burial attire for her. When they unwrapped the mat to put her body in the coffin, Ah Ji saw that her eyes shut but her face was still moist as if she were alive, and he broke into uncontrollable tears. Then he fainted by her coffin, so the boatmen brought him to by splashing water on him. They said to him, "Ah Ji, Erniang didn't have a relative in the whole town, not a husband nor a son, so don't cry yourself rotten, as you'll have to fill the role of the son and oversee the burial!" Those words brought Ah Ji to his senses, and in an instant he seemed to mature several years. He opened Erniang's money box and told a few boatmen to go and prepare the grave, arrange a band to play funeral music, and buy rice and flour so they could invite mourners for a meal.

At noon the next day, the funeral procession began. Ah Ji wore white mourning dress, and tears streamed down his face as he performed the son's rituals before the coffin, after which eight men lifted the coffin on to their shoulders. They set out from the teahouse, with over fifty boatmen from all over the river carrying wreaths leading the way, followed by the funeral band blowing horns and beating drums and cymbals. Then came a boatman setting off firecrackers, then Ah Ji carrying a picture of Erniang, followed by the coffin. Behind them were the other boatmen and townsfolk of all ages and walks of life. The procession went up River Street and along the winding street that snaked its way around the town, firecrackers exploding and horns blaring. The boatmen carrying the coffin would take three steps forward, three to the left, three to the right, then one back, before proceeding forward three steps again, all in imitation of a boat rocking on the waves. Thus the procession went forward at a snail's pace, and all those watching were so deeply moved that they burst into tears. After they reached the top of the hill in the town, they took the steep, narrow path straight up the mountain behind Gourd Town. Carrying the coffin up this path was really hard work, so all present took turns to bear the coffin, which seemed to be standing almost vertical as it was carried up the steep slope above the white-capped procession. Thus Erniang was buried way up on the mountain.

When Ah Ji had finished patting down the last shovelful of soil on the grave, he turned around to see that the hunchback from the temple gate had also come. He had bought touch paper from Ah Ji the day before and was now burning it before the grave. When he finished, he gave Ah Ji a length of cloth about six feet long, upon which he had written a funeral elegy. Ah Ji read it. It said:

> *"Although one can still find remains of the painted boats of old,*
> *That fabled sea bird leaves without a trace.*
> *There cannot be a boat passing by Gourd Town,*
> *Whose captain will not stop here to pay respects."*

Ah Ji took over the teahouse, which now was really just the teahouse building itself, sixty or seventy cane deck chairs, and all the teapots and teacups. All of Erniang's savings that had not been spent on the three hundred *jin* of Ziyang tea, now on the bottom of the river, had been spent on the funeral. Ah Ji wanted to leave the place, but whenever he saw the boatmen coming to drink tea as they had always done, he could not bring himself to go, and so he stayed on. Although he was now the owner, the sign outside still said "Sun Erniang's Teahouse." Ah Ji wanted to make sure that the teahouse would always be a part of Gourd Town and that the boatmen would always come to it. He got up early and went to bed late, and learnt to play Erniang's *pipa* and sing her songs. However, when he first performed before the boatmen, he broke into tears, and soon the boatmen were also sobbing away. So Ah Ji stopped singing and said to those present, "When Erniang was alive she sang songs to soothe you, but when I sing you weep. If Erniang knew, she would not abide it. Since she's dead and can't come back to life, then let each of us get on with his own business. So let's sing, 'Still in This World.' "

> *Still in this world, still in this world,*
> *Mulberries and willows shoot forth new leaves.*
> *Still in this world, still in this world,*
> *The dead have passed away, but we remain alive.*
> *The dead return to the Underworld,*
> *We remain in the sunshine-filled world.*

All the boatmen joined in the singing.

For the next three months, Ah Ji was busy improving the teahouse, so he did not have time to go to Seven Mile Flat, and thus did not buy any touch paper from Pockmarks, nor go to see Chouchou in the bamboo crushing room.

6.

After four months the teahouse was flourishing. All the boats from the Han River and all the rafts from the Xun River would stop at Gourd Town and come to the teahouse to drink tea. However Ah Ji found that the people around the town did not treat him with proper respect. When he met them on the street they would say, "Ah Ji, business is booming, eh!"

Ah Ji would laugh and say, "Only with everybody's help!"

Then the other person would say, "Now that Erniang is dead, you can look for a wife!"

Ah Ji still laughed, but immediately felt something was wrong, that the person meant something he did not yet understand, and so he asked, "What are you driving at?"

"Well, you accompanied her right to the end. You're smart, and you've got foresight!"

Ah Ji became angry, and even by the time he got back to the teahouse he had still not regained his cool. He knew people in the town were jealous of him and spread ugly rumors about him and about Sun Erniang. But all Ah Ji did was clean and above board. His anger only made him want to improve the teahouse even more. He worked harder and harder at upgrading the running of the teahouse. He bought a new boiler, twenty new cane deck chairs, and began to sell cigarettes, candy and fruit. Business grew even more. He decided to hire a waitress, and found one in the daughter of an old lady who lived in River Street. This girl had a flattish face, but a pretty waist, and was good with her hands and soft and gentle by nature, besides which she had a good voice. However after only a week had passed, rumors began flying wildly. It was said Ah Ji had an improper relationship with this new waitress, and that he'd done the same thing when Erniang was alive. The waitress felt so humiliated that she left without giving notice. This gave the townspeople even more cause for gossip. When Ah Ji went out into the street he could feel people were talking about him behind his back. Thus the reputation of the teahouse declined. Ah Ji went and threw himself beside the portrait of Erniang and howled in despair, particularly as he had brought so much trouble upon the teahouse.

Ah Ji closed down the teahouse for a while and went to the town government to have them investigate his case and clear his reputation. Officials went to interview the daughter of the old lady, who denied anything had ever happened between her and Ah Ji, even saying they could take her to the hospital and examine her if they wished. Then the officials interviewed the people who had been spreading the rumors only to find it was all based on hearsay. Thus the town government told Ah Ji not to worry as they were only rumors, and that he should go back and open his teahouse again. However, although he had been cleared, one hand cannot cover the mouths of thousands, and when he was really busy and offered good money for a new waitress, nobody responded. It was only at this juncture that Ah Ji understood what Pockmarks had said—that people's morals were on the decline and they were not as kindhearted as they used to be. Ah Ji now also hated these repugnant trends, but at the same time he was hated by Pockmarks. Ah Ji now felt Chouchou was the only decent person in the world and he desperately wanted to see her. He wanted to think of a way to marry her and bring her back to Gourd Town, where they could manage the teahouse in peace and prosperity.

So the teahouse was closed again, and Ah Ji left Gourd Town, taking all his savings with him, and went to Seven Mile Flat. On arriving at the Seven Mile Flat crossing, Ah Ji jumped on to the stone bank, but to his surprise noticed the channel water flowed straight down. This was the channel that Pockmarks used to divert water from the stream to drive the waterwheel, after which the water flowed down by the village into the Han River. Now water ran all over the stones in front of the village. A doubt grew in Ah Ji's mind, and when he looked at the touch paper mill in the distance, he could see the buildings were still there but the waterwheel and the crusher no longer made their awful racket. "Has Pockmarks given up the mill?" Ah Ji's heart raced. If the mill was no longer running, and Chouchou was not sitting there day after day working the bamboo crusher, it should be even easier for him to take her to Gourd Town!

In front of the mill, all was deadly silent. Ah Ji suddenly became afraid, as the silence somehow seemed eerie. Dog came running out of the mill and made straight for Ah Ji, but he neither bit nor barked. Ah Ji thought, "Could it be that in the four months of their not seeing each other, Dog had become docile?" He said to the dog, "Dog, where's Chouchou?" Suddenly, Dog became frightened and let out a long terrifying howl, which filled Ah Ji with consternation. Thereupon he saw Pockmarks and the mute old uncle sitting on a pile of stones outside the paper pulp room. They were sitting in silence tying up dried touch paper into bundles, and when they heard Dog's wild howl, they looked up and gazed woodenly at Ah Ji as he walked over, then looked down again and continued tying their bundles.

Ah Ji was used to Pockmarks' unfriendly ways, but sensed something was wrong when he did not greet Ah Ji with his usual venom and hatred!

"Uncle, why isn't the crusher crushing bamboo?" Ah Ji asked.

"Because it's not."

"And Chouchou?"

"Dead."

"Dead?!"

"Dead." Ah Ji was struck dumb, stood for a moment in a daze, then ran to the bamboo crushing room. The water trough had collapsed and the waterwheel stood still, its paddles dry and split. The square crusher stood in its place, and below it lay a pile of half crushed bamboo. In a mad fit he rushed back and yelled at Pockmarks, "Chouchou's dead?! How did she die?!"

145

But Pockmarks raised his fist and landed a blow right in the pit of Ah Ji's stomach, sending him sprawling on the ground, then went and sat still as before, and said to Ah Ji, "Calm down. Chouchou is really dead."

Ah Ji was brought to his senses. He sat on the ground sobbing, and asked how Chouchou died. Pockmarks sat head lowered tying his bundles of paper and telling the story, almost as though he were telling a tale of ancient times.

At first Pockmarks had noticed that for several days Chouchou was not herself, and soon began avoiding her father, going off by herself to vomit in the grass hut that served as a toilet. Pockmarks thought she was ill and told her to go and see a doctor, but she didn't go. The next night Pockmarks heard Chouchou moaning in her room, but when he asked what was the matter, she said her stomach hurt a bit but it was nothing to worry about, and with that went off to the toilet. Pockmarks guessed she had diarrhea and, thinking nothing of it, went back to sleep. The next morning when he called Chouchou to go out and crush bamboo, there was no answer. He went into her room and found at the top of her *kang* a bowl with a mixture made of crushed porcelain and glass, most of which was now gone. Pockmarks panicked. He knew this mixture was for inducing abortions, so he ran to the grass hut, in the doorway of which he found Chouchou lying dead, blood running from her mouth and from between her legs. When the story finished, Ah Ji broke into uncontrollable tears.

Pockmarks said, "I don't care about the loss of face from having Chouchou die, but tell me, which one of you sleazy characters seduced Couchou and made her do such a disgusting thing? I am to blame. Why did I

146

start up the touch paper mill and let all those shady people come here? I didn't look after Chouchou properly!"

Ah Ji said, "You didn't look after Chouchou properly? Wasn't it that you 'looked after' her to death?!"

"Crap," Pockmarks said. "It was a good thing she died, for if she hadn't, how would she have been able to face life? I would never have realized that it served me right for opening that mill. I'm never going to operate it again. Once I've sold the last few hundred *jin* of touch paper I'm not going to do anything! If anybody wants the waterwheel or crusher they can have it for free!"

Ah Ji said, "I want it."

"Want what? You still want the touch paper?"

"I'll buy it."

"How much do you want?"

"All of it!"

He took several wads of money out from inside his jacket and put it on the ground, then went inside and brought out piles and piles of touch paper, which he put by the channel. Then he took a broad axe and went into the bamboo crushing room. With a crack he smashed up the waterwheel and then the crusher, and piled touch paper on top of it. Then he knelt down and put a match to it all. Although bamboo relies on water to grow, when it is made into paper it is really flammable; and so once this caught fire it did not take long before black smoke started belching out and flames leapt up towards the heavens. Chouchou had sat there for several years crushing bamboo, and that bamboo had become thousands and thousands of sheets of paper which people burnt for the souls of their dead. Who would have guessed that the last, and the largest, pile of the paper would be burnt for her own soul.

147

Ah Ji's hair and eyebrows were singed, but still he knelt there like a pile of wood or stone. Pockmarks and the deaf-mute uncle were completely stunned by all this. They watched the black ashes fly up into the sky, then fall again, blackening the ground and blackening them, until tears started cascading from their eyes.

Just at that time some rafts carrying piles of bamboo went past on the Han River. The rafts were manned by another group of young men, going to a new touch paper mill in another village to sell their bamboo. When they saw the smoke and flames at Seven Mile Flat, they struck up an ancient Han River work song.

Yo, Ao————Ao, He, Ao————Ai, Hai————!

Yo, Ai————Yo————!

Ao————Ai, Hai, Yo————!

Ao————Ai, Hai, Ai————Ai————Hai————Ai

November 1985
Translated by David Pattinson

Notes:

[1] A four stringed instrument held vertically and plucked.

[2] One *jin* equals five hundred grams.

[3] *Kang* is a heated brick bed used mainly in rural families in northern China.

[4] The *xiao* is a kind of bamboo flute, played vertically.

[5] *Mu'er* is a kind of edible fungus.

[6] *Chou* means "ugly" in Chinese.

LU WENFU AND HIS FICTION

Wu Taichang

Among contemporary Chinese writers there are none more active and manifestly forceful than the generation now in their fifties or sixties. Lu Wenfu is a clear example of this group. The fact that he has been elected deputy chairman of the Chinese Writers Association and has on four occasions won national short story and novella awards testifies to the influence and status Lu's works are accorded by Chinese readers.

Lu is now fifty-nine, and his career since publishing the short story *Honor* in 1955 has spanned more than three decades. Like many other writers of his generation, he has endured much suffering, but throughout his career he has maintained a quiet dignity in his literary quest. Many fine works have resulted from his prolific literary output. His reputation was established with the appearance in 1956 of the short story *Deep Within a Lane*. The long period he lived in the ancient city of Suzhou endowed his stories with the rich flavor of Suzhou life. In opening up a window for the first time onto the life of the alleys and byways of that city, Lu Wenfu succeeded in creating vivid characters drawn from his dream world. The protagonist in that story, Xu Wenxia, a former prostitute struggling against a sense of humiliation, hesitates and suffers as happiness confronts her. Her innate virtue, tenacity and timidity arouse the reader's sympathies; her abnormal and tortuous life story confronts the reader with the wounds of the old society and the mysterious healing power of life in the new society. When the story first appeared, the original content and delicate description were appreciated by a wide readership. Another of Lu's short stories, *Master Ge*, which appeared in 1961 in China's most influential literary publication, the *People's Literature*, treated industrial themes and praised model characters as was the fashion at that time, but nevertheless it succeeded in presenting deep and original insights which set it apart from works of the same genre. The author's attention to technical detail throughout that work made it outstanding. Mao Dun, a veteran literary general and master craftsman of fiction, on discovering the significance of Lu's work, wrote a piece entitled "On Reading Lu Wenfu's Fiction" which appeared in 1964 in the nationally authoritative journal of literary criticism the *Literary Gazette*. He praised Lu Wenfu for his efforts at non-formula writing, whether the formula be that set by others or by his own previous writing. In an age of formularized and generalized writing, Mao Dun's high praise for the writer increased Lu's reputation.

While Lu Wenfu for the most part writes short stories, in the last few years he has written a number of novellas but none of these lacks the economy of the short story genre. Among writers of his age group, there are few so devoted to the short story. Economy also characterizes his output; at the most he only writes fifty or sixty thousand Chinese characters annually. In the 1950s and '60s he only published two short story collections—*Honor* and *Second Encounter with Zhou Tai*; in the '80s he again only published two short story collections—*Deep Within a Lane* and *Special Court*—as single volumes, as well as one novella, *The Gourmet*. Well aware that payment for manuscripts is dependent on their length, he nevertheless takes delight in the short story genre and writes novellas which are both rich and concise. His work in the latter genre, *The Gourmet*, ran to even less than eighty thousand characters, even though the work could have extended to a length of several hundred thousand characters. He has often said that while words may be scant in number they must be rich in flavor. On the question of how to write stories which are concise, unconventional and appealing, Lu Wenfu has many valuable and enlightening artistic insights. His 1982 collection of essays on writing theory, *A Layman's Discussion of Fiction*, is a valuable tool for understanding his writings.

In the last decade Lu's writing has received greater attention in China and abroad. After a period of silence, in 1978 he returned to writing with the publication of the short story *A Life of Dedication* and in 1979 published the short story *The Man from a Pedlar's Family*. That year these two works won national awards for outstanding short stories. Generally speaking, his literary output and the style of his writing in the last decade has changed little from that of the 1950s and '60s. The bright and simple style of his early works has, however, disappeared with the passing of that grim period, but the optimism, intelligence, humor and satire in his finely crafted writing has not disappeared with the passage of time. On the contrary these features have become more striking. The most delightful change which has occurred in his recent writing is not merely revealed in his artistic dexterity but to a greater extent in his revelation of life and in the increased depth of thought. With time his grasp on the pulse of life has become firmer. After questions are discovered in the course of life as it is lived, "in the slow accumulation of innocence rendered increasingly articulate one can search for some small detail not eroded from the memory by time" (Lu Wenfu's words). He still writes about Suzhou with its winding lanes, riverside houses and quiet lanes, but he does not locate the local conditions and customs at a remove from the destiny of the rest of contemporary China. The complexities of social contradictions and human interrelationships enmesh the streets and byways of Suzhou in a biological network.

At the beginning of 1983, Lu Wenfu's most prolific year, he published three stories in a row: the novella *The Gourmet* appeared in the literary bimonthly *Harvest*, while the short stories *The Boundary Wall* and *Nouveau Riche* both appeared in the *People's Literature*.

The Gourmet was the longest work Lu had written to date. In the space of less than eighty thousand Chinese characters, the author appears at first to be presenting a tantalizing vision of Suzhou's gardens and gourmet delicacies, but in fact there is much more—an extremely rich depiction of Suzhou's historical and present experience. Through the long inextricable entanglement of the first person narrator, Gao Xiaoting, and the capitalist and property-owner, Zhu Ziye, we are presented with an analysis of the hardships suffered by the entire Chinese nation as a result of misguided Leftist political policies, here subtly expressed through issues relating to food. This novella in its style, technique, experience and thematic content is an overall expression of the artistic achievements of Lu's literary quest at that time. When it appeared, the novel was highly acclaimed by critics, some of whom praised it as a pinnacle of Lu Wenfu's writing career, while others declared it to be a pinnacle of novella writing in the recent period. He won a national award for novella writing; screen and TV adaptations followed.

The Boundary Wall also received a national award. The mocking critique of this story is directed at present-day social abuses—the bureaucrats who threaten present reforms and their tendency to hollow high-flown talk backed up by no action. In *The Boundary Wall* we meet four characters at odds with Ma Erli: Institute Chief Wu, who has all the theory but none of the capacity to act as a leader; the all so "modern" Zhu Zhou and the "conservative" Huang Daquan, who both avail themselves of every opportunity to flaunt their avowed knowledge concerning every subject; and the "constant detractor" He Rujin, opposed to every reform while declaring himself to be impartial in his views. The atmosphere is deadly and stifling as they argue according to an addled logic and shifting positions, with each declaring their own views to be correct while shamelessly appropriating the achievements of others to their own credit. This story steeped in satire is plainly written without either embellishment or any trace of the author's own opinion. Lu Wenfu's contemporary and friend, the famous novelist Wang Meng praised this as "a novel of genius." "It makes you both laugh and cry; it conveys delight and pleasure."

In the last couple of years Lu Wenfu seems to have written few new works. The novella *Well* which appeared in 1985 in the *Chinese Writers* received high praise. The abrupt increase in his fame and royalties is possibly a result of the decrease in his literary output. The sudden illness which struck down his beloved youngest daughter in her prime was a personal tragedy for him which exhausted him as he desperately sought the right medical care for her.

Lu Wenfu's dispostion gives one the clear sense that he is a person of integrity. He is also a man of few words, but when he is feeling joyful he is a wonderful conversationalist. He is fond of wine and on one occasion when he invited me to the Deyuelou Restaurant in Suzhou we drank fine Shaoxing wine for more than three hours. He hates talk for its own sake and boasting. He has often said that "writers must stand by their words." At the beginning of this month I met him in Maoxing, a town renowned for its pottery, and when I asked him whether he had begun writing the full-length novel to which he must undoubtedly have given great thought, he simply smiled but said nothing. Seeing that smile, I felt that the long-awaited full-length masterpiece might yet appear.

Translated by Bruce Doar

The Boundary Wall

Lu Wenfu

Y ESTERDAY night there was a violent storm and a slight mishap occurred: The wall outside the Architectural Design Institute collapsed!

The collapse of the wall was not entirely unexpected. It was simply too old! In its history of over a hundred years, it had already collapsed and been rebuilt several times, but none of the repairs had been thorough and the result was that the thirty meters or so of wall bulged and humped in sections all of different heights. It was likely to come down at any moment, let alone in the middle of last night's storm!

With the wall down, things began to happen. Everyone felt the institute had changed. It was like an old man who'd just had his front teeth pulled out: when he opened his mouth, there was just a black cavern with nothing blocking the entrance, and his eyes and nose had shifted position too; or like a beautiful young lady suddenly turned into a shrunken-lipped old woman, ugly and awkward. But it was not just that it was an eyesore, the problem was that once the wall was down, this peaceful office suddenly found itself linked directly with the street outside. The innumerable crowds of pedestrians and surging tide of vehicles all seemed to be charging toward the office and the incessant clamor that now lacked a wall to keep it out poured directly in through the windows, which in the heat of summer had to be kept wide open. People had to speak much more loudly than before simply to make themselves heard, serious conferences were disturbed by unusual sights on the street, and discussions of current events would be diverted a thousand miles from the topic to idle chat about a traffic accident that had occurred somewhere. People were unsettled, their concentration was upset, work efficiency was low and they became easily tired. The demands were unanimous: Get the wall rebuilt fast!

Next morning at the brief daily meeting, the director of the institute, Wu, made simple inquiries about how work was progressing, and ideas on routine affairs were exchanged. Needless to say, the moment everyone sat down they started to talk about the boundary wall. Since the wall had come down, things had gone amiss; when they came to work, they had the feeling something was not normal, like the confusion of the year of the earthquake. Someone put it even more ingeniously and said when he came to work this morning he'd walked straight past the gate. Seeing the heaps of bricks lying all over the ground, he'd thought it was the construction site next door....

Director Wu rapped the table with his ball-point pen:

"OK. Let's discuss the question of the wall. Frankly, I knew long ago that it was going to come down. It's only been the lack of funds that has stopped it being pulled down and rebuilt long ago. But in fact it's just as well that it has collapsed; if the old doesn't go, the new can't take its place! Yes, we'll build a new wall...." Director Wu took a sip of water, "But what kind of wall shall we put up? I'm no expert on construction, but I always felt the old wall was out of keeping with the character of our unit: like a master tailor wearing a tattered gown without any buttons. On principle the new wall must be original and unique, attractive and tasteful, must unify form and substance.... Let's hear everyone's opinions."

As far as the importance of repairing the wall went, Director Wu's introductory remarks were both overly solemn and somewhat verbose. In fact all he'd needed to say was one sentence: "Everyone please think about it—how are we going to fix the wall?" But that would never do, work at the institute could not be oversimplified! The mention of construction invariably evoked a division into three factions: the modernists, whose special interest lay in research on modern multi-storey construction, the conservatives, who found it difficult to think of anything but classical architecture, and an indefinable faction who would accept a *fait accompli*, but were opposed to all changes and frequently displayed a tendency to nihilism. Although Director Wu claimed he was a mere layman when it came to construction, he did, in fact, consider himself to be far from an amateur, for he understood a great many principles. He understood, for example, practical economics; what was attractive and tasteful; what was advantageous to production, convenient for everyday life, etc. How to convert principles into blueprints was not his problem, but he couldn't neglect his role as leader and so had to rouse the two factions to a debate in which they would both bring forth their construction plans. Director Wu would then select the cream according to his principles and pass it on to the nihilists to unify. This was because they had a notable peculiarity: when they couldn't reject something, they had a great flair for effecting compromise and were also able to convince everyone. This technique of turning hostility into friendship was really very profound. Although to begin with Director Wu seemed dilatory and hesitant, equivocal and wordy, in the end he would make one feel it was a case of a man of great wisdom appearing slow-witted, and one would appreciate his prudence and reliability. Rebuilding the wall seemed a small matter, but it was nonetheless construction work and in addition it was going to be built right across the front door, so it had to be treated seriously in order to avoid possible repercussions.

Perhaps Director Wu's opening remarks had sealed people's lips, for the factions who should have begun the skirmish were temporarily silent, unwilling to reveal their firepower too early.

Director Wu was not worried. He turned to a young man seated in the corner and asked with a nod, "Logistics Department Head, what do you think?"

The so-called Logistics Department Head was in fact Ma Erli of the administration section. According to the principles of literature, in depicting a character one does not necessarily have to describe his face, but in the case of Ma Erli it is simply essential, for he had come to grief several times in recent years precisely because of this face!

Ma's face was certainly not ugly or sinister, on the contrary it was very good-looking. It was a plump oval with clear white skin, rosy cheeks and dimples when he smiled. His bright black eyes were particularly lively. Not bad eh? If he'd been a woman he could have enjoyed its benefits for a lifetime. But unfortunately his face had got its sexes mixed and found its way on to the shoulders of a man, and the thirty-seven-year old Ma Erli, an extremely capable and efficient administrator, had found himself with a baby face that did nothing to inspire people's confidence in his abilities! It was said that he was a victor in the field of romance, but when it came to some critical juncture, he invariably lost out. The sight of him filled certain of the leadership with misgivings, they doubted that he could stand up to hardship and were afraid that he wouldn't be reliable in his work. And neither fear was completely groundless.

Ma was always immaculately dressed. Even when he was going to the suburbs to plant trees, you wouldn't see him in sneakers or cloth shoes. He did as much work as anyone else, but there was never a speck of dust on his clothing. This roused the suspicion that he'd been dawdling. If he'd worn working clothes and leather working shoes, army pumps or straw sandals all day and paraded up and down in them, the results would have been quite different: "This man is prudent and experienced, hard-working and plain living." Even if his work had been mediocre, they would have commented: "One's ability may be limited, but what counts is one's attitude to work."

There were also grounds for believing that Ma Erli was not a steady worker. Reliability is often a synonym for slowness, but Ma seemed unduly agile. He was like the wheel of a bicycle—set it in motion and it goes flying.

"Xiao Ma (or Little Ma, which was what everyone called him), two window panes have been broken, you'll have to do something about it."

"OK. I'll fix it straight away."

Word was given in the morning and that same afternoon the new glass was fitted in place. No one could resist going and poking it with their fingers to see whether it was in fact cellophane, because although it was easy enough to go and buy ginseng, to buy a pane of glass was a difficult operation: even if he had been lucky enough to find some glass to buy, how could he have got the glazier to come and put it in straight away? There it was, nailed in securely with the cracks puttied over ... Oh no! They were just putting up a building next door! Don't say this slick customer had waited till they'd gone to lunch and then seized the chance to ...

Naturally all misunderstandings are cleared up sooner or later, but the cost is reckoned in time. Ma Erli had previously worked in the Housing Administration Bureau. In his first year everyone had kept a wary eye on him, afraid that this sharp-eyed, nimble-fingered young man was going to slip up. The second year they discovered that he was extremely capable, but had to be kept tight control of, for capable people were frequently liable to go beyond the limits of what was proper, it was virtually a rule. In the third year, he was lauded from above and below and all kinds of work was piled on his head. In his fourth year his leaders all declared that he should long since have been promoted to deputy section leader and should have risen one notch on the pay scale, but unfortunately the deputies' positions had all been filled, and pay increases had been granted two years ago. There, at such a vitally important juncture, Ma Erli really came off badly, and the fault all lay with that baby face!

The head of the Housing Administration Bureau was a kind-hearted old man who didn't like to treat his subordinates unfairly, so seeing that Ma Erli would have difficulty getting promotion in his own office, reluctantly parted with his treasure and recommended him to Director Wu. He told him how capable Ma was and said there was no question of it, he had the makings of an administration section chief.

Director Wu agreed to take him on, but as soon as he saw Ma he became suspicious, "Can this kind of person stand up to hard work? Will he be reliable?" The unfortunate Ma Erli began his second round of being tested....

Director Wu had asked Ma to speak first, on the one hand to get everyone talking and on the other to test his basic grounding and his experience in running affairs. So he slightly inclined his head towards the young man and said, "Logistics Department Head, what do you think?"

As expected, Ma Erli didn't know how far he should go. On the basis of his work experience and personal affiliations at the Housing Administration Bureau, he briefly considered the bricks, mortar and labor required and said, "No problem, I guarantee that wall can be up within a week!"

Director Wu gave an "Oh" of understanding. He knew from experience what was going on in Ma's head.

"You can't just consider the bricks and mortar, you have to think of the significance of the style of the wall for the character of our unit."

The word "significance" opened the floodgates and everyone began to discuss the significance of the wall, but their intentions went far beyond the question of the wall.

As expected, the topic was taken up by that erudite scholar of classical architecture, Huang Daquan. The old chap was a little naive, but there was no need to guess at his meaning.

"I raised this problem several times very early on, but unfortunately was unable to attract the attention of certain people. The collapse of the wall at this point is a profound lesson to all of us. In the course of past planning, we never attached enough importance to it, we never imagined that a trifling wall meant the difference between creating motion and creating stillness, meant creating a sense of security and unity. Now it's become obvious that the wall not only has functional value, but has a rich decorative significance too. Its place in giving a unique style to a group of buildings is of tremendous importance. Director Wu was right; this is a question of how to unite form and content."

This speech seemed to have grasped the motives of the leader, but it was in fact made with a definite object in view. He first pointed out there were means to reach that object but that he was willing to let other people use them. He had his own partialities, but he didn't want to enter the fray. The moment the words were out of his mouth, everyone's gaze turned quietly eastwards.

On a long sofa in the east of the room sat Zhu Zhou of the modernist faction. He was holding a teacup in his hands, watching the speaker with fixed concentration and listening with respectful attention.

Huang Daquan's words flowed smoothly on without a break:

"As far as traditional architectural artistry went, our forefathers really understood the wonders that can be worked with a boundary wall. There are at least a dozen different kinds of walls—flowery wall, whitewashed wall, gray brick wall, high wall, low wall, open-windowed wall, 'wind and fire' wall, screen wall, hundred pace wall, cloud wall, dragon wall—each kind of wall had its functional and esthetic value. Most ingenious was the open-windowed wall, it not only created a division between motion and stillness, but could create stillness within motion and motion within stillness. It limited men's bodies but not their eyes. It's true to say that without a wall, there's no such thing as a group of buildings. A deep courtyard must have a high wall, otherwise where's the deep courtyard? Think of the Grand View Garden in *A Dream of Red Mansions* ..." Huang had got himself roused and unintentionally wandered into the garden of the classic novel.

Zhu, sitting on the sofa put down his teacup and immediately launched off from the Grand View Garden, "Please note, we are not faced with the task of building a Grand View Garden. If we were about to restore the old Summer Palace, Huang's ideas would be worth consideration, but even then they could only be considered in part, because the style of the old Summer Palace wasn't the same as that of the Grand View Garden. We have to consider this question from the point of view of practical realities. Although classical architecture has a very romantic flavor and can make us respect and cherish our own ancient culture, it's not feasible to apply it in practical work. The urgent task in hand is to build five and six storey blocks, I don't see what significance a wall even ten meters high would have for a six storey block!"

"It has significance!" Having mistakenly wandered into the Grand View Garden, Huang turned back. He was not totally ignorant of modern architecture: "Even a six storey apartment block should have a surrounding wall, because apart from floors four, five, and six there are also floors one, two, and three. The boundary wall is chiefly for the benefit of the first two floors. The fourth, fifth and sixth floors make use of space to create the difference between motion and stillness, but the first and second floors use the wall to create an impression of distance."

The battle array of the adversaries lay exposed and the rest of the debate continued in brief phrases and sentences with no more lengthy expositions. It had become hand-to-hand combat.

"Please state clearly the distance between a building and its wall. There's really not that much space in a city."

"If the wall is right next to the windows, doesn't it block the air and sunlight?"

"Build an open-windowed wall."

"Open-windowed walls are 'motion within stillness.' Aren't you contradicting yourself?"

"They are also 'stillness within motion.' You didn't hear that part of it!"

"Just a minute. Please work out the costs for your open-windowed wall." The speaker pulled a calculator out of his back pocket.

Director Wu immediately rapped the table with his pen:

"Don't get too far off the subject. The important question is how to rebuild our own wall."

Zhu Zhou was not willing to surrender. As he saw it, the conservatives were as good as defeated and victory had to be followed up by a thorough rout of the adversary.

"We haven't got off the subject, this relates to the kind of wall we should build—whether we want an open-windowed wall or not!"

Director Wu was highly experienced in controlling meetings and never allowed anyone to throw off all restraints, so he immediately asked Zhu in reply: "In your opinion, what kind of wall should we build? Be specific."

"More specifically ..." Zhu was caught somewhat off guard because he hadn't got any specific suggestions and had only entered the fray for the sake of the argument. "More specifically ...looking at the concrete situation, the wall has two main functions: one is to cut

164

us off from the noise of the city and the other is to protect us. There's no one in the building in the evenings, only old man Hong who sleeps in the reception office and he's already getting on in years ..."

Zhu beat about the bush for all he was worth. He knew that the more concrete the proposal, the more easily it was attacked, leaving no room to defend oneself or escape.

Huang Daquan saw Zhu's predicament, looked at his watch and pressed him step by step. "Time's almost up. Where are the brilliant suggestions then?"

"To be more specific, the wall must be high and solid." Zhu had no choice but to reveal his ideas. But this proposal wasn't exactly specific either—How big? How tall? Made of what materials? He didn't touch on any of it.

Huang was too impatient. He immediately cut in, "So according to you we need a steel reinforced, eight-meter concrete wall topped by an electric fence so that we can all sample the flavor of a concentration camp!"

"That'll ruin our image irrevocably, people will shrink at the sight of it. They'll think our institute is an army ammunition depot!" Somebody chimed in.

Zhu was angry: "I didn't say we had to build a concentration camp wall. Steel reinforced concrete with and an electric fence on top were all your additions. Really! How can we discuss the question like this!" Zhu raised his eyes seeking moral support and continued:

"High and secure is right, if you want to talk about style then we should have a tall, solid wall with sharp-edged glass or iron spikes fixed on top to stop undesirable characters climbing over."

"Sharp-edged glass is the stupidity of those country moneybags. It's the equivalent of telling burglars: You

165

can climb in over the wall, but just be careful not to cut yourself on the glass!" Huang answered back sarcastically.

At this everyone laughed and the atmosphere in the meeting room eased a little.

He Rujin, not being a member of either faction, had sat there all this time not uttering a sound. When the debate was most heated he took no part, but now that things had calmed down he began, "As I see it, all this controversy is superfluous. If the boundary wall hadn't come down, no one would have thought of open windows or broken glass. Everyone felt it was perfectly natural and suitable as it was. Sure enough it's come down now, but there's not a single brick missing, so the most reasonable thing to do is to rebuild what collapsed. Is it necessary to embark on a large scale construction project? A pure waste of money! Our funds are limited; we should always put economy first. Besides, the history of the wall has set precedents for us to follow."

If this had been said at the start of the meeting it would certainly have caused an uproar, but it had been opportunely timed. Everyone had argued until they were dizzy and no one was able to offer a concrete proposal that was acceptable to all the others. As they listened to He speak it seemed as if they'd suddenly discovered the truth: he was right; if the wall hadn't collapsed there would have been no problem. Now it was down, simply rebuild it in the old way. It was just simple logic and there was nothing to argue about. The two factions nodded their heads and smiled as if an unnecessary misunderstanding had just occurred.

Director Wu gave He a disdainful glance. He didn't agree with this kind of negative attitude. His principle was to build a new, original and unconventional wall to add a bit of glory to the Architectural Design Institute. But time was already up and it would be difficult to get any substantial results from further discussion—He had no choice but to lay the matter aside for the time being: "All right. We won't say any more about the wall today. Everyone should go away and think about it. The boundary wall is an external manifestation of our institute. Things shouldn't be judged by externals, but appearances can't be too ugly all the same. Please use your imagination: we want to build something unique. The meeting's over!"

Director Wu's words brought the two factions back to their senses. They felt that He Rujin's speech amounted to nothing, he might just as well not have spoken. Determined not to let He get away with it lightly, they chased him into the corridor and launched an attack:

"What you say sounds very masterly, old pal, but in fact it amounts to attempting nothing and gaining nothing."

"According to your logic, we can disband the institute. All that is, is reasonable. What is there to design?"

Director Wu, hearing the voices fade into the distance, smiled and shook his head. Turning his head he found that Ma Erli was still sitting in the corner by the door!

Director Wu was surprised, "What is it? You still have some problems?"

"No ...nothing else. I'd just like to ask ... How *are* we going to rebuild the wall?" Ma stood up, his large eyes opening even wider.

Director Wu smiled. He'd had the same experience himself as a lively and enthusiastic young man. Once there was something on his mind, he would itch all over as if he had lice, wishing that he could remove all his clothes at once. But in fact most of the time it was quite unnecessary. Impatience only spoilt one's appetite and if you didn't let the lice bite, you might be bitten by a snake. With your clothes off you might catch cold. That was experience! But it was not appropriate to tell all this to Ma—one had to encourage the positive side of young people.

"How we finally rebuild the wall will be up to you. I've already laid down the principles and the comrades have already put forward several good suggestions. you can make a plan based on that. Rebuilding the wall is the responsibility of the administrative section, so I'm putting you in charge." Director Wu patted Ma on the shoulder, "Do your best. You're in the prime of life and capable of doing a good job!"

Ma was not very familiar with the procedure of making so-called "plans" and wasn't sure how much of a gap there was between "plans" and concrete actions, but he was delighted to be "put in charge" and felt that Director Wu had confidence in him. He hadn't been misled by his baby face. Work well for those who understand you. From now on he'd work even more enthusiastically.

Even when Ma wasn't feeling enthusiastic he got things done pretty fast, but once his enthusiasm was roused his speed was phenomenal. Nevertheless this time he was really in earnest, so he first sat down in the office and lit a cigarette while he thought things through. Before he'd finished his first cigarette, he was on his bicycle pedaling furiously towards his old work unit, the Building Repair Center.

The Building Repair Center was in a dilapidated old building that made one feel that there were numerous buildings in urgent need of renovation. Content and form really were unified!

Ma had been pedaling at a good pace, so he arrived just as their daily conference was dispersing and the director of the center, a technician and several work group leaders were just walking past the lime pool. He didn't even dismount at the gate. From across the yard he waved a hand and shouted, "Comrades, wait a minute!" By the time people had turned their heads to look, Ma Erli was beside them.

"Oh! It's you!"

Ma had worked at the Housing Administration Bureau for five years and was familiar with all the people in the Building Repair Center. For some reason, his baby face was always welcome at this basic level unit. Everyone looked on him as a lively, capable younger brother.

Ma jumped off his bicycle still puffing: "Thank Heavens I caught you, otherwise things would have had to be delayed until tomorrow."

"Xiao Ma, heard you've been promoted. Congratulations!"

Ma wiped the sweat off his forehead, "There's no need for congratulations, but if you're willing I'd like you to help me with something." He pulled out a pack of cigarettes and handed them round. "Let's sit down to talk—this isn't a simple matter!" To get everyone settled, Ma took the lead and sat down on a pile of old bricks, not forgetting to protect his clean clothes by putting his hanky down first, despite his haste.

The technician sat down, and the director squatted in front of Ma while the group leaders stood to one side smoking.

The director looked at Ma with a smile, "Well, what is it that's got you so anxious?"

"It's not a particularly important matter—the wall at the institute has collapsed."

"Is that all! You go back and we'll get it fixed for you —it's as simple as that." The director stood up. He didn't see anything remarkable in rebuilding a wall.

Ma grabbed the leg of his trousers with one hand, "I asked you to sit down, so sit down. Listen to me. Fixing the wall is not so simple. The leadership has passed the job on to me. They want me to come up with some good suggestions. I'm hopeless by myself. I have to rely on you people to!" He went on to explain all the details of the argument about the wall.

The director of the center scratched his head, "This is not going to be easy. All we do is take responsibility for laying the bricks."

The technician smiled, "It's true, the institute can't put up an ordinary wall. This is a question of a sign-board."

Ma immediately seized upon the technician and wouldn't let go. He knew this technician had a lot of good ideas tucked away and was soon to be promoted to assistant engineer. "Right, right, old pal, whatever happens I'm going to ask for your help in this. Next time you have to do something that needs a lot of running around, just make one phone call and I guarantee that within fifteen minutes I'll be there." Ma's words were pointed: The year before the technician's wife had suddenly taken ill and it was Ma who had arranged the car to take her to hospital.

The technician prodded Ma in delight, "Get on with you! Whoever sends you running around is sure to come to grief—not to mention the fact that this is quite different from calling a car. It's hard to do business with the people at your place, they discuss things for hours and can't even lay down parameters."

Ma flickered his eyes as he thought, "You can't say that, there are parameters." His brain really was agile, good at sorting the main threads of a tangled affair, "They have several fundamental ideas. The first is that it must be solid."

"Of course. It would never do to put it up today and have it fall down tomorrow." The technician picked up a tile chip and began drawing lines on the ground. He was a man who emphasized practical results and was adept at converting all kinds of demands into a workable blueprint—thickness, length, a buttress every five meters—that would be solid enough.

"Secondly it must be a high wall, but not look like a concentration camp."

"Walls are usually the height of a man with hands raised plus twelve inches. There's no need for it to be higher than that." The technician wrote down "two meters high."

"Thirdly, it must include open windows etc., something attractive that lets the air through."

The piece of tile still in his fingers, the technician shook his head, unable to continue his drawing. "That makes it difficult. Open windows on top of a two-meter wall would make it too tall and a light top on a heavy base would not be attractive. But if the windows are less than two meters above the ground, the noise from the street won't be screened out and in addition you're just inviting passers-by to stick their heads in and have a look. Problems!"

Ma waved his hand. "All right. Let's put that problem to one side for the time being. Fourthly, the wall must be burglar-proof, but can't have broken glass on top."

"Another problem!"

"We'll put that aside too. The fifth requirement is economy—it has to be cheap." Ma patted the old bricks he was sitting on. "Hey! I can solve this problem. You can sell me the old bricks from your demolishing jobs. You can charge me a nominal sum for them—you usually have to *pay* to get rubble carted away!"

Everyone laughed. The old bricks piled here were all good gray bricks. Where was the rubble?

The director shook his head. "You're a sharp one. There's no easy deal that you're not into."

The technician was still puzzling over the problematic points: "What! You still have more stipulations!"

"The consensus is that it's got to be original and unconventional."

"Well of course," the technician tapped the ground with his piece of tile, "the biggest difficulty is the open windows. Where should they go?"

A group leader spoke up, "Couldn't we put in hollow glazed bricks? We pulled down a great pile of them from old houses, they've been stacked over there ever since." He pointed to the west. "Look. If we don't get rid of them soon they'll be completely smashed to pieces."

The technician clapped a hand to his head, "Brilliant! Above one meter seventy-five we lay hollow glazed bricks—you've got your open windows and the wall's not too high. They're brightly colored too. Wang, go and get a block for Xiao Ma to look at. See if he likes it."

Wang brought one of the blocks over. It was a foot and a half square, earthenware decorative block, patterned with hollows cut through the center and glazed a deep sapphire blue. Blocks could be put together as required to form open windows of any size or shape. They were frequently found in the inner courtyard walls of old buildings.

Ma was naturally highly satisfied. Where could one go to find this kind of thing nowadays? But he still had to ask the question, "We'll be petty-minded first and lofty-minded later. How much do these things cost each? If it's too expensive we can't afford it!"

"Eighty *fen* each. How about it—it's as good as giving them to you."

Ma slapped his thigh, "Terrific! Here, have another cigarette."

The technician waved his hand, "Don't hand out the smokes. Your knotty problems have already been solved."

Ma pushed the cigarette into his hand, "What, thinking of slipping off? You haven't worked out how to keep the thieves out yet!"

The technician laughed, "Old pal, that is a problem for the gatekeeper to solve."

Ma was not willing to let it go at that. "People and walls are two different things, you're playing around with me."

"Fine, fine. I'll stop playing around. Director, you come in on this. Your place was burgled last year."

The director of the center had in fact done quite a bit of research into theft prevention, "Xiao Ma, do you know what a thief is most afraid of when he climbs a wall?"

"Who knows? I've never robbed anyone."

"They are terrified of noise. If you build a small roof on top of the wall with a roof ridge and overhanging eaves, then lay it with loose tiles, the moment your thief gets onto it the tiles will go crashing to the ground with a noise that'll have him wetting his pants."

"Great! Far more effective than broken glass —thieves all wear gloves nowadays!"

The technician took it up from the esthetic point of view. "Right! Flat topped walls are ugly too. It should have a hat—like a bamboo hat." He stamped out the rough draft he'd drawn in the earth and used the broken tile to completely redraw the whole boundary wall topped with a little roof with curved ridges. Finishing the drawing he tossed the tile away, "Xiao Ma, if this wall isn't a great success all round you can write my name upside down on it and put two crosses on the name."[1]

Everyone stood around the rough blueprint scrutinizing it carefully. The verdict was unanimous approval.

Ma was also delighted, but not to the point of complacency. When he was doing something he liked to get everything settled at one go. If he was fitting a window, he'd never forget to buy the putty; building a wall, how could he leave it on the drawing board? "Hey, don't get too engrossed in self-admiration. First put it up and then see if it's so wonderful. When can you start work?"

The director did some lengthy mental calculations and then asked the group leaders the work situation at several work sites. "We can do it like this—we'll rush things along a bit and fit you in in fifteen days."

Ma jumped up and retrieving his handkerchief from the brick wiped his hands, "How will that do? I already made a guarantee at the meeting that I'd have it up within a week!"

The director gave a sigh of regret. "See, it's not surprising that people say you're not reliable. It's not as if you don't know that the Repair Center is up to its ears in work—how could you make a guarantee like that?"

"I know the situation. I know it only too well. To tell the truth, if I weren't fully aware of the situation I'd never have dared to make a guarantee. How about it? Can you find some way of organizing it for me?" Ma took a stride forward as if he were going to force the director into the lime pit.

The director still shook his head, "There's no way, there's not enough time."

"All right. If you can't find a way, I'll arrange it. I'll give you three days' grace and you can start work on Saturday evening. Send the materials over in a truck which can also be used to take the rubble away, and send a dozen laborers to clear up the foundations. On Sunday send over a good crowd of skilled bricklayers, all you old hands included, and we'll work all day and stop when we've finished the wall. You'll get overtime, an evening meal allowance, cigarettes ...it's nothing—I can afford four or five packs of cigarettes!"

"Ah ha! You're certainly asking us to do a bit of overtime!"

"What about it? Haven't you ever done overtime before? You're not expecting me to lay on a feast, are you?"

"That's ...that's repaying our friendship—half official, half personal," the director was forced to admit.

"We're doing this all in the public interest. I'm asking you to save my face," Ma sighed, "I'm just a person who loves to keep up appearances, but always has a hard time. Everyone's afraid I'm unreliable but I still simply have to be impatient to get things done. I've just been moved to a new post and if the first guarantee I make turns out to be an empty boast, who's going to trust me in the future? Help me out, folks." Ma had begun to plead with them. People trying to get things done often had to do obeisance to the powers that be. It was pitiful to see.

It was one of the work team leaders who first slapped himself on the chest, "No problem, leave it to us!"

"Smooth sailing, Ma Erli!"

The trivial but complicated problem of the wall was thus deliberated and resolved. From start to finish it took something like half an hour.

By Saturday evening, the staff of the institute had long since finished work and gone. An electric cable was temporarily wired up outside the gate and four 200-watt light bulbs flooded the roadway with brilliant light. People arrived; trucks arrived; bricks, tiles, lime and glazed blocks were brought in, and the rubble was cleared out. In four hours all the pre-construction preparations had been completed. Then early on Sunday morning, the work began with the center director and group leaders all lending a hand. The technician took meticulous care to supervise every step of the way. Putting up the wall outside the Design Institute was the equivalent of working under an expert—you had to know the tricks of the trade. He scrutinized it from left and right, near and far, and even climbed up to the top of the office building to get a view of it from there. He checked from every angle to make sure the height was right and to decide where the glazed blocks should be laid so that the wall harmonized with the original building and was esthetically pleasing from any angle.

The office was empty on Sundays, so Ma Erli flew around in a whirl of activity, even requisitioning the services of Hong, the old gatekeeper, to give him a hand. He made tea, proffered cigarettes and hunted out odds and ends in the way of nails, aluminium wire and cotton thread, when necessary making flying trips to the hardware store. Here they shouted for Xiao Ma, there they shouted for Xiao Ma and true to his name,[2] Xiao Ma would spring like a young colt over to whoever was calling him.

The boundary wall went up at an amazing pace. People chased around shouting and calling in a bustle of activity that evoked the astonishment of passers-by.

"They must be putting up a private house!"

"No, they're having a technical examination. It's a real test of expertise to decide their grade and level."

Laying the wall was pretty easy and if they'd had new bricks it would have gone up even faster. But the glazed blocks and little roof were not so easy, particularly the roof. It was delicate work and you couldn't get everyone up there working on it either. The tiles had to be arranged carefully ridge by ridge. After every foot or so, the tiles were placed to form decorative tops and allowances also had to be made for the drainage of rain water. They'd originally planned to finish work and then eat dinner, but in the end the lights were burning until eleven at night.

Ma Erli bowed and scraped and thanked them a thousand times. He saw everyone on to the truck and then took down the electric cable, tidied up the odds and ends lying about and swept the ground. He didn't feel tired and was so pleased with himself that he couldn't resist running over to the other side of the road to admire every detail of the masterpiece.

Seen dimly through the moonlight, the boundary wall looked enchanting. It was full of poetry with its white wall, black tiles and sapphire blue windows suffused with a sparkling brilliance. The light that shone out through the patterned blocks was transformed to a shining emerald green. A soft breeze blew, swaying the tree branches and making the rays of light glimmer and dance as if there were a fairytale world hidden deep within. Above the wall one could see the black roof of the building inside jutting into the night air, and the wall suddenly seemed to change, melting into one with the main building, whose style it matched to perfection. The nearby road had changed too, it seemed to be the entrance to a scenic area or cultural palace. The more he looked, the more beautiful it seemed. He felt it was the most perfectly handled job he had ever undertaken. He didn't feel like going home, so he stretched himself out on a long sofa in the upstairs meeting room. He hadn't slept properly for two days, but this time he slept very deeply and very sweetly....

The sun rose high in the sky and a ray of sunshine crept in through the eastern window and shone on Ma Erli's baby face. He was smiling peacefully, and the faintly visible dimples gave him a most attractive, naive, childish air. But he slept too deeply for he didn't hear the exclamations of wonder and general hubbub that filled the courtyard below.

On Monday morning, people arriving at work were stupefied by the sudden appearance of the boundary wall. Although everyone had hoped the wall could be speedily rebuilt, they hadn't been in the least prepared to see it up by today. If construction had been carried out under their very eyes—adding a foot today and six inches tomorrow, with people coming and going and the ground littered with bricks and plaster, when it was finally finished everyone would have felt a great sense of relief that the chaos was over. Then regardless of the style of the wall, it would have seemed fresh and new to look at. Today, in the blink of an eye, old mother hen had turned into a duck, and it was as if it had been stolen from somewhere and brought here in the night. They weren't used to it; it was too dazzling. But the vast majority of people blinked their eyes a few times and became accustomed to it. Everyone could see clearly that this wall was better than the old one, and far better than no wall at all. But there were also some people who looked it up and down and from side to side and couldn't set their minds at rest. Despite the fact that they couldn't specify anything particularly wrong with it, they still felt that it was a bit too "uhh ..." What "uhh" was, they hadn't really thought about and were even less capable of stating clearly. That judgement would have to await the arrival of someone with authority. Should Director Wu say "Good!" most of the "uhh's" would disappear and the small number remaining, quick to grasp the situation, would praise the wall to the heavens!

Director Wu stood in the midst of the crowd looking at the wall, offering no comment from start to finish. He felt the boundary wall was what he'd imagined and yet not what he'd imagined. It was what he'd imagined because it was very unconventional, but not what he'd imagined because he hadn't envisaged *this* kind of unconventional. When he was asked to comment on the wall he just said softly, "Hmm, I never thought Ma Erli could move so fast!"

"That's just it. He's gone about this like a harum-scarum, he didn't even bother to consult general opinion," someone immediately chimed in. He primarily felt that his own opinion hadn't been sought on the question of the wall, it was really a bit too "uhh ..."

The three factions whose opinions had been solicited were also highly dissatisfied. Each felt that the wall had assimilated too few of their sound proposals. Their wonderful ideas had been messed up by unorthodox and wrong notions. They all stood beneath the wall explaining how it should have been done amidst much discussion and appraisal. Their ideas were concrete, penetrating and rich in humor.

"Call this a good-looking wall? Neither Chinese nor Western, wearing a Western suit topped by a skull cap and with a green scarf wound round its neck. Which dynasty does that get-up belong to? Does it have the slightest flavor of the modern age?" Zhu Zhou finished his appraisal and perused the crowd in search of support.

"That's right, a perimeter wall is after all a wall, what do you want to give it a great roof for?" The people who found the wall a bit too "uhh" began to express themselves more explicitly. All that offended their eye was localized in that small roof. But in fact it could hardly be called a roof, it was just shaped like a roof, that was all.

Zhu was extremely complacent. He went over to the wall to measure its height and rub his hand over the protruding brick pillars. He felt the height and solidity of construction were just what he'd had in mind. It was just that the open brickwork windows and that little roof were too preposterous. It was the conservatives who were the cause of their being there! He turned his head and called to Huang Daquan:

"Huang, you should be satisfied this time—the flavor is entirely classical!"

Huang shook his head, "What are you talking about? He hasn't completely grasped the spirit of my conception. The roof ridge shouldn't be a flat line, it's too monotonous. He could have built two decorative squares in the center to symbolize good luck, that would have given it variety without being too ornate. Why did it have to be so tall? ... Zhu, go and stand over there and don't move, I want to take a picture. I'll call it, 'Even with wings you couldn't fly over.' "

"You're right. It's too tall."

"There should have been corner eaves sticking up at either end."

"They didn't lay quite enough glazed blocks."

Everyone who had felt the boundary wall was a bit "uhh" helped pick fault with it. Their ability to criticize had always been greater than their creative abilities.

He Rujin didn't make any specific comments on the wall, but approaching from a different angle brought up a question likely to have the masses rising in anger.

"Let's temporarily ignore whether this wall is good or bad. What I want to ask is does it conform with our principles of economy? How much labor did that little roof require, how much each were those glazed blocks? I'm afraid this will have used up every cent of our administrative budget. Our thrift bonus this quarter is likely to be twenty cents each!"

He Rujin's words evoked a wave of excitement, "That's right! He should have just built the wall and had done with it, why did he have to go and trim the top with lace!"

"This is just ..." the speaker glanced around and found no sign of Ma, "this is just Ma Erli's work style, the man is wasteful and extravagant. By the look of it he's a spoilt young rich boy, spending money like water."

"Director Wu, was it you who made him build it like this?"

Director Wu hastily waved his hands. "No, no! I just told him to think about it. I never thought he'd act first and then ask for approval. Ma Erli ..." he shouted, but Ma was still sleeping on the sofa and didn't hear.

"Old Hong, did you see Ma Erli arrive this morning?" enquired one of the others who had joined the search for Ma. He wanted to call the chief offender to question there on the spot.

The old gatekeeper Hong was furious, "Stop your screaming and shouting, he hasn't rested for two days, unlike you!" Old Hong was disgusted by all the artful talk. He sided with Ma because he'd seen him working endlessly while the wall was being built, clothes soaked through. It wasn't everyone who could do that. Sitting at the gate he'd also heard the comments of passers-by —they all said how attractive the wall was. He personally had an even deeper affection for the wall, for from now on he could sleep in peace. If a burglar tried to climb in, some of the tiles on the eaves were sure to go crashing to the ground!

Director Wu frowned. He waved his hands for silence and told everyone to go and get on with their work, at the same time calling Zhu, Huang, He, and others to attend a brief meeting upstairs.

Zhu pushed open the door of the meeting room and discovered Ma Erli sleeping peacefully on the sofa!

"Heavens! We've been looking for you in vain everywhere, and the whole time you were here having a good sleep. Get up!"

Ma rubbed his eyes and scrambled up. Still half asleep, he hazily weathered the hail of censure.

But it wasn't so bad. Although there was a lot of criticism, no one suggested demolishing the wall and rebuilding it. The boundary wall passed the summer and autumn unscathed. Delicate grasses began to grow around the foot and wisteria began to climb across the surface.

That winter, the Architectural Design Institute played host to the annual architectural conference to which various scholars and specialists from different parts of the country were invited. Because there weren't a lot of participants, the conference was held in the ground floor meeting room of the institute. No sooner had the experts entered the gate than their attention was attracted by the boundary wall. They looked it up and down, full of praise. Once the conference had got under way, the wall became the main topic of conversation. They said the boundary wall solved one of the major problems of city construction! Today's city architecture was too monotonous; everything was constructed on a standard matchbox pattern, unvaried and unornamented, totally lacking our own unique traditional flavor. There were also places which blindly went back to the ways of the ancients, building curving eaves with upswept corners, carved rafters and painted crossbeams with the result that hotels turned out like temple halls. The good thing about this wall was its traditional style. Yet it was not a blind replication of the classic but executed according to criteria of practical economy. It also harmonized with the building itself. They hoped that the comrades would carefully think things over and come to a scholarly conclusion.

The participants from the institute were all pleasantly surprised. They had never imagined a golden phoenix would appear out of their hen's nest!

Director Wu pondered, "This is all because the guiding thought was clear and unequivocal. From the start I made explicit demands, at the same time rousing the masses to comprehensive discussion...."

Zhu Zhou was also pondering, "Too true, the practical value of the boundary wall can't be overlooked. Right from the start I maintained that it must be taller, more secure...."

Huang Daquan was quite simply delighted with himself, "If it hadn't been for me arguing for what I knew was right, who knows what unearthly shape the wall would have gone up in. Architects just can't afford to forget their origins. Our ancestors understood the magical effects of boundary walls long ago. They had scores of names for them, let alone ..." Huang Daquan considered this speech should be written into the opening paragraph of the conference proceedings, summary, it would do as a foreword.

He Rujin had suffered momentary unhappiness, but then immediately felt his contribution had really been enormous. If he hadn't insisted on economy, Ma Erli would never have gone looking for old bricks and tiles and would never have found the glazed blocks. Without the glazed blocks the wall would have been nothing out of the ordinary.

Ma Erli didn't take part in the conference, he just busied himself rushing in and out of the room arranging tables and chairs and bringing tea and water. He'd taken into consideration the fact that the room would be very cold and from somewhere or other had produced four glowing charcoal braziers. With one placed in each corner, the room immediately became as warm as springtime. Everyone felt cosy and relaxed....

Translated by Rosie A. Roberts

Notes:

[1] It was a common practice, when denouncing someone, to put the characters of one's name upside down or sideways and cross them out with red strokes during the Cultural Revolution.

[2] In Chinese *xiao* means "little" or "young," the original and common reference of *ma* is "horse."

SHEN RONG AND HER FICTION

Gladys Yang

Shen Rong's father was a judge in the Supreme Court before 1949. In New China this "bad family origin" was something to live down. This may have strengthened the determination to forge ahead which has characterized her career.

A native of Wushan County in Sichuan, Shen Rong was born in 1935. At the age of fifteen, stirred by the revolutionary changes around her, she left junior middle school after only one year to be a salesgirl in a bookshop for workers. In 1952 she transferred to the *Southwest Workers Daily* in Chongqing. She studied Russian by following broadcast lessons, and in 1954 was admitted to the Foreign Languages College in Beijing. Just before graduation she married a journalist, Fan Yongkang, now a senior editor of the *People's Daily*.

In 1957 she started work as a translator in the Radio Station. She drove herself so hard that her health broke down and she went to Shanxi to convalesce, staying in the home of a woman brigade leader. Her love and admiration for Chinese villagers dates from that time. In 1964 she returned to Beijing where, not fit enough to go back to her job, she did some writing and painting. Her first works were plays, and one was in rehearsal when the start of the Cultural Revolution quashed it.

Between 1969 and 1973, when most cadres were sent down to the country, she went with her colleagues to Tongxian County. There again she lived with a peasant family and worked with them in the fields. As her health improved she joined a team which went from village to village explaining the Party's policies at that time. They were called in to settle all manner of disputes, which increased her understanding of the peasants.

Her first novel *Perpetual Youth* was published in 1975. Her second, *Light and Dark* (1978), deals with the struggle against the Gang of Four. She also wrote two novellas, *Eternal Spring* and *White Snow*. However, the work which brought her fame was *At Middle Age* (1980), a bold, accurate reflection of new social problems.

When this novella was assigned to our magazine *Chinese Literature* to translate, one young colleague waved it in the air and called: "Hey, here's something different! It's about INTELLECTUALS." Hitherto the protagonists of Chinese fiction had almost always been workers, peasants, or soldiers.

This story is not a traditional chronological narrative. It starts off with the heroine Dr Lu lying semi-comatose after a heart attack, then uses recollections, the words and behavior of Dr Lu's patients, colleagues and husband to build up a series of pictures from the past which reveal her gentle but determined character, her conscientious attitude to work and her love for her patients and family.

Dr Lu represents the middle-aged professionals now playing a key role in modernizing China. They work long hours, often under poor conditions. Their salaries are very low, their living quarters are cramped, and, when this story was written, they had few labor-saving devices to make their housework less onerous or give them time for research. Dr Lu sacrifices her health to cure her patients, yet has a sense of guilt for not looking after her husband and children better. (Shen Rong, too, says she neglects her family to make more time for her work.)

Another doctor and her husband are preparing to leave for Canada. In addition to the hard conditions which all intellectuals must face, they have had to put up with political discrimination because of their connections overseas. Now that the government has relaxed the restrictions on emigration, a number of well-qualified doctors have left. This brain drain is deplorable in view of the shortage of trained personnel. Some readers therefore criticized Shen Rong for portraying this couple sympathetically, but her aim was to highlight the shocking conditions of overworked, underpaid professionals in order to arouse more concern for them.

Other critics thought *At Middle Age* painted too black a picture. Some took exception to her satirical sketch of a "Marxist-Leninist old lady," a high official's wife who mouths political platitudes, demands preferential treatment, does no useful work herself and makes things difficult for other people. But readers in general applauded this exposure of an "old revolutionary" who had lost all revolutionary feeling. The novella won a best story award and over three million copies have been sold. Foreign readers may find certain passages saccharine but would do well to read it. In 1983 it was made into a popular film, which Shen Rong hopes will soon be out of date as the treatment of intellectuals improves.

Since then she has written a novella each year as well as short stories and essays reflecting a wide spectrum of society. Here I can only touch on a few examples.

The Secret of Crown Prince Village shows a deep insight into peasants and grassroots cadres and is shot through with humor. Before the agricultural reforms the county authorities often ordered communes under their jurisdiction to grow crops for which their land was unsuited, and frowned on side-line production, calling this "capitalistic." As a result the peasants' output was low and they were underfed and apathetic. To remedy this, the shrewd brigade leader Li of Crown Prince Village makes a great show of "grasping class struggle" to trick the authorities. For instance, in order to start a profitable beancurd mill he holds a struggle meeting to denounce an ex-landlord who declares that the project is like "a toad lusting after the flesh of a swan." Then by quoting Chairman Mao's saying "We support whatever the enemy opposes," Li gains the commune's permission to go ahead. Using various ruses to bypass arbitrary instructions, and arousing his brigade members' enthusiasm by material incentives, he makes Crown Prince Village prosperous. When finally the policy changes, the authorities approve his methods of boosting production.

A Rose-Colored Evening Meal is a poignant account of a family reunion to celebrate the rehabilitation of an old artist after twenty years in disgrace. It reveals the remorse of his elder son who broke with his father when he was declared a Rightist, and shows how normal family relations were disrupted by the ultra-Left line.

A Distracting Sunday exposes the all too common practice in China of "finding a back door," or pulling strings to benefit oneself. Mu, the Party Secretary of a university, is about to take his grandson to the park when he receives a stream of visitors. All urge him to allow a graduating student Ding to stay on in Beijing instead of going back to his own province. This Ding got into college through the back door and has now been bribing people right and left, going so far as to become engaged to the ugly daughter of a vice-minister, Mu's old superior. In spite of all this pressure, Mu determines to oppose backdoorism. This straightforward tale with its optimistic ending displays Shen Rong's skill in character vignettes.

Waiting for Phone Calls illustrates the psychology of newly retired bureaucrats, bored men with few hobbies or interests. Shen Rong is adept at finding topical themes which reflect recent social changes.

Snakes and Ladders (in Chinese entitled *True and False*) describes a series of meetings called in a Foreign Literature Research Center to criticize a valuable article on Western modernist writing which a Party official has condemned. The author Xu, an ex-Rightist, is very worried. This is after the Third Plenum of '78 when the Party called for independent thinking and for seeking truth from facts. Still the researchers are too accustomed to obeying those in authority to speak out frankly. Their meetings consist mainly of long silences, verbal acrobatics, phoney self-criticisms or statements like, "I agree with what everyone's said and I've nothing new to add." Only the daughter of a high official feels safe to defy the Party commissar. Finally the head of the center, after a mental struggle, defends Xu's scientific analysis of Western modernism and urges his colleagues to liberate their minds because there is no need to lie any more.

In the 1980s literary magazines proliferated. There are now hundreds of them, and Shen Rong, as a most popular woman writer, is always being asked for manuscripts. She may retort, "You can't squeeze stories out of me like toothpaste out of a tube." Once when she had nothing new for an editor he asked for some of her early unpublished work. "No," said Shen Rong, "those are rejects." He replied, "It's your name we want." But she still refused. When two publishers wanted to put out selections of her writings both including the same novelette, she stopped them. They pointed out that this would earn her more money, but she countered that it would be unfair to those readers who bought both selections.

Her somewhat blunt way of speaking has laid her open to charges of arrogance, and may have delayed her admission to the Party. She applied many years ago, but was not accepted till 1986. I have never found her arrogant. However, like most Chinese writers whose work is in great demand, she is not overly amenable to editorial advice. In 1982 she wrote her first piece of reportage, *Forty Years of Shared Griefs and Joys*. As this was about my husband and me, I know how conscientiously she wrote it. I also know that when advised to cut the last paragraph she issued the ultimatum, "If you mean to do that I'll give it to some other magazine." The editors did not insist.

Shen Rong's life is packed. Though her two sons have grown up and her daughter is at high school, she has to work hard to keep house, entertain her many Chinese and foreign visitors, attend meetings and make time for reading and writing. She is often asked to give talks, and frequently travels to different parts of the country to keep up with the rapid changes there and grasp the new trends in China's modernization.

In recent years she has preferred to write novellas or short stories rather than novels, because the publication of a book is a lengthy business whereas shorter works in magazines can reflect social developments much faster.

When she has time to relax she watches video material to improve her English. Self-taught, she can now after careful preparation deliver a talk in English. On our last visit to her, when all the children were home for a festival, I was struck by their lifestyle, a happy combination of East and West. She showed us the handsome green bathroom she has installed, surely the finest in any flat in Beijing. We danced to Western music, her two-year-old grandson entertained us all by his fluent recitations of Tang poems, and the meal was Sichuan cuisine at its best.

In recent years she has traveled extensively to North America, Japan, Singapore and Europe. Intrigued by the black humor and the Theater of the Absurd of the West, she has produced spoofs about China. Her gentle satires dealing with everyday topics are dramatically effective. A collection of these has recently been published in Hong Kong.

Ten Years Deducted, an award-winner introduced in this selection, is influenced by the modernist school. But although surrealistic it is rooted in Chinese life; hence the psychology of its characters is truthful.

The Cultural Revolution or "ten years of turmoil" had devastating consequences for all age groups, quite apart from the huge economic losses incurred. Schools and libraries closed, depriving a whole generation of a regular education. Young people were sent to work in the countryside, where girls were reluctant to marry, not wanting to stay there for life. When at last they returned to the cities, too old to go to college, they were looked down on as old maids. Rehabilitated cadres discovered that years of chaos had played havoc with labor discipline. Most of their subordinates simply muddled along in offices bogged down by redundancy and bureaucracy, so that it was very difficult to restore order. Middle-aged intellectuals, long deprived of facilities for research, found it hard to understand the new technical material from abroad....

Now that life tenure has ended, advancing age seems a menace leading to retirement or marking an end to promotion. To justify their own inertia many people sigh, "If only I were ten years younger ..." In this story wishful thinking makes them believe in a non-existent directive to turn the clock back ten years. Shen Rong implies that

191

they should give up illusions, tackle the work in hand and live in the present.

Readers of the story felt a thrill of amusement, recognizing their own feelings or the mentality of acquaintances in it. It has been made into a popular film.

Shen Rong in her early fifties seems much younger. Dressed attractively in a bright sweater and jeans, her hair fashionably styled, she looks full of energy. Her literary output has been considerable. This year the Huacheng Publishing House in Guangdong will publish her collected works in five volumes. She is continuing to forge ahead, and is now at work on a full-length novel.

January 1988

Ten Years Deducted

Shen Rong

WORD wafted like a spring breeze through the whole office building. "They say a directive will be coming down, deducting ten years from everybody's age!"

"Wishful thinking," said a sceptic.

"Believe it or not," was the indignant retort. "The Chinese Age Research Association after two years' investigation and three months' discussion has drafted a proposal for the authorities. It's going to be ratified and issued any day now."

The sceptic remained dubious.

"Really? If so, that's the best news I've ever heard!"

His informant explained,

"The age researchers agreed that the Cultural Revolution wasted ten years of everyone's precious time. This ten years debit should be canceled out...."

That made sense. The sceptic was convinced.

"Deduct ten years and instead of sixty-one I'll be fifty-one—splendid!"

"And I'll be forty-eight, not fifty-eight—fine!"

"This is wonderful news!"

"Brilliant, great!"

The gentle spring breeze swelled up into a whirl-wind engulfing everyone.

"Have you heard? Ten years deducted!"

"Ten years off, no doubt about it."

"Minus ten years!"

All dashed around to spread the news.

An hour before it was time to leave, the whole building was deserted.

Ji Wenyao, now sixty-four, as soon as he got home, yelled towards the kitchen,

"Minghua, come here quick!"

"What's up?" At her husband's call Fang Minghua hurried out holding some spinach she was washing.

Ji was standing in the middle of the room, arms akimbo, his face lit up. Hearing his wife come in he turned his head, his eyes flashing, and said incisively,

"This room needs smartening up. Tomorrow go and order a set of Romanian furniture."

She stepped forward in surprise and asked quietly,

"Are you crazy, Old Ji? We've only those few thousand in the bank. If you squander that ..."

"Bah, you don't understand." Face flushed, neck dilated, he cried, "Now we must start a new life!"

Their son and daughter, as if by tacit consent, hurried in from their respective rooms, not knowing what to make of their father's announcement. Was the old man off his rocker?

"Get out, this is none of your business." Old Ji shooed away the inquisitive young people.

He then closed the door and, quite out of character, leapt forward to throw his arms around his wife's plump shoulders. This display of affection, the first in dozens of years, alarmed her even more than his order to buy Romanian furniture. She wondered: what's wrong with him? He's been so down in the dumps about reaching retirement age, he's never demonstrative like this in the daytime, and even in bed he just sighs to himself as if I weren't there beside him. What's got into him today? A man in his sixties carrying on like those romantic characters in TV plays—she blushed for him. But Old Ji didn't notice, his eyes were blazing. Half hugging, half carrying her, he lugged his impassive wife to the wicker chair and sat her down, then whispered jubilantly into her ear,

"I'll tell you some top-secret news. A directive's coming down, we're all to have ten years deducted from our age."

"Ten—years—deducted?" Minghua let fall the spinach, her big eyes nearly popping out of her head. "Well I never! Is it true?"

"It's true. The directive will be arriving any minute."

"Oh my! Well I never!" She sprang to her feet to throw her arms round her husband's scrawny shoulders and peck at his high forehead. Then, shocked by her own behavior, she felt as if carried back thirty years in time. Old Ji looked blank for a moment then took her hands and the two of them spun round three times in the middle of the room.

"Oh my, I'm dizzy." Not till Minghua pulled free, patting her stout chest, did they stop whirling merrily round.

"Well, dear? Don't you think we ought to buy a set of Romanian furniture?" Ji looked confidently at his rejuvenated wife.

"We ought." Her big eyes were shining.

"Oughtn't we to make a fresh start?"

"We ought, we ought." Her voice was unsteady and there were tears in her eyes.

Old Ji plumped down on the armchair and closed his eyes while rosy dreams of the future flooded his mind. Abruptly opening his eyes, he said resolutely,

"Of course our private lives are a minor matter; the

main thing is we now have ten more years to work. This time I'm determined to make a go of it. Our bureau is so slack, I must take a firm grip on things. On the back-up work too; the head of our general office is not a suitable choice at all. The airs our drivers give themselves, they need to be straightened out too...."

He flourished his arms, his slit eyes agleam with excitement.

"The question of the leading group will have to be reconsidered. I was forced to appoint the best of a bad lot. That Zhang Mingming is a bookworm with no experience of leadership. Ten years, give me ten years, and I'll get together a good leading group; a young one with really new blood, chosen from today's college students. Graduates of twenty-three or twenty-four, I'll groom them myself for ten years and then...."

Minghua took little interest in the overhauling of the leading group, looking forward to the wonderful life ahead.

"I think I'll get another armchair too."

"Get a suite instead, more modern."

"And our bed, we'll get a soft one in its place." She reddened.

"Quite right. After sleeping hard all our lives we should get a soft bed to move with the times."

"The money ..."

"What does money matter." Ji Wenyao took a long-term view, filled with pride and enthusiasm. "The main thing is getting another ten years, ah, that's something no money could buy."

As they were talking excitedly, getting along so well, their daughter opened the door a crack to ask,

"Mum, what shall we have for supper?"

"Oh, cook whatever you want." Minghua had forgotten completely about the meal.

"No!" Old Ji raised one hand and announced, "We'll go out and eat roast duck, I'm standing treat. You and your brother go first to get a table, your mother and I will follow."

"Oh!" His daughter gaped at seeing her parents in such high spirits. Without asking the reason she went to call her brother.

Brother and sister hurried off to the roast duck restaurant, speculating all the way there. He said perhaps an exception had been made in the old man's case, and he was being kept on. She thought that maybe he had been promoted or got a bonus. Of course neither of them could guess that the deduction of ten years was worth infinitely more than any promotion.

At home the old couple were still deep in conversation.

"Minghua, you should smarten yourself up too. Ten years off makes you just forty-eight."

"Me? Forty-eight?" she murmured as if dreaming. The vitality of her long-lost youth was animating her plump flabby figure, to her bewilderment.

"Tomorrow buy yourself a cream-colored coat for spring and autumn." Old Ji looked critically at her tight grey Mao-suit and said decisively, almost protestingly, "Why shouldn't we be in fashion? Just wait. After supper I'll buy myself an Italian-style jacket like Zhang Mingming's. He's forty-nine this year; if he can wear one, why shouldn't I?"

"Right!" Minghua smoothed her scruffy, lusterless grey hair. "I'll dye my hair too and treat myself to a visit to a first-rate beauty-parlor. Ha, the young folk call me a stick-in-the-mud, but put back the clock ten years and I'll show them what living is all about ..."

Old Ji sprang to his feet and chimed in,

"That's it, we must know how to make the most of our lives. We'll travel: go to Lushan, Huangshan, and Jiuzhaigou. Even if we can't swim we'll go to have a look at the ocean. The fifties, that's the prime of life. Really, in the past we had no idea how to live!"

Not pausing to comment Minghua went on thinking aloud,

"If ten years are deducted and I'm just forty-nine, I can work another six years. I must go back and do a good job too."

"You ..." Old Ji sounded dubious.

"Six years, six years, I can work for another six years," she exulted.

"You'd better not," Ji said. "Your health isn't up to it."

"My health's fine." In her eagerness to get back to work she really felt quite fit.

"If you take up your old job who'll do all the house-work?"

"We'll get a maid."

"But that lot of women from Anhui[1] are only too irresponsible. You can't trust one of them to take over here."

Minghua began to waver.

"Besides, since you've already retired you don't want to make more trouble for the leadership, do you? If all the old retired cadres asked to go back, well, that would mess things up." Ji shuddered at the thought.

"No, I've still six years in which I can work," she insisted. "If you won't take me back in the bureau, I can transfer somewhere else. As Party secretary or deputy secretary in some firm—how about that?"

"Well ...those firms are a very mixed lot."

"All the more reason to strengthen their leadership.

We old people are the ones to do ideological and political work."

"All right."

Ji noddd, pleasing her as much as if the head of the organization department had agreed. She chortled,

"That's fine then! Those researchers are really understanding. Ten years off, a fresh start—that's beyond my wildest dreams."

"Well, I dreamed of it." Quite carried away Ji cried out vehemently, "The Cultural Revolution robbed me of ten of my best years. Ten years, think what I could have done in that time. Ten wasted years, leaving me white-haired and decrepit. Who's to make good that loss? Why did I have to swallow such a bitter pill? Give me back my youth! Give me back ten years! Now this research association is giving me back that decade of my youth. Good for them; this should have been done long ago."

Not wanting her husband to recall painful memories, Minghua smiled and changed the subject.

"All right, let's go and have roast duck."

Zhang Mingming, forty-nine that year, couldn't analyze his reaction. It seemed a mixture of pleasure and distress, of sweetness and bitterness.

Ten years off certainly pleased him. Working on scientific research, he knew the value of time. Especially for him, a middle-aged intellectual approaching fifty, the recovery of ten years was a heaven-sent opportunity. Look at researchers overseas. A scientist in his twenties could win an international reputation by presenting a thesis at an international conference, then go on to head his field while in his thirties, his name known throughout the world—there were many such cases. Then look at him: a brilliant student, one of the most promising in his college, with just as good a grounding as anyone else. But unluckily, he had been born at the wrong time, and sent to do physical labor in the countryside. When he got down again to his interrupted studies, the technical material was strange to him, his brain didn't function properly and his hands trembled. Now with this extra ten years he could make a fresh start. If he went all out and research conditions improved, with less time wasted bickering over trifles, why, he could cram twenty years' work into ten years and distinguish himself by scaling the heights of science.

He was pleased; just as pleased as everyone else, if not more so.

But a colleague slapped him on the back and asked, "Old Zhang, what are you so bucked about?"

"What do you mean?" Why shouldn't he be bucked?

"Deducting ten years makes Ji Wenyao fifty-four. So he won't retire, and you won't take over the bureau."

Quite true. That being the case, Ji won't retire. He doesn't want to. He'll stick on as bureau head. And what about me? Of course I won't be promoted, I'll remain an engineer doing scientific research in the lab and library. Yet two days ago, the ministry sent for me to tell me that Old Ji would be retiring and they'd decided to put me in charge. Does that still hold good?

He really didn't want an official post. The highest he had ever held was that of group head, and convening a group meeting was the height of his political experience. He had never expected an official title, least of all the imposing one of bureau head. He had always been a "bookworm." In the Cultural Revolution he had come under fire as "a reactionary revisionist bent on becoming an expert." Since the overthrow of the Gang of Four he had spent all his time in his lab, not talking to a soul.

But somehow or other, when it came to choosing a third-echelon leading group he had been chosen. In each public opinion poll his name headed the list, just as he had always come top in examinations. When he was summoned to the ministry, it sounded as if the whole business had been settled. In that case he couldn't understand where or how he had shown any leading ability, to be favored by the authorities and trusted by the rank and file. Thinking it over he felt most ashamed. He had never had any administrative ability, let alone any leadership qualities.

His wife Xue Minru, moderately good-looking and intelligent, was an admirable wife and mother. She took a keen interest in her husband's affairs and knew the disputes in his bureau very well. Her comment had been:

"It's because you're not leadership material that you've been chosen for a leading post."

Zhang was puzzled by this statement. What does that mean, he wondered. Then he thought: maybe there's some truth in it. Because I've no ability to lead or any definite views of my own, and I've not jockeyed for position, no one need worry about me. Perhaps that's why I've been given this opening.

Of course there was also an "opposition party." It was said that at one Party meeting in the bureau his problem had been disputed all afternoon. What the dispute was about he wasn't clear. Nor what his problem was either. After that, though, he felt that he had become a "controversial figure." And this "controversy" wouldn't be resolved nor would his "problem" be cleared up till the day he became bureau head.

Gradually, as these public opinion polls and arguments went on, Zhang became accustomed to his role as someone due to be promoted and a "controversial figure." Sometimes he even imagined that he might really make a good bureau head, though he had never held such a position.

"Better take the job," said Minru. "It's not as if you'd grabbed at it. When you're bureau chief, at least you won't have to squeeze on to the bus to go to work."

But now he wouldn't get the job. Was he sorry? A little, not altogether. What it boiled down to was: his feelings were mixed.

He went home at a loss.

"Back? Good, the meal's just ready." Minru went into the kitchen to fetch one meat dish, one vegetable dish and a bowl of egg and pickles soup. The meat dish wasn't greasy and the green vegetables looked very tempting.

His wife was an excellent housekeeper; considerate, clever and deft. During the three hard years when their neighbors contracted hepatitis or dropsy, she kept their family fit by cooking coarse grain so that it tasted good, boiling bones to make soup and using melon rind in place of vegetables. Now farm produce was plentiful, but fish and meat had risen so much in price that everybody claimed they couldn't afford them. However, Minru knew how to cook tasty inexpensive meals. When Zhang saw the supper she had served, he lost no time in washing his hands, sitting down at the table and picking up his chopsticks.

"What succulent celery," he remarked. "Is it expensive? The papers say celery keeps your blood pressure down."

Minru simply smiled.

"These pickles are good too; they give the soup a fine flavor."

Still she just smiled and said nothing.

"Bamboo shoots with pork ..." he went on praising this simple meal as if he were a gourmet.

She laughed and cut him short to ask:

"What's got into you today? Has anything happened?"

"No, nothing," he made a show of surprise. "I was just admiring your cooking."

"You never do normally, so why today?" she was still smiling.

Feeling driven into a corner he retorted:

"It's because I don't normally that I'm saying this now."

"No, you're hiding something from me." She could see through him.

With a sigh he put down his chopsticks.

"I'm not hiding anything, but I don't know what to make of it myself or how to tell you."

Minru smiled complacently. Her husband might be an expert researcher, a top man in his own field, but when it came to psychoanalysis he was no match for her.

"Never mind, just tell me." She sounded like a teacher patiently encouraging a child.

"Today word came that they're going to issue a directive to deduct ten years from everybody's age."

"Impossible."

"It's true."

"Really?"

"Really and truly."

She thought this over and looked at him with big limpid eyes, then chuckled.

"So you won't be bureau head."

"That's right."

"Does that upset you?"

"No. I can't explain it, but I feel put out."

He took up his chopsticks again to fiddle with the rice in his bowl as he went on,

"To start with I'm not leadership material and I didn't want this job. But they've made such a mess of things these last few years, it seems I ought to take over. Still, this sudden change makes me feel a bit ..." He was at a loss for words.

Minru said incisively,

"If you don't get the job so much the better. You think it's a cushy post?"

Zhang looked up at his wife, surprised by her decisive tone of voice. A few days ago when he'd told her about this impending promotion, she had shown genuine elation. She'd said, "Look at you—you didn't grab at the job and now these laurels have been put on your head." Now the laurels were lost she wasn't upset or angry, as if there had never been any talk of promotion.

"As bureau head, head of the bureau, you'd have been expected to solve every problem big or small —could you have stood it?" she asked. "Allocation of housing, promotions, bonuses, private squabbles, financial affairs, finding jobs or kindergartens for people's children. How could you manage all that?"

True, no one could manage it all.

"Stick to your speciality. An extra ten years will make all the difference to what you can achieve."

Yes, it would certainly make all the difference.

Zhang felt easier in his mind, with a sense of light-hearted well-being.

He went to bed expecting to sleep soundly. But he woke in the middle of the night with a feeling of faint regret and deprivation.

Thirty-nine-year-old Zheng Zhenhai shot out of the bureau and cycled swiftly home. There he took off his old grey jacket and tossed it on to a chair, conscious of inexhaustible energy. This deduction of ten years seemed to call for prompt action to solve many major problems.

"Hey!"

No one answered his call. His ten-year-old son was fooling about as usual in the alley, and where was his wife who usually responded? Out visiting? Hell! What sort of home was this?

His home-made armchair was so misproportioned that his spine didn't reach the back, while the low arms and high seat made sitting in it positively tiring. All because she had to keep up with the neighbors, she had insisted, since they couldn't afford to buy armchairs, on his making a set himself. What a philistine! It was sickening the way every family had armchairs like this, as standard as a cadre's uniform. So philistine!

Whatever had made him choose her? Such a vulgar family with no interests in life except food, clothing, pay and perks. Family upbringing was all-important. She was the spitting image of her mother: the same crude way of talking, and fat as a barrel since the birth of the boy, with no good looks, no figure, no character. Whatever had made him choose someone like her?

Hell! It came of being in too much of a hurry. A bachelor nearing thirty couldn't be choosy. Now with ten years off, he was only twenty-nine! He must think over this problem seriously. Yesterday she'd squawked and flounced about because he'd bought a carton of good cigarettes, threatening to divorce him—they couldn't go on like this. Divorce? Go ahead! Twenty-nine was just the right age to find a wife, a slender college graduate of twenty-two or twenty-three with a refined, modern outlook. College graduates should marry other college graduates. She was half-baked, just from a technical school. He could kick himself for making such a mistake.

He must re-organize his life, not muddle along like this. Where the hell had she gone?

In fact, after the office she'd bolted out of the bureau to head for a shop selling women's clothes.

The thought of ten years off had thrown Yuejuan into raptures and fired her imagination. A woman one year short of forty, she was suddenly restored to a girl of twenty-nine. For her this heaven-sent stroke of luck was a boon not all the money in the world could buy.

Twenty-nine—to be so young was glorious! She glanced down at her faded, drab, unprepossessing dress with a stab of pained resentment. Hurrying into the shop she pounded up to the section displaying the latest fashions, her eyes scanning the dazzling costumes hanging there till a scarlet dress trimmed with white gauze struck her. She asked to try it on. The salesgirl looked her up and down, her impassive face cold and stony, her cold look implying contempt.

"Well? Aren't I fit to wear this?" Yuejuan fumed inwardly, as she often had in recent years when shopping for clothes, because whenever something took her fancy, Zhenhai always ticked her off: "That makes you look like mutton dressed like lamb." What was wrong with that? Did she have to dress like an old woman? Generally she went home in a rage without buying anything, to squabble with him all night. How unlucky she was, landed for life with such a stick-in-the-mud.

Why stop to argue with the salesgirl? I'll pay for what I buy, you hand it over and mind your own bloody business! What did the silly fool know? Had she heard about the directive? This is just the dress for someone of twenty-nine. The Chinese are too conservative. In other countries, the older ladies are, the more they prink themselves up. Eighty-year-olds wear green and red. What does it matter to you what I choose to wear? However you glare at me, I'm taking this.

Having paid up, Yuejuan went into the fitting room. In the long mirror, the scarlet dress which hugged her plump figure so tightly seemed a rather outsize mass of fiery red, but really hot stuff, really smart. Well, she'd have to start slimming. Ten years could be deducted from her age by a directive from on high, but to deduct ten pounds from her weight she'd have to sweat blood. She'd long since stopped eating animal fat and ate only the minimum of starchy food, even cutting down on fruit. However was she to slim?

She huffed and puffed her way home, threw open the door and burst in like a ball of fire. Zhenhai leapt up in horror from his armchair to ask,

"What's come over you?"

"What do you mean?"

"Where on earth did you get that dress?"

"I bought it. So what?" She raised the hem of the dress and circled round like a model with a coquettish smile.

He at once poured cold water on her.

"Don't imagine that gaudy colors are beautiful—it depends on who's wearing them."

"Why shouldn't I wear them?"

"A dress like that is out of place on you; you're past the age for it. Just think of your age."

"I have thought; that's why I bought it. Twenty-nine! Just the right age to dress up."

"Twenty-nine?" Zhenhai was taken aback.

"That's right, twenty-nine. Minus ten years makes me twenty nine, less one month. I insist on wearing reds and greens—so there!" She was gesticulating like an affectedly coy pop singer careering about the stage.

Confound the woman, at her age, so broad in the beam, what a sight she was carrying on like this because of ten years off! Zhenhai shut his eyes, then opened them abruptly to glare at her.

"The authorities are issuing this directive so as to give full play to cadres' youthful vitality and speed up modernization, not so that you'll dress up!"

"How does dressing up affect modernization?" She sprang to her feet. "Does the directive forbid us to dress up? Eh?"

"I mean you can't dress up without taking into account your appearance and figure...."

"What's wrong with my figure?" Touched on a sore spot she struck back. "I'll tell you a home truth. You think me fat; I think you are scrawny, scrawny as a pullet, with deep lines like tramways on your forehead, and you can't walk three steps without wheezing. Bah! I wanted an intellectual for a husband. But with you, what better treatment have we had? You're an intellectual in nothing but name. No decent clothes, no decent place to live in. Well? Now I'm twenty-nine, still young, I can find a pedlar anywhere in the street who's better off than you, whether he sells peanuts or sugar-coated haws."

"Go ahead then and find one."

"It's easy. We'll divorce today, and tomorrow I'll register my new marriage."

"Let's divorce then."

With that the fat was in the fire. Normally Yuejuan

kept talking of "divorce" while to Zhenhai the term was taboo. Now that devil was using it too. Of all the gall! This wouldn't do.

It was all the fault of those damn researchers. She butted her husband with her head and raged:

"Deducting ten years has sent you round the bend. Who are you to want a divorce? No way!"

"You think by deducting ten years you can have your way in everything—you're crazy!"

"Little Lin, there's a dance tomorrow at the Workers' Cultural Palace. Here's a ticket for you." Big Sister Li of the trade union beckoned to Lin Sufen.

Ignoring her, Sufen quickened her step and hurried out of the bureau.

Take off ten years and she was only nineteen. No one could call her an old maid any more. The trade union needn't worry about a slip of a girl. She didn't need help from the matchmakers' office either. Didn't need to attend dances organized to bring young people together. All that was done with!

Unmarried at twenty-nine, she found it hard to bear the pitying, derisive, vigilant or suspicious glances that everyone cast at her. She was pitied for being single, all alone; scoffed at for missing the bus by being too choosy; guarded against as hypersensitive and easily hurt; suspected of being hysterical and warped. One noon when she went to the boiler room to poach herself two eggs in a bowl of instant noodles, she heard someone behind her comment:

"Knows how to cosset herself."

"Neurotic."

She swallowed back tears. If a girl of twenty-nine poached herself two eggs instead of having lunch in the canteen, did that make her neurotic? What theory of psychology was that?

Even her best friends kept urging her to find a man to share her life. As if to be single at twenty-nine were a crime, making her a target of public criticism, a natural object of gossip. The endless idle talk had destroyed her peace of mind. Was there nothing more important in the world, no more urgent business than finding yourself a husband? How wretched, hateful, maddening and ridiculous!

Now she had been liberated. I'm a girl of nineteen, so all of you shut up! She looked up at the clear blue sky flecked with small white clouds like handkerchiefs to gag those officious gossips. Wonderful! Throwing out her chest, glancing neither to right nor left, she hurried with a light step to the bicycle shed, found her "Flying Pigeon" bicycle and flew off like a pigeon herself through the main gate.

It was the rush hour. The crowded streets were lined with state stores, collectively run or private shops. Pop music sounded on all sides. "I love you" "You don't love me" "I can't live without you" "You've no place in your heart for me ..." To hell with that rubbish!

Love was no longer old stock to be sold off fast. At nineteen she had plenty of time, plenty of chances. She must give top priority now to studying and improving herself. Real knowledge and ability could benefit society and create happiness for the people, thereby earning her respect, enriching her life and making it more significant. Then love would naturally seek her out, and of course she wouldn't refuse it. But it should be a quiet, deep, half-hidden love.

She must get into college. Nineteen was just the age to go to college. There was no time to be wasted. If she did well in a television college or night school, she could get a diploma. Still those weren't regular universities, not up to Beijing or Qinghua Universities. Her life had been ruined by the interruption to her education. Strictly speaking she had reached only primary school standard, because in her fourth year in primary school the Cultural Revolution had started; but after skipping about in the alley for several years she counted as having finished her primary education. In middle school she felt as dizzy as if in a plane, unable to grasp nine-tenths of what was taught, yet somehow or other she managed to graduate. Sent down to the country to steel herself by labor, she had forgotten the little she'd learned. When the "revolution" ended she had gone back to the city to wait for a job, but none materialized. She contrived to get into the service team under the bureau, though that was only a collective, not a state-run enterprise. Reckoning up like this, it seemed there was only one way for her to spend the rest of her life—find a husband, start a family, wash nappies, buy oil, salt, soya sauce, vinegar, and grain, change the gas cylinder, and squabble.

Was that all there was to life? It wasn't enough for Sufen. One should achieve something, leave something behind one. But with her primary school education, unable to grow rice or to mine coal, she was neither worker nor peasant, an "intellectual" with no education, a wretched ghost cut off from humankind.

She'd started from ABC, spent practically all her spare time attending classes, and most of her pay on school fees and textbooks. Chinese, maths, English, drawing—she studied them all. But this method of catching up was too slow, too much of a strain. She wanted a crash course. Her age was against her. If she couldn't get quicker results, even if she ended up fully proficient it would be too late for her to win recognition.

She concentrated on English, hoping to make a breakthrough; studied different textbooks, radio materials, TV classes and crash courses all at the same time. After a month she discovered that this breach was already besieged by countless others. All aging bachelors or unmarried girls like her, trying to find a short cut to success. And this wasn't a short cut either. Because even if you gained a good grasp of English, what use would it be in China which is still backward as far as culture is concerned? Translate English into Chinese? Chinese into English? There were plenty of good translators among the graduates from institutes of foreign languages. Who was going to look for new talents among young people waiting for employment?

She transferred to the "Correspondence College for Writers." Why not write stories or poems to disclose all the frustrations, uncertainties and aspirations of our generation? Let the reading public and the youth of the twenty-first century know that for one brief phase in China the younger generation was unfairly treated and stultified by history. Through no fault of their own, they had lost all that should have been theirs by right and had been burdened with a heavy load they hadn't deserved. They would have to live out their lives weighed down by this crushing burden.

To talk of writing was easy. But how many works written by her age group had any appeal? When you picked up your pen, you didn't know where to start. She'd torn off so many sheets from her pad that her family were desperately afraid that she was possessed. Apparently not everyone could be a writer.

Then what about studying accountancy? Accountants were in great demand....

She couldn't make up her mind. She vacillated, frustrated and unsure of herself, not knowing what she wanted or ought to do. Someone advised her, "Don't be senseless. At your age, just muddle along." Someone else said, "Once you're married you'll feel settled."

But that was the last thing she wanted.

Now this stupendous change: flowers were blooming, birds singing, the world had suddenly become infinitely beautiful. Subtract ten years and I'm just nineteen. To hell with all hesitation, frustration and wretchedness. Life hasn't abandoned me, the world belongs to me again. I must treasure every single moment and waste no time. Must set my goals in life, not turn off the right track again. I mean to study, go to college and get myself a real education. This is my first objective.

Yes, starting today, as of now, I'll press on towards this goal.

Cycling along and smiling all over her face, she headed for the textbook department of the Xinhua Bookstore.

The next morning the whole bureau seethed with excitement. Upstairs and down, inside and out, all was bustle, talk and laughter. Cardiac cases climbed up to the fifth floor without wheezing, changing color or getting heart palpitations, as if nothing were wrong with them. Men of over sixty who normally talked slowly and indistinctly now raised their voices and spoke so incisively that they could be heard from one end of the corridor to the other. The doors of all the offices stood wide open and people wandered about as if at a fair to share their excitement, elation, dreams and illimitable plans.

Suddenly someone suggested,

"Let's parade through the town to celebrate this new liberation!"

At once everyone went into action. Some wrote slogans on banners, some made little green and red flags. The head of the recreation committee fetched out from the storeroom a drum the size of a round table and the red silk used for folk dances. In no time they had all assembled in front of the bureau. Written in yellow characters on the red banners was the slogan, "Celebrate the Return of Youth." The small flags voiced their inmost feelings: "Support the brilliant decision of the Age Research Association," "Our new youth is devoted to modernization," and "Long live youth!"

The big drum beat a rousing tattoo. Ji Wenyao felt his blood was seething. Standing at the top of the steps he meant to say a few inspiring words before leading this grand parade, when suddenly he saw dozens of retired cadres rush in. Charging up to him they demanded,

"Why weren't we notified of this deduction of ten years?"

"You ...you've already retired," he said.

"No! That won't do!" the old men chorused.

Ji raised both hands and called from the top of the steps:

"Quiet, comrades. Please ..."

They paid no attention, the roar of their voices rose to the sky.

"Ten years deducted applies to everyone. It's not fair to leave us out."

"We must carry out the directive, not just do as we please." Ji's voice had risen an octave.

"Where's the directive? Why hasn't it been relayed?"

214

"Show us the directive!"

"Why don't you let us see it?"

Ji turned to the head of the general office.

"Where's the directive?"

The man answered bluntly:

"I don't know."

They were in this impasse when shouts went up from some newly recruited workers in their late teens:

"Ten years taken off—nothing doing!"

"Have we grown up for eighteen years and landed a job, just to be sent back to primary school—no way!"

The children of the bureau's kindergarten trooped up to Ji too like a flock of ducklings. Clinging to his legs and grabbing his hands they prattled,

"Ten years off, where can we go?"

"Mummy had to have her tummy cut open when I was born."

In desperation Ji called again to the head of the general office:

"The directive—hurry up and fetch the directive."

Seeing the man at a loss he thundered:

"Go and get it, quick, from the section for confidential documents."

The man rushed off to hunt through all the directives there, but failed to find it.

Well-meaning suggestions were made:

"Could it have been put in the archives?"

"Could it have been lent out?"

"Dammit! Suppose it's been thrown away!"

In all this confusion Ji kept a cool head. He ordered:

"Everybody's to make a search. Look carefully, all of you, in every corner."

"Shall we call off the parade?" asked the head of the general office.

"Why should we? First find that directive!"

Translated by Gladys Yang

Note:

[1] Since the early 1980s, large number of rural girls from Anhui have been leaving their home towns to find house-keeping positions or baby-sitting work in urban families in large cities. Anhui is one of the poorest provinces in East China.

WANG ANYI AND HER FICTION

Ying Hong

It was at the height of the Beijing summer that I sat in a tiny room, chatting with Wang Anyi. I remember vividly that it was drizzling that day.

The rain fell in steady streams, drumming out a sprightly rhythm against the window pane. It prompted me to start talking about *Drizzling Rain* which she had written a few years before and which had been widely acclaimed at the time. I also got on to the subject of *The Small Village of Bao* which had startled many critics and had been described as a "completely new departure" for her. At the same time we discussed *The Three Loves* written after her writing had lost a certain exquisiteness and "self-expressive quality" and which had consequently provoked quite a controversy.

I talked for a long time and about many things, but she merely listened, smiling or quietly pouring out a glass of water for herself from the thermos flask. All done without a word spoken. No wonder a friend once remarked to me: "It seems as if Wang Anyi locks all her words into a drawer." Later it occured to me that that drawer full of words must be her soul.

I told her that every time I read her novels, it would for some reason remind me of the saying: "The world is tiny, but the heart boundless." In a world in miniature, every tiny convolution of those amplified souls had sent her in quest of the new and unfamiliar, to dig them out one after the other and carefully examine them.

Finally she spoke. She seemed at a loss as to what to say, but her sincerity could not be doubted. This sincerity is as important to her as life, whether in her capacity as a writer or as an ordinary person. "I honestly don't know what to say. Perhaps the best thing would be for you to ask questions and for me to answer them," she said.

So that's how it was. Wang sat opposite me, staring at the glass in her hand, and then began to pour forth a torrent of words. It became faster and faster scarcely leaving her time to draw breath: "In terms of purpose and theme my works are consistent. All along I have been trying to discover what 'man' is, what 'love' is. Naturally there may be people who think that my previous works have an innocent, more appealing quality to them. I think this opinion is quite normal. Probably everybody likes reading descriptions of purity and beauty; moreover it seems as if the more one is knocked about by life, the more one prefers things which are pure. But looking at it from another angle, a person's works, like him or herself, also grow older and more mature. Of course I realize that children are more lovable than adults, but everyone has to grow up, it's an irresistible law of Nature. Since people have to grow up, how can you expect their works not to 'grow up' too?"

Indeed, Wang uses her works to draw a distinct line, for herself as well as for others, which is all part of the path along which her creativity has led her. Along this path we can see signs of three stages, all different in tone. Representative of the first stage is her earliest work *Drizzling Rain*. These works have the emerald freshness and brightness of a landscape after rain. They are the song of an innocent young girl, poured out from the depths of her soul. This soul is a delicate yet sincere

218

vessel, and with it, as well as her purity and gentleness she faces life. Life's opposites; beauty and ugliness, light and dark are all revealed as very clear-cut to her innocent eyes. Yet this simplicity of view is not monotonous, for it is blended into the work to such an extent that it creates a mood of youthfulness, particularly for younger readers.

In her second creative stage, she broadens her scope somewhat, shifting her attention from young girls to a much wider range of very ordinary characters, as in novellas like *Passing Time*. These are still tenderly written and full of minute description, yet it is simply that they have now absorbed the author's feelings of sympathy for the destiny of her characters. The emphasis of her works dating from this period is no longer on liveliness and intensity of mood. Instead their style is simple and straight forward, rather like that of a Chinese painting. With their simplicity and concision, these works afford the reader much food for thought. Although relatively mundane details of everyday life begin to figure largely in her works at this stage, her writing has still in fact gained a depth which it did not have before. The woman writer Bing Xin has been very encouraging about the "probing" quality of Wang's work, as well as its gradual maturation. The characters which Wang was describing at this time were not the petty and despicable individuals of the nineteenth century Russian novel; rather, they reflected the hardships in the lives of a broad spectrum of people, as well as describing their intellectual poverty and stolidity of character. Of course, these characters embody and reflect a much deeper layer of historic consciousness, mirroring thereby the profound nature of Chinese history and life.

Just like a chrysalis that overnight turns into a butterfly, so did Wang Anyi become unrecognizable for a time when she produced *The Small Village of Bao*. This is her third stage. Gone are the tender young heroines; gone too is the freshness of mood, the quiet elegance and charm. In this new world, the significance of reason and emotion is hidden beneath a superficial layer of language. Using words that carry not the least hint of subjectivity she casually tosses forth a whole string of "slices of life." The invisible thread that runs through all these snippets is the distillation of the author's reactions towards life, history, and culture. In *The Small Village of Bao, Small Town Love* and other works, she consciously explores uncharted areas, such as culture and sex. This change, however, can still be seen as a continuation of her previous works, because her thought is still centered on life itself: the subject of her explorations is still man, life, and love.

Lao Kang Is Back, featured here, can almost be regarded as an interlude between her second and third stages. It was around the time of its publication that she commented on the aim of her novels: "I hope that my novels can condense within a very short time a very long history, that they can within a very small space condense a very large world, and that they can within the most concrete of things contain the most abstract of philosophies." The Wang Anyi who wrote *Lao Kang Is Back* is a very leisurely storyteller. In her descriptions of intellectuals, whose lives are full of frustrations and end sadly, she uses a very prosaic tone. Within a very narrow space, history is concentrated into a simple story and into the descriptions of very ordinary characters. Even where her principal character Lao Kang is concerned, her sketches are brief and not deeply etched. Descriptions of people meeting, talking, and living together are all somewhat prosaic. Yet on giving the matter a little thought, one realizes that such an ordinary background is replete with very strong historic significance.

The detail of Lao Kang mechanically writing the character for rice is repeated many times in the course of the story, yet Wang Anyi does not use it for theatrical effect, nor does she provide much in the way of argument and exposition about it, she simply makes her readers ponder on it and learn from experience. She is, of course, trying here to convey very profound messages, yet in keeping with the style of the whole story, she is in no way deliberately abstruse. Through the casual remarks of the housekeeper, the author expresses her own attitude towards the lives of hundreds and thousands of people like Lao Kang: "Let's put it this way: Man is breath, with it he can live, without it he dies." If one thinks about it carefully, this phrase implies deep feeling towards both the tragic fate of Chinese intellectuals of the time and Chinese history.

Wang Anyi was born into a family of creative artists: her father was a theatrical director and her mother a writer. As long ago as the 1950's her mother Ru Zhijuan wrote the short stories including *Lilies* and *The Tall White Poplars*, all of which would have a profound impact on the reading public and establish her in Chinese literary circles. Therefore, when Wang Anyi began subsequently to make a name for herself in the literary world of more recent times, with her first batch of novels including *Drizzling Rain*, there were some people who wondered whether her works did not owe something to her mother. Whenever this subject is raised, Wang always replies in a tone of some disgust: "As far as writing goes, I don't wish to be lumped together with my mother. I am Wang Anyi and in this respect a wholly independent human being."

This is indeed the case, for in their writing, mother

and daughter have trodden two completely different paths. Thus the experience of life, the attitudes, and the styles displayed in their works are very dissimilar. What is most interesting is the trip that mother and daughter made together to the United States in 1983. On their return they each wrote in diary form about their experiences and together published a book entitled *120 Days in America*. Having read this book very carefully I have discovered that the observations and impressions of mother and daughter, as well as their methods of recording the same events frequently differ to a great extent.

Wang's life story is as simple as this, not filling more than a few lines on a curriculum vitae. After graduating from junior high school in 1969, she was sent to work in a production team in Huaibei in Anhui Province. In 1972 she passed the entrance exam for the Xuzhou district song and dance ensemble. In 1978 she came back to Shanghai to work as an editor on a magazine. Of all the events in this simple history, undoubtedly it is the time which she spent in the production team, and in the song and dance ensemble playing the cello, that had the greatest influence on her later creativity. These experiences are the inexhaustible spring from which she has always drawn, and will continue to do so in the future, as material for her writing. However, as far as any change in the thought and artistic conception of her writing is concerned, it was probably after she had traveled on the continent on the other side of the Pacific for four months that she discovered she had a reservoir of very different material to draw on. It was the first time she had left her own country for a totally strange new world. Some people observed that after her return both she and her writing had undergone a dramatic change, which culminated in *The Small Village of Bao*, which took the literary world by storm and won for her great public acclaim.

What sort of a change are we talking about then? It seems as if Wang Anyi herself finds it difficult to explain: "To put it briefly, when I went out into the world and saw how huge it is and how numerous are its inhabitants, only then did I have a slightly more accurate idea of my own value. No longer would I become upset and confused because of some small happiness or sadness; my mind has broadened somewhat, I shall no longer have merely my own insignificant self to consider but all living creatures under Heaven."

At the time of our meeting she had just got back from a two-month visit to West Germany. She told me that what had interested her most about this visit was the religious culture of the West. For someone like herself, a Chinese who has grown up in surroundings almost totally devoid of religious influences, this is undoubtedly an extremely mysterious and difficult question. Therefore, during this trip, in almost every town she visited she first went to look for a church. She visited countless churches up and down the country, wishing to experience for herself the very different atmospheres of each, and also as to work out carefully the differences between the various denominations. As I listened to this flow of words describing these new and vivid impressions, I felt sure that it would all find its way into her future writing.

As an ordinary woman, Wang is no different from many of her fellow Shanghainese. She lives a very ordinary life. She has her own small home, and she attends every day to household affairs and fulfils her duties as a housewife. She is also very particular about her clothes, and seems to have a predilection for red pullovers. Her clothes are fashionable and display a youthful vigor. They are not in the least mundane, but are rather an indication of her good breeding. Her husband is a composer and pursues his art as ardently as she does hers, yet as far as their work is concerned, they are independent of each other. Since becoming famous, Wang Anyi is often asked in interviews about her husband, but each time she tactfully refuses to comment, saying merely: "The two of us have a rule that as far as our respective work is concerned, we are totally independent."

June 1988
Translated by Katharina A. Byrne

Lao Kang Is Back

Wang Anyi

PEOPLE told me that Lao Kang was back, staying at his brother's house, and they said he was seriously ill. Some of us made plans to go and visit him, but because we were so busy, and the trip was so long, and there were so many of us, we could not manage to agree on a time. We put it off for over a month, and still we did not get around to seeing him. And since nothing further was heard, after a while we sort of forgot about him.

We had not seen each other for twenty whole years —and that is pretty close to half a lifetime. Life is too rushed and troubled to leave time and inclination for reminiscing; when you do look back it is as if, in the blink of an eye, you are thousands of miles from where you were. Happenings of the past may be clear in memory, but they seem as remote as events of another lifetime, as spectral as dreams.

When Lao Kang and I were classmates we were little over twenty, and each of us harbored oceanic aspirations. Lao Kang's aim was to write a history of Chinese music. Such an aim was not extravagant, nor was it trifling, but it would be quite difficult to realize. He had long before earned the reputation of a "walking library," and by his sophomore year, he had accumulated a soap box full of index cards. He always said that China was the earliest country to keep historical records, and he was resolved to carry on that tradition. There is no question that he worked painstakingly to gather materials, but he seldom took his time putting pen to paper. He did not even come up with a short article that could be published in the school paper, let alone a book. It was disappointing. By this time one of his ambitious classmates had written a grand chorale called "River of Joy" that had taken first place in choral music at the Seventh International Youth Festival. We asked him what was up, and he just said, "In a little while, in a little while." He had not written a single word, even when he was labeled an overlooked Rightist in the anti-Rightist campaign and sent to Qinghai. There was no unpleasantness between him and me, but you could hardly have called us close. Anyway, he did not have many close friends, being such a bookworm. He was fairly normal as bookworms go, not being one to crack a lot of jokes or behave in a crazed manner. For this reason my recollections of him are faint—there is nothing especially stirring in them. But I feel sorry that he was made out to be a Rightist so early. And his crime was no more than a few words of displeasure at current conditions, words that had little of the fervor of public protests against Xian Xinghai[1] made by the "clique of three members"[2] —so he did not leave much of an impression. Later on, people more innocent than he was met with even more tragic misfortunes, so the sympathy I felt for him faded.

But after all we had been classmates once. Now that twenty years had passed, having been classmates meant more than simply having gone to school together. It implied recollections of those wonderful days twenty years ago. That is why my wish to see him was a sincere one.

One day I had business to do near his brother's

house, so I went straight there after I was finished.

Lao Kang's family was originally from Zhenjiang, not Shanghai. It was his older brother who had brought him here for his schooling, so every weekend he used to go to his brother's house to pass the time. His brother had played first violin in an orchestra, but now he was retired. Now and then he wrote a piece of music, and sometimes he wrote articles. Sometimes he could be seen at meetings or rehearsals, and when we saw each other, we nodded. We were by no means strangers, and I knew the new place he had moved to.

His brother lived on the twelfth floor of a newly built apartment building. I went up in the elevator, made a left turn as I got out, and found myself right in front of his door. I rang the electric doorbell next to the door, but there was no answer. I was ringing a second time when the door opened quietly, and a sixty-year-old country woman looked at me questioningly. I figured this was the family housekeeper. Her Shanghainese had a marked northern Jiangsu accent.

"Nobody in the family is here."

"Nobody?" I was very disappointed, you know, since I'd come a long way to get here. There would not be many chances to stop by.

"There is an invalid here," she added.

"I am here to see the invalid," I wasted no time telling her. I was extremely glad that I had not come for nothing.

"You want to see the invalid?" She looked at me in extreme puzzlement, then turned and let me in.

I went in. It was one of those tiny, newly built apartments, but the occupants had redone the interior before moving in. They had put a fabric covering on the walls, laid down a new tile floor, and put tiles and a

227

mosaic in the bathroom. A ceiling lamp had been hung, and there were a few oil paintings on the walls, all of which gave it a surprisingly luxurious look. I walked down the short, narrow hallway, looking to the right and the left. The room facing south was closed, and the one facing north was open. A man was seated with his head resting on a table, dozing. More than likely it was Lao Kang.

"Lao Kang," I called. There was no answer; he kept on dozing.

I called again.

There was still no answer, and he did not look much like Lao Kang. I was beginning to doubt if it was him. I turned and saw the old housekeeper behind me, crossing her hands over her apron and looking as if she had something to say.

"Is this your employer's brother?" I asked her.

"Do you know him?" she asked in return.

I nodded.

She said, "Go ahead and try calling him." With that she left, and I could hear the sound of running water in the bathroom.

I called again, but he still did not answer. Feeling perplexed and uneasy, I moved slowly over to his side. I discovered that he was not sleeping. He was just resting his head on his arm, and with the other hand he was tracing some sort of mark. His face was totally strange to me; it was abnormally gaunt, I had never seen such a gaunt face. There seemed to be no features in it, only a brow, cheekbones and jawbones fused together and covered by a layer of translucent skin. Without thinking I shuddered a bit.

"Is that Lao Kang?" I asked.

He did not look at me, and did not seem to have

heard. He was tracing something on the table with his finger.

I walked near and raised his shoulder so his face was level with my eyes. This made him look at me, but his expression was blank.

"Do you recognize me?" I asked.

He was expressionless. There was not enough muscle in his face to allow for an expression, but anyway I could tell he was expressionless.

I let his shoulder down, and he leaned his head back on the table and went back to tracing some sort of mark. As far as I could tell, he was making the strokes for the character "rice" (米).

I started to tremble, and slowly backed out of the room. The old housekeeper, in the bathroom washing clothes, saw me come out and asked, "Does he recognize you?"

I shook my head.

"He's been like this ever since he got back from Qinghai. Still, he knows how to eat and go to bed, and he knows how to go to the toilet. Well, you really can't say he knows. As long as someone takes him by the hand, he can do it. He never makes a mess." She seemed somewhat proud of him.

"Do you know what illness he has?" I asked, lifting my hand to wipe my brow. I had been perspiring.

"They say a blood vessel in his brain burst. It was odd the way it happened. He did not fall or knock his head against anything. He was just sleeping peacefully when it burst."

"It was probably a stroke."

"It was fate too. He was just about to come to Shanghai. They say his work transfer and change of abode were all taken care of. Right then his blood vessel burst, and this is what he ended up like." She rubbed a piece of clothing strenuously between her hands, sending suds flying in all directions.

"Are you here just to take care of him?" I asked.

"I came because I felt sorry for him. I had it nice in the Dragonflight Building: a family of four, with two adults and two kids. The older child is already at university and only comes back on Saturdays. I had it nice and easy. Really I'm here because I felt sorry for him." As she spoke her hands were busily at work under a pile of suds.

"You're not very busy here either."

"Not busy? It's like watching a kid: I can never get free of him. At the Dragonflight Building I did laundry for two other families. The man in this family said he'd make it up to me in my pay. I said I wasn't out for money!"

She was a little reluctant to see me go, and said she had forgotten to make me some tea. I told her quickly that there was no need and pulled myself away. Outside I discovered I did not have my bike key. I remembered putting it on the table a moment before, while lifting his shoulder, so I went back for it. He was still pillowing his hand on the desk, taking no notice of me and tracing the character for "rice" with his finger. I had no idea of the meaning of this.

I thought about Lao Kang all the way home. I could not understand what had reduced him to the state he was in. In the twenty years he had lived alone in Qinghai, none of his classmates had corresponded with him. He had preserved complete silence on how he passed those twenty years. I went home and ate, took a nap and joked with my daughter, but I could not put Lao Kang's emaciated form out of my mind. I could not get myself to relax. I kept wanting to seek someone out and talk about it, but when I got ready to open my mouth, I felt there was no way to convey what I thought, so I did not say it. I simply made plans to go visit him again, hoping I could see his brother.

I set aside time on a holiday and took a box of cakes to Lao Kang's.

Unexpectedly his brother was not at home; I was told he had gone to a meeting. His sister-in-law had also gone out to take her kid to a piano lesson. Lao Kang was napping on the wire mattress of a folding cot. The housekeeper snapped out of her midday drowsiness the minute she saw it was me. It was our second meeting, so we were more familiar with each other now. Right away she brewed tea for me, cleared me a chair and told me: "He ate a bowl and a half of rice for lunch. He ate rib meat, and vegetables and beans. He even had soup. He can eat well enough, as long as he's fed. He falls asleep after he eats and sleeps straight through till three o'clock. After that he just sits there."

"Is he still the same way, not recognizing anyone?" I asked. I was hoping his condition had improved.

"He does not really recognize people."

"Not even his older brother?"

"When his brother calls him, he seems to listen. When I call him now, he seems a little better."

"I guess he has some slight awareness of what goes on around him."

"When I tell him to eat, he knows to pick up his bowl, and when I tell him to sleep, he knows to take off his socks and clothes. He's pretty easy to handle."

"Be sure to take good care of him."

"Do you think I would neglect him? My boss has me buy nice things for him to eat; he says there wasn't much to eat in Qinghai. Now it's time he enjoyed a little comfort. Every day I try to fix something unusual for him. Yesterday I bought pork liver, and today I fixed spare ribs and tomato sauce."

"Does he seem to like it?"

"He knows what good food is! Why, he ate plenty of those spare ribs today. Yes sir, he knows!"

I let out a sigh.

"Mister!" she said to me. "If you ask me, a person who lives like this is not good for anything, is he? All he can do is breathe."

I had no answer for her.

"Well, that's what I think. A person is not much more than a lungful of breath. If there's still breath in him, he's alive; if there isn't, he's dead." The corners of her mouth sagged as she spoke. Early afternoon sunlight beamed in through the west window, shining on her forehead with its receding hair. It had a glossy look.

He turned over on the wire springs.

"He's awake." She rose and went to help him up. In obedience to her movements, he sat up and rose to his feet, then let her lead him slowly to his seat by the table. He sat down directly across from me. His gaze swept blankly past me and fell to the table. Not long after sitting down, his hand began making tracing movements on the table: it was still the character "rice."

As the nursemaid folded up the cot she said, "Ah, he's always like this." She put the folding cot away in the closet, walked over and helped Lao Kang up, saying: "Let's go to the toilet!"

Lao Kang followed her obediently. Before long, the sound of water could be heard from the restroom. I stood up, determined to take my leave. I had no wish to see the nursemaid put him through his daily paces for me. I said I was going, and sure enough the housekeeper betrayed a sense of disappointment. I still had not drunk my tea, she said. Nevertheless, I left.

I did not want to visit him again, but I was preoccupied with wondering what his life had been like the past twenty years. It did not look as if he had started a family. And how had he fallen ill so quickly? Besides that, what was the meaning of the character "rice" he kept tracing over and over again? The only thing to do was to ask his older brother all these things. And by a remarkable coincidence, I went to see a movie the same day at the cultural hall and ran into his brother. I nodded to him and struck up a conversation:

"I've been to your place twice, but I haven't met up with you."

"So you're the one! I couldn't tell who it was from what the maid said." He kindly invited me to sit with him in the snack bar, so we went there. The movie would not start for ten minutes or so.

"What's wrong with him? Something terrible has happened to him!" I asked, before we even got settled in our chairs.

He remained silent, felt for a cigarette, lit it.

"Didn't he start a family?"

"No." He shook his head.

"How were things for him there?"

He let out a puff of smoke. Holding the cigarette between his first two fingers, he fidgeted with the matchbox, using his thumb and little finger. The answer came out slowly: "First he did labor, and then he was transferred to a county cultural office." He mentioned the name of the county, but I had never heard of it.

"Which county?" I wanted to hear it again.

He told me a second time. It was an awkward

sounding name; I would not have known which characters to use in writing it.

"Did he come back during those years?"

"He came back twice. He couldn't help losing some weight, but he was in pretty good spirits."

"Did he write you fairly often?"

"In his letters he always said he was doing all right. I sent noodles to him a few times, but he kept saying I didn't need to send them, so I stopped. Now that I look back, I keep feeling I let him down. Later I heard someone say life in Qinghai was terribly hard."

"But still, you really couldn't have done much for him," I consoled him.

After the Gang of Four fell I did some running around for him, and finally it worked. His case was redressed and his rehabilitation announced. He was about to come back to Shanghai. His luggage was all packed and he even sent me a telegram. I went to meet his train, but he wasn't on it. I thought maybe something else had come up that was holding him. I never expected that back at home I'd receive an emergency telegram from his unit, saying he was critically ill. We were talking of going to Qinghai, when, wouldn't you know, another cable came, saying he was out of danger, and a person would be assigned especially to escort him to Shanghai that day. Of course we didn't go. Afterwards I regretted it a little. Maybe I should have gone once, just to see what sort of life he led in that place. We have no way of knowing."

"Did you ask his escort anything?"

"The escort was a young man who had been sent to the cultural office only a few months before. He never knew my brother well. He just said my brother was a very kind and honest person. I did not need him to tell me that." He gave a strange laugh. "He brought along a worn-out bedroll, a shabby suitcase, and a few hundred *yuan*. That was all."

"Was he like this when he first got back?"

"Just like this. He seemed even more numb. Now that he has been home he is a little better."

"What is his illness, anyway?"

"A stroke. It happened the evening before he got on the train. It was probably brought on by overexcitement."

I lapsed into silence. He too was silent.

Our silence lasted awhile, then I asked, "What does he mean by writing the character 'rice' all the time?"

"We thought it was strange too. It really is strange. He has forgotten everything else, but he remembers a senseless word like 'rice.' My wife says maybe he suffered so much in the famine years that he won't let the word 'rice' slip from his memory. My kid says it probably stands for a young woman named Rice. He even got out the *Book of Surnames* and looked it up to prove it. There really is the surname Rice. I think it isn't a character at all; it's just a simple design. He probably got used to drawing it mechanically, without even thinking. Look, it actually is not such a simple design. It is two crosses with the same center." He wet his middle finger in some spilled tea next to him and traced the design for me to see.

I was feeling pretty gloomy. I asked him for a cigarette, lit it off his, and fell into a fit of coughing.

"Maybe it really is a word. It certainly has been branded into his mind. What on earth does it mean? But I guess I just can't bear to look further into it." He made a grim attempt at a smile.

I coughed.

"To understand all this, I should really take a trip there. But it is too far away. And the county where he was is a very out-of-the-way place. I'm afraid there is not much chance of going."

"We old classmates have not shown enough concern for him these past few years," I said remorsefully.

"If you're speaking of that, I'm even worse. These past years people have had a hard time protecting themselves. To tell the truth, he and I are not full brothers: we were just born to the same mother. I brought him to Shanghai; maybe I harmed him without realizing it."

I paused, and finally asked a question I'd been thinking of the whole time but had not dared to utter: "Did the doctor ... say ... how long ... he could ... survive?"

"The doctor said ... said he could ... for a long time." He stubbed out his cigarette in silence.

The bell in the auditorium rang. Neither of us moved.

All in all, I knew nothing of what he had lived through over the past twenty years, and even less did I know what that cursed word "rice" stood for. I knew only that within his whole being, only this single character "rice" was flourishing and alive. Luckily this word "rice" lived, so he was not totally dead yet. There was still a stirring of breath. Suddenly I thought of what the old housekeeper had said about being alive, and came to a realization of how much lay behind her words. She had, after all, managed to keep alive to a good old age.

The bell rang for the second time. We heard it and stood up almost simultaneously.

"Let's go see the movie," he said.

"Yep, let's see the movie," I said.

We walked out together. Sunlight was spread like

mercury across the leaves of the trees.

October 1985

Translated by Denis C. Mair

Notes:

[1] Xian Xinghai (1905-45), famed musical composer, chief works including *The Yellow River Cantata*, *Go to the Enemy Rear*, and *On the Taihang Mountains*.

[2] This is one of many examples in which intellectuals or officials were accused of forming a clique against the revolutionary cause and its pursuers, and were thus persecuted during the Cultural Revolution. Few of such accusations have stood the test of time.

WANG MENG AND HIS FICTION

Gladys Yang

Young Bolshevik, Rightist, teacher, settler in a border region, original writer, member of the Party Central Committee and Minister of Culture[1]—the successive roles of Wang Meng illustrate the vicissitudes of life in the first thirty years of New China.

He was born in Beijing in 1934. During the anti-Japanese war he joined the patriotic student movement and at nineteen was admitted to the Communist Party. After Liberation he taught in a primary school, then worked for the Youth League.

Long Live the Youth, finished in 1953 but not published for twenty-six years, was the first contemporary novel about school students preparing to build up the country. Addressing itself to the question: "How should we spend the best years of our lives?" it conveys the comradeship and revolutionary enthusiasm of the early fifties. Here the influence of such Soviet works as *How the Steel Was Tempered* is evident. His view that literature should educate readers is revealed in this and most of his subsequent work.

In 1956 the policy of "letting a hundred flowers blossom" called for more diversity in literature and art, and emboldened Wang to write *The Young Newcomer in the Organization Department*. Its protagonist is an ardent young Party member who opposes the bureaucracy of the district Party committee to which he has been assigned and tries—in vain—to unseat an inefficient factory manager. This straightforward, lively narrative struck readers as truthful and courageous, and as a pioneer work in exposing social problems, and it has won itself a special place in modern Chinese writing. However, during the anti-Rightist movement of 1957 it was condemned as a "poisonous weed," and in 1958 he was labeled a Rightist. He was unable to publish anything more for over twenty years.

In 1961 his Rightist label was removed and, though not rehabilitated, he taught modern literature in Beijing Normal College.

In 1964 he took his wife to settle in a commune in Yili, Xinjiang. The night they reached. Urumqi, he wrote a poem dedicating himself to the service of that border region. He used his aptitude for languages, which has more recently enabled him to teach himself English, to learn Uygur, making friends with the local people whose wit and folk wisdom appealed to him. In his preface to *Anecdotes from Department Head Maimaiti* he wrote that humor is an essential element of existence. He has also described it as an expression of equality, a protest against hierarchy. Even now he is always ready to laugh at himself. His sense of humor and his humanity helped him to survive those difficult years and turn them to good account. In Xinjiang he gained valuable experience, a broader context in time and space, and a keener analytical judgement. He is short-sighted and sometimes absent-minded in practical affairs. For example he once went out to buy cotton cloth, but by mistake, put the coupons for this in a letter which he posted to his sister. However, in observing society he misses very little. His mind has been compared to a computer storing up information. Looking back in 1980 on that period in Xinjiang he wrote: "I came to know true greatness and nobility of spirit. At the bottom of the social strata and in the most distant of places, I experienced the joys and misery of ordinary people and saw from their perspective the chicanery of those years, the arbitrariness of power, saw who was right and who was wrong ...as clearly as one would see a raging fire."

In 1979 he was fully rehabilitated, returned to Beijing and started publishing a stream of strikingly original works. These are quite different in style from the straight-forward narratives of his 1950s stories. He concentrates on his characters' inner world, their mental processes and mental conflicts; and in order to mirror the depth and intricacies of China's post-Liberation development, he has evolved new literary techniques which draw on native tradition as well as Western literary modes.

He pioneered stream-of-consciousness writing in China. This aroused very mixed reactions. Some readers objected that stories such as the *Eyes of Night* and *Voices of Spring* were unrealistic, and hard to understand. They thought it inappropriate to borrow "decadent," out-dated forms of expression from the Western modernist school. The concensus, however, was that he had not simply transplanted Western modes of writing about the sub-conscious, which are rooted in idealism; his portrayals of the Chinese people's struggle to advance had their roots in real life and aimed at impelling it forward. His complex structure and technique gave the author more scope for his imagination and for profound character portrayal, making possible a more fully realistic reflection of life. Other writers have since adopted his methods.

In 1981 he won awards for three short stories and his novella *The Butterfly.* He was also appointed to the secretariat of the Chinese Writers Association, later becoming vice-chairman of the Beijing branch.

The Butterfly takes its name from an old fable in which a philosopher dreams that he is a butterfly, but on waking wonders if instead he is not a butterfly dreaming that it is a man. Life is equally bewildering, sudden reversals inducing a nightmarish sense of unreality. This story is a brilliant example of his chronological technique. He uses fleeting impressions, free associations of ideas, symbolism and serious philosophizing to depict a high official's vicissitudes and mental processes from the late 1940s to the late 1970s. By so doing, this impressionistic story conveys that period most faithfully. Finally the rehabilitated official comes to terms with his situation and prepares to work even harder. Like most of his stories, this ends on a note of sober optimism and leaves readers with a clearer understanding of modern China.

In *The Butterfly*, *Voices of Spring* and *Eyes of Night*, Wang Meng's protagonists make physical as well as metaphysical journeys. They are placed in fluid, unfamiliar contexts and try to grasp the symbolic, bewildering scenes around them. In the process they think over their traumatic experiences and make more sense of them. Works such as *Eyes of Night* and *Voices of Spring* are akin to poems, for they express moods without presenting clashes between different characters as in traditional fiction or drama. The novelist Feng Jicai commented that the *Eyes* described feelings he himself had been unable to put into words.

Wang adopts other styles as well to suit his subject-matter. He makes use of satire in *A Spate of Visitors* and *The Barber's Tale* to castigate the abuse of official power. The former shows the pressure brought to bear on a factory director who has fired the nephew of a high official. It ends on an encouraging note when the director refuses to reinstate the young man and turns the inefficient factory into a provincial model.

The Barber's Tale is in the tradition of Chinese comic monologues. The narrator, a barber in a shop patronized by high officials, recalls the political and social changes he has seen since the birth of New China when he was "in love with the new society, the revolution," when "leaders were close to the people" and a provincial governor cleaned the wash basins in his shop. By the late 1950s things had changed; some of his old customers disappeared and, not understanding why, he had to join in denouncing them. During the Cultural Revolution humanitarianism made him help a persecuted Rightist, but this man after his rehabilitation ignored him. The story ridicules high officials alienated from the people and deplores their callousness, but the barber's attitude is tolerant. He decides not to fawn on old cadres, not to avoid them or be antagonistic. "If everyone avoided them, not telling them what he thought, what would happen to our country and our Party?" This implies the need for a more democratic dialogue between the authorities and ordinary citizens.

Snowball, presented here, is a gentle, subtle satire. It starts with an appreciation of the many conferences held every year "in the best seasons in the best places," when the participants can go sight-seeing and feast at public expense. Since such conferences are snowballing despite widespread protests and repeated calls from the government to cut down on them, they cost the state huge sums of money which China can ill afford. The narrator comments "It's not a bad deal"—shedding light on his character.

At nine thirty on the last evening of the conference

someone raises a hue and cry. An officious woman, Zhuge Yun, who has spent her time not on academic discussion but on ingratiating herself with senior academics, has discovered that the driver Little Li is not in his room. Someone explains that he has gone out to swim. For an able-bodied man to stay out till after nine is hardly cause for alarm, but Zhuge is insistent and the others apparently succumb to her fear that he has been drowned or eaten by sharks. As their dire suppositions snowball, the narrator stops taking the business calmly, swayed by Zhuge's display of "powerful concern for others." All, including the decrepit, go off to search for Little Li. Failing to find him, they mill around till eleven when he turns up after a game of poker. The conference organizer criticizes him so angrily that he sheds tears of remorse.

Later it emerges that no one except Zhuge had seen any need to search for the driver. Her insistence, taking the form of moral blackmail, had made the whole thing snowball.

The ending is ambiguous. What was Zhuge really thinking that night? Why did she intrude into the driver's room?

The conference participants have not been portrayed as high-principled characters. What motivates them to join in that futile search? The answer seems to me to be: conformism.

In a society influenced by centuries of feudal ethics and conventions, each individual feels required to conform to certain norms instead of taking an independent line. The pressure of social opinion is very strong. This has its positive side, making for unity and stability. But if ultra-Left policies snowball, it may lead to mass hysteria and fearful aberrations. The moral seems to me to be:

243

individuals need the courage to use their own judgement and oppose any trends holding up social progress. But, typically, Wang Meng leaves each reader to reach his or her own conclusions.

Wang is well-known abroad as a major Chinese writer with profound insight into his country's history and its present problems. He is also becoming known as a convivial humorist, a master of repartee. Asked his hobbies by the editors of a *Who's Who*, he gave them as swimming and drinking. Perhaps he should have added: joking. Before going on trips abroad, he likes to have names and addresses of friends with whom he can relax after formal functions. Between 1978 and 1986 he wrote over one and a half million words. In 1982 he became an alternate member of the Party Central Committee. In June 1986 he was appointed Minister of Culture. High position has not made him assume official airs. Dropping in on us recently he asked the typically Chinese question, "How do you manage with no children here to help you?" We answered, "Fine, except when it comes to changing light bulbs." He promptly replied, "Which one? I can do that for you." Many lower officials would not have volunteered. Of course his post leaves him with little time for writing, but he has not given it up. His latest novel *Moving Parts* (1987) is about an intellectual before Liberation. Attracted by Western culture, he is too weak and confused to resist the domination of his feudal family, which breaks up tragically in the 1940s. This story, told trenchantly and humorously, reveals the characters' warped psychology and exemplifies the tremendous difficulty of reforming China's social customs.

Some of his recent stories, essays, and poems were conceived in barbers' shops or airport waiting-rooms. In this connection he quotes the English proverb: Where there's a will there's a way.

1988

Note:

[1]Wang Meng was appointed Minister of Culture in 1986 and relieved of the post on the Ninth Meeting of the Standing Committee of the Seventh National People's Congress in September 1989.

Snowball

Wang Meng

In the summer of 1982 I went to a scenic city on the east coast for the annual conference of the local redology[1] society. You know, there have been many such conferences in the past few years, always held in the best season in the best places: Mt. Huangshan, Guilin, West Lake, Lake Taihu. You get to see the sights with your friends from the conference, and it's not a bad deal.

This conference lasted ten days, with papers and discussions in the morning and afternoons free. I was nearly sixty, but I still liked to swim and spent nearly every sunny afternoon at the beach. After ten days, sure enough, I had both tanned and unwound considerably.

After packing up my few belongings on the last night, I was feeling relaxed and went to the room of a new young friend from the conference to chat. I said I had had the pleasure of reading his recently published paper, "The Story of Nu Wa Patching the Heavens and Elements of the Fantastic in *A Dream of Red Mansions*," which I had found insightful, but that I was unable to make the connection between *A Dream of Red Mansions* and the fantastic.

The young are always so earnest. He took up the argument with considerable excitement, and though he was calling me teacher and dean at every turn, it was clear that my view had made him mad. An old codger like me can be just as fanatical as the young, and I did not hold back either.

Just as our debate was reaching a most strenuous pitch, we heard outside the nearly hoarse cry, "Little Li, Little Li, Little Li …"

Little Li was the driver for the conference, and though those shouts sounded a little strange, our minds were fully occupied with Jia Baoyu and his ladylove, and we simply ignored them.

We opened the door to an urgent knock to find Zhuge Yun with seven or eight conference participants behind her.

Let me introduce Zhuge Yun here. She was in her forties, short, wore thick glasses and came from a university in the sticks. She had been extremely energetic and solicitous at the conference. I often saw her running around getting camphor oil for Professor Zhang or a laxative for Professor Yang. At first I thought she was a conference organizer; only later did I find out she was just a participant like me. Her enthusiasm moved me deeply.

"I'm telling you, Little Li is lost," she said at once, brow furrowed.

"How can he be lost?" the author of "Elements of the Fantastic" and I asked at the same time.

"We've been looking for him for half an hour. Do you two know how late it is?"

I looked at my watch; it was 9:30. The hands and face of the watch, indicating 9:30, had enlightened me no further, yet I had begun to detect in Zhuge's voice her dissatisfaction with us.

"Zhuge Yun was the first to notice that Little Li was lost," an enthusiastic old woman chimed in.

"I went past his room at nine," said Zhuge impatiently, "and knocked at the door, but no one answered, so I pushed it open. The light was on, and his shirt, undershirt, pants and underpants were lying on his bed."

"Then he went swimming. I saw him walk by in his swimming trunks," the author of "Elements of the Fantastic" said.

"Wonderful. You saw him. What time, and where?"

"After supper, probably around 6:40."

"Great! 6:40. And what time is it now? Also, did he go swimming alone or was he with someone?"

"Let's see ...yes, he was alone."

"One person, all alone, goes off to swim in the sea at night and has already been gone three hours. You don't think there's anything wrong with that?"

"Maybe he went out afterwards."

"Where would he go? A, he doesn't have relatives here, and B, he has no friends here, I've already checked."

"I hope nothing's happened to him," said the enthusiastic old woman anxiously.

"Right. It's that one chance in a million we have to worry about," said Old Zhu, the conference chairman, wringing his hands.

"You said it. The heartless elements, the heartless, heartless elements!"

"I've heard there are sharks here!"

"Aren't there eight or ten drownings a year? ... In any case, no one has seen him since 6:40." Everyone was talking at once.

I began to recognize the seriousness of the situation. I still felt that the chances of something having happened to Little Li were small, but I couldn't, I dared not, I just didn't have the right to guarantee that nothing had happened to him. As a newly promoted leader of an institution of higher learning and a probationary Party member, I couldn't, even if the chances were one in a million that some danger had befallen the young man, remain indifferent to a comrade's fate. Something more precise than facts and a thousand times more important than logic was operating in the discussion between the author of "Elements of the Fantastic" and Zhuge on Little Li's whereabouts, and that was Zhuge's powerful concern for others and her sense of responsibility and mission, which made her ten times, a hundred times better, stronger and more invincible than the two of us in that discussion. In fact, if anyone had suggested then that Little Li was probably safe and sound, he would have been suspected of thinking only of his own sleep that night and not caring about his comrades. So my expression grew grave, my muscles tense, and my eyes wide as I said, "Have you looked in every room of the hotel?"

"We did that before coming to you here!" said Zhuge, making "you here" sound like an "independent kingdom" that was rife with problems and needed to be "mixed with sand."[2]

My young adversary in the *A Dream of Red Mansions* debate was looking at everyone angrily; obviously he hadn't figured it out yet and was convinced that Zhuge and the rest were getting all worked up over nothing. But I couldn't yield to his mood; I couldn't fail to recognize my own role and responsibility, so I jumped to my feet and said, "OK, let's go down to the beach and look for him!"

As expressions of satisfaction crossed the faces of Zhuge and her followers, the author of "Elements of the Fantastic" seemed suddenly to have caught on. He leapt into action. "Right. We can split up to look for him. I think we should meet back here in half an hour. If we haven't found him, first, we notify the police, and second, we notify the navy and ask them carry out an underwater search. In addition, I suggest that we call Shanghai and notify the officials of our society...."

I wasn't fully prepared for this sudden one hundred and eighty degree change in his attitude. It seemed Zhuge hadn't expected it either; she stood there blinking.

"OK, Let's split up." Having unintentionally taken charge, the author of "Elements of the Fantastic" divided us into groups and assigned our routes. Everyone assented, and Zhuge was just left blinking.

The ten of us, including one professor who was seventy-four and an associate professor who had suffered a myocardial infarction and carried nitroglycerin tablets with him at all times, set off, calling, "Little Li, Little Li, Little Li ..." The shore resounded with cries to wake the dead, especially the doleful cries of the comrade who had had the heart attack and was shouting himself hoarse.

At 10:15 everyone returned without a clue. When the author of "Elements of the Fantastic" mentioned his three emergency measures again, everyone just looked at each other in dismay. So I said, "Why don't we wait a little longer? If Little Li isn't back by midnight, it still won't be too late to take those steps, and we may avoid undue alarm.

When everyone agreed, I thought I saw the author of "Elements of the Fantastic" smile.

Some of the conference participants were elderly or infirm, and many of us were in the habit of going to bed early, but that night no one went to bed; we were walking around as restless as ants on a hot skillet, especially Zhuge Yun, who stood in the courtyard tire-lessly recounting in a high-pitched voice how she had discovered the young man was missing and organized the search. I was dead on my feet and lay down on the bed with my clothes on.

At 11:03 Little Li humming "On Sun Island," came walking down the corridor in his swimming trunks.

Everyone rushed toward him. I roused myself and ran out too; I wanted to let everyone know that I hadn't been asleep.

"Little Li, where were you? We were looking every-where for you!" everyone said at once.

"What, didn't you say no one needed a car tonight?"

"We didn't want a car. We were afraid you had fallen into the sea and been eaten by a shark!"

"No, I just swam for half an hour and then got out. I've been playing poker with the hotel staff ever since!"

"Preposterous!" Old Zhu, the conference organizer, normally such a cautious man, suddenly exploded with an anger so great his veins stood out and he began to stammer. "You stayed out so la-la-la-late. Why didn't you le-le-le-let us know? Everybody was wor-wor-wor-worried sick."

Little Li had no idea what was going on, but he sensed the seriousness of the situation and hung his head and shed a few tears.

Several months later I ran into the young friend who had written the paper on Nu Wa and *A Dream of Red Mansions*. He told me that after the conference he called on the participants and conducted a survey. The results showed that not a single person felt there had been any need to drag everyone out to look for Little Li that night, but in the face of Zhuge Yun's insistence, her determi-

251

nation, and her lofty motives that left no room for doubt, everyone, out of essentially the same consideration, had joined in. The behavior of one had influenced the next, and the whole thing had snowballed.

"But what about you? You were worse than any of them that night."

"I had no choice."

I shook my head.

Later, another question occurred to me. "Did you ask Zhuge Yun as well? Do you know what she was really thinking that night?"

He shook his head.

Translated by Cathy Silber

Notes:

[1] Scholars of the classic novel *A Dream of Red Mansions*.

[2] Mao Zedong had referred to Beijing as an independent kingdom during the Cultural Revolution. Sending industrial workers into work units considered to have too many intellectuals was called mixing them with sand.

LEE CANED

KATHY

Jia Pingwa

Feng Jicai

Ah Cheng

ZHANG JIE, A CONTROVERSIAL, MAINSTREAM WRITER

Gladys Yang

Zhang Jie was born in 1937. During the anti-Japanese war her parents separated and her mother, a teacher, brought her up in poverty in a village in Liaoning Province. In high school she developed a passion for music and literature including translations of Western novels of the eighteenth and nineteenth centuries. However, she was persuaded to study economics as being of more use to New China. Upon graduating from the Chinese People's University she worked for some years in the National Bureau of Mechanical Equipment, which familiarized her with Chinese industry. Then she joined a film studio and wrote two film scripts, *The Search* and *We Are Still Young*. She is now a full-time writer, one of China's most popular authors.

She did not begin to write till she was forty, just after the fall of Jiang Qing and her close colleagues known as the Gang of Four. In 1978 she joined the writers association; in 1980 she joined the Chinese Communist Party; and in 1982 she became a salaried member of the Beijing Branch of the China Federation of Literary and Art Circles.

Before 1977 Chinese writers had been urged to gear their writing to the current ultra-Left political line, and subjects such as democracy, love unrelated to the revolution, or the value of the individual were virtually taboo.

The Third Plenary Session of the Party in 1978 condemned the previous ultra-Left line and called for a realistic approach to China's problems. This encouraged writers to write more honestly and tackle a wider range of themes. It was under these circumstances that Zhang Jie began to write.

Her earlier themes were mainly the problems of youth and love. She had divorced her husband because he maltreated her, and that was considered a stigma. She thus had personal experience of the discrimination against women about which she writes so pungently. Her story in this collection does not address itself to women's problems, but the obnoxious bureaucrat who is its protagonist is described as never confiding in his colleagues or even his wife. Then comes the revealing throw-away line: "In any case, his wife was no more to him than a wisdom tooth one simply acquired at a certain age."

The first story she wrote, *The Child from the Forest*, won a prize in 1978 as one of the best short stories of the year. The next year, *Whose Life Is Most Beautiful* won another award. However, the story that brought her into the public eye was *Love Must Not Be Forgotten*, published in 1979. The Chinese media used to imply that an individual's highest fulfilment came from serving the people, but Zhang argues that this is not enough; personal relations and marriage are crucially important. In China all men and women are expected to marry. Moral values are a mixture of socialist ethics and traditional conventions. And nowhere is the influence of tradition stronger than in the field of marriage. The mother of the narrator of this story was a divorcee passionately though platonically in love with a married man, who returned her love at a distance. Her daughter therefore questions the current marriage conventions and decides to remain single, despite social disapproval, if no kindred spirit appears. Many young readers supported this stand. Critics, however, accused Zhang of undermining social morality because of her defence of love—even in the purest form —outside marriage, and because she was a divorcee.

Zhang Jie is physically frail, mentally tough. She finds it stimulating to be under fire. When interviewed she welcomes provocative questions. But malicious charges of immorality because of her own platonic love for a married man made her wretchedly indignant. She contracted coronary heart disease, aggravated by the difficult conditions in which she had to work. She and her mother and daughter Tang Di lived for years in a small two-room flat. The little passageway was stacked with books and magazines on top of which usually lay a snow white cat. One had to edge past to the sunless bedsitter shared by Zhang and her daughter. Two drawers of the small desk were used by Tang Di, who also practised the piano there. And visitors poured in. Zhang often had to leave Beijing to find quieter surroundings. Only recently, after marrying the man she had loved for years when he finally got a divorce, has she been given larger living quarters.

Leaden Wings, first published in 1980, has as its central theme the modernization of Chinese industry. In 1981 the *Christian Science Monitor* called it China's "first political novel," supporting Deng Xiaoping's program for reform and criticizing ultra-Leftists and conservatives whose old policies resulted in appalling waste and inefficiency as well as low living standards. The novel is set in the Ministry of Heavy Industry where the old guard and reformists oppose each other. It gives a picture of a society in flux, and Zhang airs her views on the need for more democratic and scientific approaches, recognition of the value of the individual, and an overhauling of social morality by throwing out the vestiges of feudalism.

The publication of this book met with whole-hearted approval from young people in industrial ministries. Some officials were scandalized because she said that economic reform must bring about social and political reform, and that Marxism must develop with the times. She was summoned to hear accusations that her novel was "anti-Party, anti-socialism." In an interview with me which she taped, she refuted these charges, declaring, "I wrote that book precisely because I'm for socialism and China's modernization." On her way home she passed our local free market and felt it her duty as a Party member to stop a peddler from charging exorbitant prices.

She later revised *Leaden Wings* three times in the light of criticism of its form and contents, admitting that she had written too hastily—260,000 words in four months. Even so, the German translation of this first edition sold out in only three days. In 1985 the revised edition won the Mao Dun award, China's most prestigious literary prize. However, Zhang was in hospital at the time, unable to attend the ceremony.

The Ark, her next major work, written in 1981, describes the daily struggle for survival of three professional women separated from their husbands, and the social disapproval with which they have to contend. Some readers acclaimed this as China's first feminist novel, though she denies that she is a feminist—she attacks social injustice of every kind. Some critics denounced her for encouraging women to let their resentment against men embitter them, so that they behave in an unwomanly way and are not really happy. Others claimed that she distorted socialism by painting too black a picture of women's difficulties.

Zhang Jie declares that *The Ark* and *Leaden Wings*

are the works with which she is "least dissatisfied."

The story in this collection "The Time Is Not Yet Ripe" won the National Best Short Story Award for 1984. Though not one of her major works it is one of the best written, not long-winded like so much modern Chinese writing or in the flowery melodramatic style of some of her other stories. Its portrait of a hypocritical Party bureaucrat manoeuvring for power is skilfully drawn. The central committee is planning to retire elderly cadres and in three months to promote younger men who are technically more competent. Yue, a university graduate, section chief and secretary of his Party branch, sees this as his big chance. But his former classmate Cai, who is professionally superior to him, is being considered for deputy director. Party membership is usually a requisite for appointment to such a responsible post, and Yue has consistently blocked Cai's admission. He now craftily employs more delaying tactics, talking self-righteously all the time about his principled stand. He has no genuine concern for the work, but to better his personal status is willing to do down colleagues and deceive his superiors. However, finally Cai is the one promoted.

This satire faithfully reflects the policy of reforming leading bodies and the bureaucratic opposition which has to be overcome. Just as topical today as when it was written, it shows her understanding of the bureaucratic mentality while expressing her conviction that, in spite of all man-made obstacles, China's economy will forge ahead.

Zhang Jie's international readership is growing, and she receives many invitations to go abroad. She has visited America and Europe, receiving exceptionally wide coverage in West Germany. She appears to advantage on TV, one of her interviewers describing her as "vividly attractive." And she finds foreign travel stimulating. In 1985 she stayed for a month in a students' dormitory, living on three packets of instant noodles and three bottles of yoghurt a day while she wrote nearly 100,000 words about her first trip to Europe. In 1987 she went back for nearly seven months, accompanied part of the time by Tang Di who, fluent in English and Spanish, can interpret for her mother.

I believe these trips to the West have influenced her style and subject matter. In recent years she has tried her hand at black humor. One example is *What's Wrong with Him?* written in 1986. It presents a series of neurotics, describing the social conditions which have unhinged them. A far cry from her early sentimental style and passages of purple prose, it is mordant and fantastic. When I told her that I found some passages revolting, she said, "I agree. But many social phenomena are revolting and it is our duty as writers to expose them."

Whatever themes Zhang Jie may choose in future, we can be sure that she will retain her strong sense of justice, and her hatred of bureaucracy and the vestiges of feudalism in China. She will continue tackling sensitive issues to educate her readers, regardless of some critics' outcries against her.

In *My Boat* she envisages herself putting out to sea and braving angry waves:

...I renovate my boat, patch it up and repaint it, so that it will last a little longer. I set sail again. People, houses, trees on shore become smaller and smaller and I am reluctant to leave them. But my boat cannot stay beached for ever. What use is a boat without the sea?

In the distance I see waves rolling towards me. Rolling continuously. I know that one day I will be smashed to bits by those waves, but this is the fate of all boats—what other sort of end could they meet?

December 1987

The Time Is Not Yet Ripe

Zhang Jie

BREATHE in—breathe out.

A pearly mist faintly tinged with green was hanging above the lake. The air was as fresh and bracing as ozone.

Breathe in—breathe out.

All of a sudden, Section Chief Yue saw before him a mass of lotus blooms. Had they opened overnight? He ran round this lake every morning, yet hadn't noticed them before.

Breathe in—breathe out.

The day had started out muggily and now it seemed as if it might be going to rain. Dragonflies skimmed the water; others circled above his head.

Breathe in—breathe out.

Yue had run half a lap already, yet his pace and breathing were still steady and even. He loped along, effortlessly overtaking one by one the elderly people who, though ostensibly jogging, were little faster than walkers.

Their ranks had expanded in the last couple of years. Some, you could see at a glance, were newly retired and slightly paunchy officials, who retained their old mannerisms. Jogging under the willows by the lake, each step they took seemed as weighty as if they were solving some complex case.

Some of them he came across every day. Each time he overtook them, Yue would nod respectfully with a smile. And their answering smiles elated him like a green light at a crossing.

After passing the hexagonal pavilion, Yue saw Little Duan tottering along in front, his old blue gym shoes flip-flopping on the cement path, his lean flabby legs quivering under his baggy shorts. On the back of his faded purple track suit was printed the number 7. On the front were the characters indicating the name of their old university—one of the most prestigious in all China.

Their splendid Alma Mater had graduates all over the country.

There had been only twenty-one of them in their class, yet he seemed to run into them everywhere. There were three in his own bureau: Little Duan, Cai Depei and himself.

Well, no wonder. Having specialized in the same subject, most of them were naturally assigned to similar posts. Since their graduation in the 1960s, their practical experience had equipped them to work independently; and now that the Central Committee set store by intellectuals they were doing all right, their social status had risen. Whenever he went down to a grass roots unit, he always found a couple of his old classmates in senior positions. Still, a section chief in the provinces could not compare with him, a section chief in a government ministry.

Yue had ascertained that he had done the best of their whole class. And now the Central Committee had a long-term plan for training leading cadres and intended to promote younger people, a "third echelon," aged between thirty-five and forty-five.

As luck would have it, Yue was just forty-five.

His generation was fortunate. They had completed their formal education, and though sent to work in cadre schools in the Cultural Revolution had come through unscathed. For over a dozen years there were no pay rises, but since 1978 they had received four increases. And now the Central Committee was stressing the importance of middle-aged technicians, owing to the drastic shortage of competent cadres. The timing was just right!

Someone had intimated to Yue that he would be promoted to deputy director of their bureau. And this seemed to be borne out by certain events.

He had, for instance, been made responsible for coordinating the designing of equipment for a major project, work involving many research institutes and factories. Though Director Chai was nominally in charge, it was Yue who had the actual say. Chai was nearly seventy. In a few more months he would no doubt join the ranks of the retired officials beside the lake.

Again, Yue had recently been invited to attend enlarged meetings of the bureau Party committee....

These reflections made him assume a graver expression. Like an actor entering into his part.

He caught up with Little Duan. They had called him "little" in college because he was the youngest in the class. Though he was growing bald now, Yue still addressed him this way. Since becoming section chief, he had taken to prefacing the names of many of his subordinates with "little." Apart from sounding fatherly, it also marked his seniority.

Duan grinned at Yue.

"Jogging?" asked Yue, neither too heartily nor too

coldly. Without waiting for an answer he loped on. This was deliberate. From now on he ought to keep his distance from his old connections. If he put off doing this till his promotion it would seem to abrupt. They might accuse him of putting on airs. For the sake of the work he must keep them at arm's length, or they might sound him out about the intentions of the leadership, and that would never do. To tell them would be a breach of discipline; not to do so would hurt their feelings.

Duan had no understanding of this. Were Yue to be promoted to deputy premier, he would still buttonhole him for a chat, whether he had anything special to say or not. He did not notice Yue's calculated aloofness but put on a spurt to catch up.

"Say, where were you yesterday evening? I came to see you but you weren't in."

"I was out on business." Yue didn't ask what he had wanted—it couldn't be of any consequence.

Undeterred by Yue's cryptic reply, Duan asked, "Didn't Huifen give you a message?"

"She was already asleep when I got back."

"Trust women to hold things up."

Yue shot him a sidelong glance. Little Duan's way of running was all wrong. Instead of moving backwards and forwards like pistons, his arms revolved like spindles in front of his chest.

"Did you hear? A few days ago two cadres from the personnel division came, apparently to check up on Cai Depei as our bureau has been considering him for deputy director."

At first Yue failed to take in this news, so at odds was it with his own wishful thinking. When it did sink in it nearly knocked him over. He had been so sure of getting

263

that post himself.

He sagged, overborne by a dismay which left him unable to answer, utterly crushed. No need to worry about the top echelon. In less than five years they would all have to step down. But the men appointed to the third echelon would stay put for twenty years, by which time he would be finished. Losing this last chance he felt driven to distraction.

Though this shocking disclosure had left him more dead than alive, he recovered sufficiently to analyse its credibility.

He couldn't believe it. For the simple reason that it came from a bookworm with no real grasp of the overall situation. Little Duan was entirely capable of turning things upside down. He completely lacked insight. By comparison, Yue, though not all that brilliant himself, at least had the experience of over twenty years in the Party.

Still, he couldn't help having misgivings. Two men from the personnel division *had* come. If it had been to check up on Cai Depei, Yue would surely have heard about it before Little Duan.

Mind-boggling as this was, he had to behave as if nothing had happened. He said off-handedly, "I hadn't heard."

Even if he had, he would never have spread such news casually.

Rifts suddenly appeared in the slate-grey sky, almost as though the roasting red sun inside had cracked it. Lurid sunlight shone through the clouds. The sultriness made Yue's scalp tingle as if with prickly heat.

But one overriding thought recalled him to composure: This threat couldn't be averted by a fit of temper. He had to keep cool to analyse the situation.

As soon as a "third echelon" was called for, Yue had reviewed all the members of their bureau aged between thirty-five and forty-five. He had assessed their political stand, qualifications, technical skills, leadership qualities, the leadership's opinion of them, even the records of their family dependants. As to the speed and accuracy of this investigation, Yue, the head of the technical section was every bit as good, if not better, than the personnel division. For he had carried it out completely on the sly. Not even his wife Huifen had had any inkling of it. In all previous political movements a lot of people had ended up in trouble through careless talk. As the ancients said: A loose tongue leads to disaster.

A thorough sifting revealed that the cadres who were professionally competent and had the ability to lead were, unfortunately, not Party members, while some Party members were lacking in ability. His own qualifications were seemingly the best. He might not measure up to the most skilled technicians, but at least he came from a first-rate university. Compared to comrades in the first echelon, his Party seniority was nothing, but he had joined the Party twenty-six years and seven months ago. He had steered clear of trouble in all the political movements, and no serious problems had cropped up in the section under him.

"Old Yue, Cai Depei has mass support, so I think he's got a good chance of being promoted. What do you think? The only possible snag is that he's not in the Party yet."

Right! Even Little Duan could see that.

Breathe in—breathe out.

Yue's steps and breathing, temporarily uneven, recovered their normal rhythm.

Breathe in—breathe out.

That was the crux of the matter. Only in exceptional cases were non-Party members appointed to leading posts.

It was an unwritten law. A good thing too, or what a mess they'd be in. Yue now knew his best course of action.

"Little Duan, the decision is up to our Party committee."

Duan shot him an appraising glance, wondering whether this was official jargon or was what Yue really believed. It was the same look he gave pedlars weighing out vegetables in the free market; no matter how closely he watched the scale in their hands, they always managed to cheat him just the same. Deciding that Yue had spoken casually, he went on confidently, "So why don't you help him? He's under your Party branch; hurry up and get his application passed. In another three months he'll be forty-six, too old for the third echelon. As his classmate you know all about him, you were our Party secretary in college. Hasn't he been applying to join the Party for the last twenty-five years, ever since he was in college?"

Yue was disconcerted. Even Little Duan had seen the next move to be taken.

Duan was watching him expectantly and had put on a spurt to keep up, his arms rotating like spindles, his steps even jerkier. Sweat from his forehead was dripping down his sallow cheeks.

Strange, what business was it of his? What was he so worked up about? Still he had pointed out that the crucial thing was the three months' time limit.

"Precisely because we're classmates I can't butt in. The truth is, Little Duan, you still haven't overcome that old weakness of yours. We have to act in a principled way and pay attention to politics instead of being swayed by personal feelings. What does the Party Constitution say? We join the Party because we believe in communism, not for the sake of selfish interests or special privileges."

Yue had spoken earnestly, his solemn eyes fixed on the winding path ahead. He only blinked when sweat dripped from his eyebrows.

Duan had nothing to say. He kept his eyes on the path too, listening to his shuffling feet. Compared with Yue's regular steps, his own seemed to reveal unprincipled liberalism. Yue was running along calmly, as if confident of a prize at the end of the track.

"You ought to know me better than that. Since our college days have I ever been swayed by personal sentiment?" Yue seemed to be appealing for understanding.

True. In their five years at college, Duan recalled, Yue had done his best to help all his classmates in turn to straighten out their thinking. Not for five days or five months but for five whole years he had sacrificed his own academic prospects to help them make progress. To this friend who gave them frank advice they had confided everything, even what love-letters they had been writing. But by graduation not one of them had managed to join the Party; a poor return, they felt, for Yue's concern.

Remembering this, Duan felt doubly contrite. Yue was right: he hadn't changed. Neither had Yue.

Once home again Yue sat motionless till his wife asked, "Aren't you going to have a wash?"

He had to stand up then. Huifen had already eyed him several times. If he sat there any longer she was bound to ask, "What's wrong? Aren't you feeling well? It's ten past seven, high time to get washed and have breakfast."

Yue could never relax, at home or in the office, if there was someone else around. His plump, easy-going wife never gave much thought to serious matters, and only concentrated on being a good housewife.

Yue went into the toilet and glanced at himself in the mirror. It struck him that he had suddenly aged. He moved closer to the mirror. Yes, the wrinkles on his forehead and round his eyes seemed much deeper than before. In dismay he reached up as if to smooth them away. The stubble on his chin pricked his hand. Maybe after shaving he would look less haggard.

He poured hot water into the basin, moistened his face with a towel, squeezed some shaving cream on to his brush and lathered his cheeks and jaw. Then he started to shave.

Three months ... they were crucial, might make all the difference. He heaved a long sigh, thinking hard.

Damn, his wrist shook and the razor gashed his face. Blood reddened the lather. When he wiped it off he saw that the cut was a small one. He bent under the tap to rinse it with cold water, then quickly shaved around it and washed his face.

He must stall for three months, he thought.

He picked up a comb to comb his thick hair, but stopped abruptly, holding it in mid-air. There was a white hair at his temples, very conspicuous among the black.

What was the matter with him today?

He'd found white hairs before, but they hadn't made him so conscious of his age and the passing of time. Now of all times he mustn't give the impression that he would soon be an old man.

Yue put down the comb and tried to pull out the

white hair, but, slippery with brilliantine, it eluded him. He tugged several times, but only pulled out some black hair. Never mind, he had plenty of hair, not like some of his colleagues turning bald prematurely.

His arm was beginning to ache, but he wouldn't enlist Huifen's help. Why should anybody else know about this? In any case, to him his wife was no more than a wisdom tooth one simply acquired at a certain age.

Finally he pulled the hair out, flicked it angrily on the floor, then emerged from the toilet.

His wife and sons had finished their breakfast, leaving his share on the dining-table. He sat down, straightened his chopsticks then polished off the food. Having wiped his mouth he took down his black, artificial leather briefcase from the clothes rack behind the door. "I'm off now," he announced, addressing no one in particular.

Huifen came out of the kitchen to call him back. "What's the hurry? Take these salted duck eggs to Depei." She thrust a dozen blue-shelled eggs in a net bag at him.

"Why take him those? He can buy some himself if he wants them." Yue stepped back frowning. What a fool he'd look, a section chief carrying a net bag of salted eggs to the office.

"What time has he got for shopping? A bachelor can't pick and choose what he eats." Again the net bag was thrust at him.

Yue could only say, "Then find a plastic bag, so that I can put them in my briefcase. I'd look a sight dangling a net bag of eggs."

"What does it matter? Everybody does it." Huifen rounded her big eyes. But being easy-going she didn't insist, and brought him a plastic bag.

It had probably been a bag of milk powder. White powder dropped out as she shook it. "Did you talk to Sis?" she asked.

Wouldn't the plastic bag dirty his briefcase? "Forget it." Yue took a big envelope out of his briefcase, stuffed the net bag into it, then put it back.

He ignored Huifen's question. Wanting no part in that business, he hadn't proposed the match to his sister-in-law. His motives were strangely mixed.

Marry his sister-in-law to Cai Depei? Could she be happy with him? He had divorced his first wife. If she agreed—and he could tell that she had a good impression of Cai—how should he treat him in future? Cai had recently been promoted to be a seventh-grade engineer. So what? Their outfit swarmed with engineers and technicians; but a seventh-grade engineer with a Party card, that would be someone to be reckoned with.

"Little Duan came yesterday evening and said ..."

"I know, I met him out jogging."

"As secretary of the Party branch, can't you help Depei join the Party?"

"He's still not up to it, so what can I do? I can't order our Party members to vote for him, can I?"

"What do they have against him?" she asked with concern.

"Well," Yue hesitated. "He just isn't ready for it yet." This was a valid pretext which could be used at any time about anyone. Everybody could be faulted in some respect. Who could claim to be a thoroughly remoulded proletarian intellectual?

But the fact was quite the opposite of what Yue made out. No one, in the Party or out of it, had anything against Cai, whose name headed the list of candidates to be admitted to their Party branch. Only Yue, Party secretary, kept putting off holding a meeting to discuss it.

"Well, for one thing ... he's arrogant, lacks political consciousness and a good mass line.... And why did he get a divorce? Divorced his wife out of the blue without reporting the reason to our Party branch.... Oh yes, there's been plenty of talk."

Yue could keep this up for hours. Practice makes perfect! Like a donkey turning a grindstone, plodding round and round in circles.

"Is that all?" cried Huifen. "Well, you can surely win over those Party members who hold that against him."

What nonsense! If everyone joined the Party it would cease to be a distinction. It would only produce more rivals.

"You want me to drag him into the Party? I can't do such an unprincipled thing," he retorted self-righteously.

"Well, he helped you write your graduation thesis. If not for him you'd have flunked."

Ignoring this, Yue looked again at his watch—the third time in two minutes. "It's late," he said. "I must go now."

Huifen couldn't understand why, even to her and his classmates, her husband should behave like a bureaucrat. She blurted out, "Seems to me your classmates are all making out better than you!"

This touched a raw nerve in Yue.

You couldn't have it both ways. Who could have known that a time would come when technical proficiency was what counted? It was too late now. He couldn't go back to college to make up the classes he'd missed. Couldn't summon back the last twenty years. Could only keep going on the path he had chosen. Cai

271

Depei on his sunny highway was heading for further promotion, so why should he squeeze Yue out? And he didn't mean to block Cai all his life, not after this appointment of new leading cadres.

"That's no way to talk. If I hadn't steered them the right way, would they have made such a good showing? I've done my best for the Party, training all these skilled technicians." Resentfully stuffing his briefcase under one arm, he marched out with an air of martyrdom.

In spite of the load on his mind, when Yue stepped into his office he surveyed every corner as usual. Because this was *his* office he examined it carefully, as if preparing to welcome some inspector.

Good, everything was just right, in its proper place.

The little girl on the calendar was smiling, head tilted like a film star and looking out of the corner of her eyes. The caption underneath read: "I'm mama's only child." On another wall was the slogan "Learn from Zhang Haidi." The wall for an inch around this was slightly lighter in color, as previously a larger slogan "Learn from Comrade Lei Feng" had been there. That didn't look so good, but never mind, he would probably put up a bigger one soon. Yue liked slogans because they showed at a glance, more effectively than circulars or reports, the central tasks of the time.

As he put his briefcase down on a chair by the window, the salted duck eggs clinked against each other. He smiled at it as if he were contemplating his rival's skull.

He sat down at his desk rubbing his hands, then picked up the telephone, rapidly dialed a number, and asked Liu Danian to stop by.

This done, he took from a drawer a de luxe edition

of the *Documents of the Third Plenary Session*, and put it in a prominent position on the desk. He then pulled out a sheaf of documents, putting some on his right, the rest in front of him. Next he picked up a red and blue pencil, lit a cigarette and made a show of going carefully through this material.

There was a knock at the door.

"Come in," called Yue without looking up. He greeted Liu with a nod. "I'll be through in a minute." Having underlined certain passages in red he put down the pencil and turned to ask Liu to sit down, offering him a packet of cigarettes. "Have one. They're from Yunnan."

Liu lit up. "Recently the price of cigarettes has come down. They thought raising prices was the way to make a profit, but then found people stopped buying."

Normally Yue made no response to remarks like this. Today, however, with a tolerant smile, he commented, "After all these years of planned economy, we still lack experience in market adjustments."

Liu took a deep drag on his cigarette. Yes, it was good tobacco.

"You can see, I'm up to my ears in work." Yue indicated with a vague gesture the documents and notebooks on his desk. "So I never got round to asking after your father."

Liu stopped smoking and sat up straight. "He's in a bad way," he said in a worried voice. "After his operation last year he picked up, but recently my mother wrote saying he's had a relapse. I'm afraid the cancer is spreading. And it's not easy to get him hospitalized."

Yue nodded sympathetically, then switched on the fan and turned it in Liu's direction.

"Don't worry. I've got an idea, see what you think. A few days ago we received a report from one of the plants manufacturing equipment for our new project; but we still need to know how long it's going to take them." He took the report from a drawer and handed it over. "There seem to be some problems they need our help with. Could you go there and see what's going on? You might also liaise with the other units involved. It would take you at least three months. And during that time you could make arrangements for your father. My wife has a classmate, a doctor in your hometown who's a hospital director. I can write and ask him to help. I don't know, though, if it would be convenient for you to leave home."

Liu rose eagerly to this bait. "What could be better! A trip for the bureau combined with family business, how considerate of you to think of it."

"How else could you manage? With your father's illness dragging on, your mother needs help. You can't ask for a long leave of absence, and someone has to visit that plant. Only ..." Yue hesitated, looking troubled. "This business is rather urgent. As this is a key project, the ministry keeps ringing up and asking for progress reports. I just hope there's no hitch through any fault of ours. Can you set off in the next couple of days?"

"No problem, don't you worry."

"Good. Then hand over your work today, and go home to get ready. I've got to attend a meeting on housing now. It's going to be another rough session. We've made a fair allocation, but there's no satisfying certain people, they're demanding flats for their children and grandchildren. Old Wen in our section still only has two rooms for his family of five, three generations and a grown-up son and daughter. It's just not good enough! If he doesn't get a flat this time, I'm going to take it up with the Party committee."

Everyone in the section knew that Yue had worn himself out, talked himself hoarse, trying to get Old Wen a flat. He himself, though a section chief, still had only two rooms. Luckily both his children were boys, which simplified matters.

After seeing Liu out, Yue equipped himself with a notebook and went off with an easy mind to the housing meeting.

After the meeting he announced the outcome to his section. He had at last managed to get a three-room flat for Old Wen. The latter nearly kowtowed in his gratitude, as if Yue had personally built the flat and presented it to him.

Old Wen's delight bolstered Yue's self-confidence. He told them earnestly, "This is the result of implementing the Party's policy on intellectuals. We must all work harder to speed up modernization"

He returned to his office exhausted yet elated, as if he had just run a marathon. Having brewed himself a mug of excellent jasmine tea, he settled down contentedly to skim through the round-up of foreign news and the *People's Daily*.

The telephone rang. He picked up the receiver, his eyes still on the paper. He never missed out on a single day's news. Even towards the end of the Cultural Revolution, when everyone was disgusted by the lies of the Gang of Four which the papers were full of, he had still read them conscientiously.

"Hullo, who's there?"

"Chen Jinghui speaking."

"Oh, Director Chen! What can I do for you?" Yue asked respecfully, putting down the paper.

"I want to know what you've done about admitting Cai Depei to the Party."

Yue's scalp seemed to tighten. So Little Duan hadn't just made it up! Director Chen was in charge of personnel. If he asked specially about Cai Depei, it must be after discussion with the Party committee.

What was the best way to handle this? He'd better watch his step.

"Yes, we mean to accept him ..."

"Right," Chen cut him short. "I understand he has a good record."

Yue's heart contracted. "Yes, we've given him a form to fill in."

"When was that?" The director sounded rather displeased.

"Oh, six or seven months ago." Yue had to give an honest answer.

"Why haven't you discussed it then?" Chen was no layman in this kind of thing; he got to the point.

Yue laughed apologetically. "We haven't been able to convene a meeting of the whole branch. The work keeps us too busy because we're so short-staffed. There's always somebody away on business, stopping us from having a quorum. The committee member who's sponsoring him is out on business again at the moment." He secretly congratulated himself on sending Liu Danian off first thing that morning.

"How long will he be gone?"

"About three months."

"That long?"

"Yes."

"You must expedite matters so that we can make better use of our middle-aged intellectuals, according to the Central Committee's directive."

"Yes. As soon as his sponsor comes back we'll call a branch meeting."

"What's Cai's attitude?"

"Quite correct. He says that in spite of the delay he'll work as hard as he can for the Party.... In fact in our section we treat him just like a Party member."

Director Chen laughed. Was Yue trying to teach his grandmother to suck eggs? "All right then, see to it." With that he rang off.

Putting down the receiver, clammy with sweat, Yue stared blankly at the slogans on the wall. Well, he'd managed to get by this time, but what next? Was he one up, or was Cai? It was hard to tell what the next three months would bring. If only this nerve-racking period would flash past in an instant.

But the three months passed uneventfully, with no further pressure from Director Chen. And Yue heard no more talk about Cai's promotion. The weight on his mind lessened with each passing day.

At last Liu Danian came back and reported that the problems had been solved and the equipment would be ready on time. But his father's illness was going from bad to worse.

"Don't worry," Yue told him, "We'll find some other way out."

Liu couldn't understand why Yue looked so grateful and patted him so cordially on the back. He had only done his duty, hadn't he? Strange!

Yue did not convene a branch meeting immediately, but if pressed by Director Chen he intended to say, "I've notified everyone to attend a meeting the day after tomorrow. We hope you'll come to it too."

The director appeared to have forgotten all about the matter.

One Wednesday morning in October, Yue was summoned to an enlarged meeting of the bureau Party committee. He went there confident that he would soon be a full member of that committee. After a discussion of the current major tasks, Director Chen announced, "All Party committees have instruction to waste no time in appointing younger and better qualified cadres to their leading bodies, to speed up modernization. Our bureau Party committee has considered the situation. After examining a number of comrades, we all agree that Comrade Cai Depei comes closest to the Central Committee's criteria. He has been well educated by the Party, is of good political caliber, is in his prime and has rich practical experience. He has a sense of responsibility, works very hard, and is one of our key cadres. We should recruit him as a reserve cadre for the third echelon and train him systematically for eventual promotion to the post of deputy director...."

Finished, done for! Yue gave up all hope.

His cigarette burnt his fingers. He darted a glance at Director Chen, afraid the latter might know what he was thinking, then tried to look indifferent, listening intently. Chen went on, "Comrade Cai Depei is just over forty-five, but that age limit isn't too rigid; and though he's not a Party member that's not because the time is not yet ripe for him, it's because we have let things slide." He glanced sharply at Yue.

Hell, if he'd known non-Party members could be promoted and that the age limit wasn't a strict one, he needn't have worried all this time for nothing!

He'd been taken for a ride!

Fuming inwardly, Yue impassively accepted this fait accompli. What else could he do? He'd muffed it, missed his chance.

When had he slipped up? He couldn't figure it out.

Perhaps it was because of his carelessness, because he'd had too much faith in his past experience.

Straight after the meeting he told Liu Danian to convene a Party branch meeting for Friday morning, to discuss Cai Depei's application to join the Party.

Before the Party branch meeting Cai met Yue in the toilet.

Yue told him confidentially, "Relax, there's no problem, I've seen to it that everything will go smoothly. Whatever criticism the comrades raise, your attitude should be to correct any mistakes you have and guard against those you haven't." After a moment's thought he added, as if passing on a precious tip, "On no account try to justify yourself. Take along a notebook and write down everything that's said. Oh yes, and in conclusion promise that, whether you're passed or not, you'll go on trying to remould your world outlook and to measure up to the standard of Party membership...."

Cai nodded nervously and thanked Yue sincerely. "I will. You've shown so much concern for me over twenty years, since our college days, all the help you've given me ..."

"Don't treat me like a stranger, we're old classmates," Yue retorted. "I'm really pleased that your application is finally going to be passed. I only wish our whole class could have the honor of joining the Party." He didn't mention a word about Cai's coming promotion, as if it had never been mooted.

As they left the toilet Yue said cryptically, "Oh, I nearly forgot. Come to my place this evening, Huifen's preparing a meal to celebrate, and her sister will be there too. We've got a private matter to discuss with you." This said he walked with solemn dignity into the meeting-room to cast his sacred vote.

Translated by Gladys Yang

ZHANG KANGKANG AND HER FICTION

Wu Taichang

A striking phenomenon in Chinese writing of the recent decade is the prominent rise and the vigor of young writers. Among the many young writers, it is women writers whose demonstrated talent and potential have attracted particular attention, and among them thirty-eight-year-old Zhang Kangkang is outstanding.

She was born in the renowned southern city of Hangzhou, where she attended elementary and middle schools. In 1969 she went to live on a state farm in the Beidahuang region of northeast China, where she remained for eight years. There she planted vegetables, hewed timber, worked in a brick kiln, engaged in scientific research, worked as a reporter in a progaganda department, and wrote for a local art troupe. Her work was intense and arduous, but she managed to find the time to read and write. In her letters to relatives living afar, she wrote down her impressions of the mysterious Beidahuang. In her memoirs, she says: "When we saw that the environment there offered nothing and that there was no help to be had from society, our only course of action was to expend several times the psychic and physical energy required of others, in order to make even the very slightest advance in our work."

She got off to an earlier start than most writers of her generation. Her first short story, *The Lamp*, appeared in

1972 in the supplement of a Shanghai newspaper. Shortly afterwards she took advantage of a long convalescence to write a novel, entitled *Border Line*, reflecting the life of educated youth living in China's border regions. As a result of this work, published in 1975 by a Shanghai publishing house, she made her debut in literary circles, but she readily admitted to the shortcomings of this work: "This novel of mine appeared on the eve of a great historical turning point, and, because of my own limitations as regards both knowledge and ideology, it was largely unrealistic."

In 1979 her short story *The Right to Love* appeared in *Harvest*, the literary bimonthly edited by Ba Jin, and consequently she was acknowledged to be an influential young writer. Unlike the "scar literature" fashionable at that time, her short story was not content merely to "expose and denounce." Instead it raised human rights issues which were profound in their significance and explored questions of human value and morality. One American scholar has gone as far as asserting that *The Right to Love* was the work which signaled a new era in Chinese literature rather than the 1977 national prize winning story *Teacher* by Liu Xinwu. In 1979 she was admitted into the Heilongjiang Provincial Writers Association, and became a full-time writer. In that year she also wrote the short story *White Poppy Pod*, which was published in the *Shanghai Literature*. This story describes the new lease of spiritual life gained by a released prisoner. Some critics found fault with the work for being a "quest for a personality abstraction," but the author reveals a partiality for the character she creates throughout the work.

1980 was a fruitful year for Zhang Kangkang. In a number of influential magazines she published three short stories—*The Tolling of a Distant Bell*, *Summer*, and *Philosophy in a Hen's Egg*—and the novella *Light Morning Mist*. Of these *Summer* and *Light Morning Mist* respectively won national prizes for excellence in short story and novella writing in 1980, when she became a member of the Chinese Writers Association. In 1982 she became a member of the International PEN Society (China Chapter) and in 1987 she became deputy chairperson of the Heilongjiang Provincial Writers Association.

Her novella *Northern Lights* (published by Tianjin Baihua Wenyi Publishing House in 1981) was a milestone in her career, indicating that she had achieved maturity as a writer, as well as being a significant account of China's social and intellectual development. In artistic technique she made use of dreams and soliloquy in the stream of consciousness style, while her choice and use of language reveal a refinement of her previous philosophical content and indicate a trend to greater writing freedom.

Between 1983 and 1985 she published few works. Her personal life underwent a number of twists and turns. She threw herself into study and read great quantities of literature, philosophy, economics and other subjects. Occasionally she wrote essays. Most people concentrate on her achievements in fiction and overlook her essays, but her essays are in fact excellently written. Her essays, "Thoughts on the Underground Forest," "Anecdotes from the Home of the Swan," and "Olives," have received high praise. Her first anthology of essays, *Olives*, was published in this period by Shanghai Literature and Art Publishing House.

It became clear in retrospect that she had in 1984 been giving thought and consideration to a full-length novel reflecting the lives of educated youth. This was

Invisible Companions, published as a single volume by Writers Publishing House in 1985 and then serialized over the fourth and fifth issues of the *Harvest* in 1986. When this novel, which runs to three hundred thousand Chinese characters, first appeared it was acclaimed by critics. The *Literary Gazette* ran a long review which said that "this work is filled with the writer's awareness of literary consciousness and with her pioneeringly significant esthetic realization....Not only has she connoted much concerning man and human nature in her writings, but has written much about the significance of good and evil for mankind, thus comprehending in her field of enquiry the possible and future adjustments necessary for man, his interpersonal relations, and his relationship with society as a whole." Many critics are of the opinion that this work represents the crystallization of her long term speculations and investigations of man, human nature and the entirety of human society. The writer herself regards this work as important, and in the *Literary Gazette* published a long piece in which she discussed "the power of the self-examined consciousness and the psychological novel," described in detail the process of writing this novel, and offered her own explanation of the novel's meaning. Writers regard *Invisible Companion* as a uniquely original achievement among the spate of novels treating the theme of educated youth which have appeared in recent years. The Writers Publishing House is at present organizing a symposium on this particular work in conjunction with the Heilongjiang Provincial Writers Association.

We recommend to readers *Bitter Dreams* (which appeared in the original Chinese in the third issue of 1985 of the *Chinese Writers*) as the most noteworthy of Zhang Kangkang's recent short stories. Mental illness and mental clinics are everyday social phenomena in the West where their existence is acknowledged and taken seriously, but China has long overlooked such research. *Bitter Dreams* can be described as the first contemporary literary work to touch on this topic, and in the midst of its description of an age of dramatic changes in the economic situation of Chinese society, and in human personality and consciousness, we find a psychological portrait of an ordinary person. The story tells us how in fact the reforms make a psychological impact and have an effect on the circumstances of every member of society. In the clash between traditional feudal consciousness and an ossified doctrinaire "system of public ownership" on the one hand, and the new concept of modern society's equal advantage for all on the other, a large number of Chinese have lost their psychological equilibrium. This is an illness afflicting society which requires a treatment that can remedy the relationship between man and society, and in the course of it, individuals will discover their own weaknesses. The conclusion of the story seems to deny the fact that this is a piece of realistic writing and when I questioned the author on this point she told me with a smile that the work is "merely a metaphor."

She has published many collections of her work —*Summer* (an anthology of short stories), *Anthology of Zhang Kangkang's Novellas*, *Pagoda*, *Dialogue with a Terrestrial*, *Fiction Writing and Artistic Perception* (a collection of theoretical articles) and *Invisible Companion*. Her works have been translated and published in many languages, and of them *Northern Lights*, *The Right to Love*, and *Invisible Companions* have appeared in German, French, Japanese, Russian, English, and Korean editions, as well as attracting attention from foreign sinologists. Why have her works been so well received internationally? The reason why the acclaim she receives overseas for her works is often greater than that accorded her in China is, I believe, that her writing is intimately involved with high-minded and major humanitarian themes.

Translated by Bruce Doar

Bitter Dreams

Zhang Kangkang

IT was May when the early lilacs, with their petals just falling off, and the lushness of the river banks had both begun to tempt more and more townsfolk to brave a fierce sun and head for Sun Island.

The attractions included a tall pavilion by the water and the man-made Sun Hill. At the top of the hill a grotto had been hewn out of the rocks and at the foot of the hill stood figures of deer, geese, and cranes. These were all creatures of the forest and grassland. In the past they had been a common sight on the farms in the area so there was nothing particularly extraordinary about them. As for the pavilion, there was nothing rare about it either; it merely imitated style of those in Hangzhou and Suzhou. No, he had most certainly not come to the island in search of these novelties, nor to savor the holiday atmosphere. Although he had had to get up early, there had been no need to set the alarm. Night and day were one and the same as far as he was concerned. In utter despair he would watch the dawn break, but as soon as it had got light, a black curtain would draw itself across his eyes, dark smudges appear under his eyes and his whole body be overcome by fatigue. Insomnia. It had been plaguing him for at least a month now.

What with getting on and off buses and boats he had felt giddy, dazed. Nor did it help that he was one of the unfortunates doing the fetching and carrying, covered in sweat, and having instructions yelled at them the whole time by those in charge. At quarter past nine he had finally got his share of the picnic: peanuts, sausage, four preserved eggs, a tin of sardines and two bottles of Sun Island beer, all packed into a large buff envelope. When everything had been handed out it was found that too much sausage had been brought along, so the organizers and oddjobmen naturally had a little more than everyone else. Wasn't the once-a-year trip to the island made simply for the sake of the packed lunch? If you didn't come in person do you think there would be anyone to take it back for you?

He had not wanted to come, not with these herds of people about. Some had dragged along the whole family. His one comfort was the free picnic, which he now clasped tightly to himself.

Then his eyelids came to feel heavy and uncomfortable, as they did when the dry, dusty spring winds blew on them and made him blink and rub until blisters appeared. His legs too felt weighed down, and as he walked this gave him the appearance of a small boat that had sprung a leak and was now sinking, bobbing occasionally as it did so.

He wished for nothing better than to find a spot among the trees to have a nap. The sun was warm, the wood tranquil, the grass invitingly soft. If he was lucky he might be able to snatch a few minutes of sleep.

Yes, why not have a go? At any rate, having only just received his share of the bounty he could not very well return home immediately. However, he could not find one vacant tree or bush anywhere. There were people everywhere, playing cards, having a game of chess, plucking at stringed instruments or learning to dance.

The swirling dust kicked up by the dancers' high-heeled shoes was settling itself evenly over every one of the copious feasts set out under the trees, stretching into the very heart of the wood. Under every tree was the scene for a holiday paradise. If one were to have looked down at it from an aeroplane, it would probably have resembled a gypsy camp, with everything in complete disarray. In his present state it was a sight guaranteed to annoy.

His eyelids began to droop again. His one thought was of finding a tree under which he could spread out his coat. It was a moment of critical importance, for if he let slip this feeling of drowsiness, no matter whether it has a carpet, sofa, or bed to his hand, that would be it.

He walked on quickly. He passed one clump of trees and then another, but there were always people. Everywhere there were people. He spotted a patch of grass, but poking out from it was a disheveled head of hair and a palette, whilst from inside likely-looking bushes came the sound of passionate kissing. He was depressed in the extreme, suspecting that the island had been occupied by creatures from another planet. The only spot that was free was at the side of the main road, yet how could he lie there and sleep, sprawled out in front of all the visitors? How could he let his colleagues know that he could not sleep? Even if he was tired to death he could not.

Just at that moment he happened to glance sideways and all at once his eyes took in the sight of a white house set amongst a grove of emerald green poplars. On all four sides of this white house was a broad porch, perhaps more accurately a veranda. All was quiet. Now wouldn't it be wonderful if he could find a spot behind there to lie down for a while? First, however he picked up a stone and threw it across, to see if there were any dogs.

This house was extraordinarily white. Its pointed, Russian-style roof gave it the appearance of a patch of snow-covered ground, with a layer of silvery powder sprinkled on top. In the bright sunlight the whole effect was dazzling to the eye. The walls seemed to be built of bricks of frozen snow, smoothed over with a layer of translucent glaze. The supports of the veranda were like so many silvery birch trees, rooted in the white marble floor.

Nailed on the wall was a white board with the following legend in blue:

Dr Tong Dazhuang.

A unique course of treatment without drugs for disorders of the nervous system, e.g., insomnia, palpitations, depression, headaches.

He read it once more, his eyes coming back over and over again to the words "without drugs."

He was feeling light-headed with happiness and had to gulp back his excitement. Thank God! His lips formed the words, yet there was no sound.

...Naturally he should give it a try. A clinic that offered a drug-free course of treatment for neurasthenia, that did not use librium or any other relaxant in order to induce sleep. But what did it use? Breathing exercises, or some newly-discovered gadget? Anyway, it did not use drugs. This must be one of the world's greatest, wisest psychiatrists! How many chemists had he been to in the past month or more to have prescriptions made up? They had been counted out pill by pill, tablet by tablet so that you'd have thought the chemist was afraid he might commit suicide, given half the chance. Twice in three days he had been to the hospital so his colleagues must have begun to suspect something. If by chance they found that he had been to fetch sleeping tablets, heaven knows what might be said or done behind his back!

At once his tiredness left him and it was with eager anticipation that he climbed the first step.

...What was more with that sort of drug, once you had become addicted to it, if you didn't keep taking it, it would be even more difficult to sleep. He couldn't go without taking it for even a day. If he tried to cut down, he still couldn't sleep, but if he took too much, my God! The next day it would be almost impossible to get up and go to work. He would feel addleheaded, giddy, barely able to balance properly on his bicycle. Take last night for example; all he had been able to do grin and bear it. But it couldn't go on for ever. Such a clinic was a real godsend.

It was strange that today, if there was a demand for a thing, then something would immediately spring up to supply that demand. It just depended on your luck, whether you found it or not. He had been about to climb the fourth step, but suddenly shrank back. Tong Da Zhuang? Had he ever heard of this person? No. It had to be a private clinic. It could be run by quacks for all he knew. At fairs he never bought bean starch jelly from those privately run stalls. How could one be sure that it hadn't been made with water that someone had, say, used to wash their feet in! No, there was no such thing as an honest tradesman.

His foot remained poised a moment. Through the white-screened window he could make out the figures of people, noiselessly walking to and fro.

Resolutely he strode onto the last step, crossed the porch and opened the screen door a crack. To his utter surprise he found the room full of people, all sitting around the sides.

A slight sound attracted his attention and suddenly there was a young woman wearing a pointed green gauze turban. She stretched out her hand towards him smiling radiantly and said: "Please take your place in the queue, sir." He heaved a sigh of relief. It was all right after all, if so many people were waiting and you had to queue up. "Can't you sleep either?" He whispered to a young man in the queue in front of him.

"Only so many people can be seen to in one day, so you'll have to wait a while, but you can also make an appointment." The young man replied without looking round.

That was a pointless answer, so forget it. He wasn't one to argue with psychiatric cases. Yet it seemed that insomniacs were not that few in number either. The whole town had probably come down with the complaint, it was just that no one said anything. Look at himself for example, none of his colleagues knew that he was suffering from loss of sleep, did they?

He suddenly felt enormously relieved. He had come to the conclusion that the whole town was suffering from insomnia, otherwise how could business be so brisk? Looking about he saw that the room was spacious, large enough to accommodate thirty or forty people. Upholstered benches were ranged around the sides, with small tables for armrests. A few people were leaning over them, writing something. The walls were a buttermilk color, with a few oil landscapes hanging here and there. On one wall, not far off the ground hung two glass-fronted metal cases. Inside there was:

Business Permit

....

....

Sun Island Chamber of Industry and Commerce, 1984

Master's Degree Diploma

....

....

Center for Graduate Studies, Dongfang Medical Institute, 1982

He carefully read the documents through twice and once again felt a twinge of doubt: Since this doctor was a graduate of a famous college, what was he doing here in the back of beyond, running this show? Why wasn't he in the capital, or at least the provincial capital? He couldn't have made a mistake, could he? Surely it was all above board? Surely it wasn't just a money-grabbing enterprise? Surely....

The more he thought about it, the more his doubts grew, and the more he felt that he had been deceived. He felt like taking himself off at once, but at that very moment a voice said "Please sit down ..."

It was his turn.

That girl, she was handing him a piece of paper and a pen. She smiled as she did so and said in a smooth voice:

"Could you first pay a registration fee of two *yuan*, please?" He started. So he hadn't guessed wrongly. Money! Did he have any money? No. There was none in his pocket, nor at home, and even if he did have some at home, he wasn't going to carry it around on his person. He was poor, but he still had his pride. Any way, nobody was that well-off. If you don't have any money on you then you can't spend it on goodness-knows-what. He had a family to keep after all. Hastily fumbling in his pockets he said reddening, "I've ...I've forgotten to bring any money with me." He got up and was about to leave. "I won't see the doctor today," he mumbled.

"Just a moment," the little nurse hurried after him. Just then, light footsteps sounded on the small, wooden spiral staircase. He saw a young woman, slim and fashionably dressed, accompanying a portly old gentleman in a grey mackintosh down the stairs. The latter was leaning on a red walking stick and in his wake came a man with a black briefcase tucked under his arm.

The woman stopped at the top of the stairs, shook hands with the old man and said with a smile: "I still think you should retire, take up fishing, travel ..."

"Well, I'll think about it," the old man gave a long sigh, "Thank you." Suddenly there were people clamoring all around him. Since there weren't any buses on Sun Island, surely they were not going to carry him away?

As he gazed at the woman's trim figure he hesitated. But if VIPs were coming here ...if they believed in it all ...

The nurse pressed the pen and paper into his hands and said softly:

"It doesn't matter if you haven't brought any money. Something else of value would do."

With a look at her bewitching smile he decided to give it a try, regardless of the consequences. After all, it was only two *yuan*; worth it if he could gain some relief. He did a careful mental calculation, then took out the tin of sardines. Even if he was a tin short when people came to dinner, he could always do a quick stir-fry of something else and no one would be the wiser. As he was about to start writing he realized the paper was actually a form, headed "Medical Record." There were so many sub-headings you would have thought they were conducting some sort of poll or doing a census. A shaft of hope ran through him as he began to fill in the questions carefully.

Name: Ding Xiaoshen
Previous Names: None
Age: 35
Schooling: Middle school graduate
Sex: Male
Occupation of Parents: Workers
Brief Curriculum Vitae: Graduated 1966 from Harbin No. 11 Middle School; 1968, went to work on a state farm; 1978, returned to Harbin
Work Unit: General Affairs Section, Northeastern College of Art
Job Description: None (previously held post of vice-head of No. 9 unit, Red Star Farm)
Awards and Achievements: 1971, commended for activism in the study of the works of Chairman Mao; 1973, commended as a Model Student
Party or Youth League Status: No longer a Youth League member; 1973, joined....
Marital Status: ....
Family Members: ....
Blood Type: ....
Medical History: ....

There were still other questions to be answered yet he felt an urge to describe in detail his experiences of the 1970's. He realized suddenly he no longer felt in the least bit tired. So this was what was called a medical record; strange, to say the least.

Climbing to the top of the spiral staircase he found

a spacious, well-lit room with French windows on all four sides. The likeness to a greenhouse was enhanced by the pale green net curtains, decorated with pink lotuses set amongst a cluster of huge leaves. These lotus flowers had no stems, but seemed to be floating idly on the surface of the water. Outside the window rows of birches and poplars blocked his view, yet he could still hear the birdsong from amongst the foliage. In each corner of the room were vases of white lilacs and some other flower whose name escaped him. There was no desk as one would have expected of a doctor's surgery, no stethoscope, no sphygmomanometer, not even a single medicine bottle. The only furniture was two weirdly shaped sofas placed in the center of the dark green floor. The whole scene was accompanied by exquisite music floating up from somewhere below and reverberating gently a few inches above the ground.

It didn't seem as if he had come to see a doctor at all, rather that he had walked into the home of some friend. If only he could stay here for just a while, for in such a tranquil atmosphere he was bound to be lulled into sleep. Just then, she entered with a light step and sat down opposite him. Instead of a white overcoat she was wearing a pale yellow sweater. Her jet black hair was coiled up in a style he had never seen before, yet was infinitely more stylish and elegant than that of the dancing teachers at the college. It was difficult to tell her age: the creases at the corners of her eyes made her look at least forty, but then she would smile and all of a sudden she seemed twenty.

"Are you the doctor?" he asked.

"Yes."

"Tong Dazhuang that is?"

"Of course."

He closed his eyes as a surge of disappointment swept through him. Tong Dazhuang was a woman, this hospital was being run by just two people, and he had taken her to be merely the nurse in charge upstairs.

Two *yuan* gone down the drain, and there was nothing at all he could do about it.

The doctor spoke: "Thank you for coming to my clinic. Before we start treatment I have just one small request to make of you." He had a sinking feeling in the pit of his stomach. More money?

"As my only condition, I require my patients to tell me as accurately as possible of the earliest occurence, origin and usual symptoms of their disturbance. In other words, I need to have the complete faith and cooperation of my patients in order to gain results." Her voice was compelling, coming across clear and evenly as she spoke.

So it was like this all the time. Well that was all right, just as long as no more money was required. There was nothing difficult about just talking after all.

"I require my patients to be totally frank about their illness. Otherwise my diagnosis may be wrong," she added emphatically, looking at his file.

At the impact of these words his brain suddenly went numb. He felt as if it was swelling up like a balloon but the very next moment it had shriveled up again like a dried orange. How could he be "totally frank" when chronic insomnia had made him forgetful. Thinking back would be as painful as trying to get at a fish bone lodged in one's throat, or as unpleasant as searching for a watch in the murky waters of a sewer. It seemed as if it was going to be more difficult than he had thought.

"I think you've got something on your mind. It'll help if you can talk about it." Her smiling gaze seemed to brush across his face.

Feeling uncomfortable he shifted once or twice in the armchair. "Something on your mind," of course he had something on his mind. In fact, it wasn't just something, it was everything. A chicken-coop for a house, being put upon all the time at work. A son in feeble health, a harridan for a wife ...

He gave a deep sigh, buried his head in his hands and exclaimed: "Yes, yes, I have something on my mind. I've tried for the Open University three years in a row, but I failed each time, and got nowhere near the pass-mark. Now people look down on me for having no education ..."

She nodded kindly. It seemed as if she knew exactly what he was talking about.

"But is it my fault?" he said on a fierce note. "Where was I supposed to get books from during those ten years? Night school was enough to cope with, let alone the Open University. Back at work in the city during the day I would always be dead tired and then I'd come home and have to make dinner and see to the children ... Is it any wonder that I couldn't study?"

He couldn't tell whether she was smiling or not when she said: "Well, in that case, don't bother with university. A degree isn't everything. Why get worked up about it? Somewhere it says that seventy percent of the school-leavers of '64-'66 haven't been to university, so you're not alone."

He gave a nod, rubbing his hands nervously and still frowning. It wasn't a case of getting worked up about it or not, he already was worked up. He waited for her diagnosis. Her face was grave as she closed the file. A pair of black eyes gazed at him, their expression deep, unfathomable. "I thought I made it clear at the beginning that I wish my patients to be totally frank with me," adding quickly: "But there you are, as vague as anything, hemming and hawing with the result that we aren't getting anywhere. Please understand that it is only when a person's wishes and desires become subject to intolerable constraints that nervous disorders arise. It is only when they are released from those constraints that the suffering can be alleviated or even done away with altogether." Hearing this Ding felt the hairs on the back of his head prickle and a cold shiver ran through him. She seemed to be able to look into his very soul and see the anguish hidden there. How, he did not know. But now that he was here, he could not seem to avoid her eyes.

That damned globe! At the time it had reminded me of a blue skull. That chap was so self-important when he brought it round as a goodbye present, just the way I had behaved many years back when confiscating that old book of his. But what did he himself have to be proud about? Five, ten years ago I would have compared more than favorably with that chap. I knew what hard work was. Could he manage to walk carrying two sacks of beans piled up on his shoulder? When we were out in the fields turning up the soil bit by bit with a spade, he did nothing but chase wolves around. Had he ever been honored as a model for young intellectuals? What he had been best at was stealing out of sight and reading books behind a haystack.... And now he had the nerve to come dressed in a suit and red tie. How come?

Because his father was a professor, that's why.

The way he moved the globe around and around,

pointing things out, as if he were giving a lecture. "That's where I'm going, California University in the United States, to read for a doctorate. I passed all the exams and now I've come to say goodbye and give you this globe as a leaving present to remember me by." And that was how it was. He was off to become a doctor, a professor, with the whole world on a plate.

And what about myself? Forty-three *yuan* a month as a man Friday with no education, diploma, or qualifications, and seemingly no way of getting them either. It wasn't fair. How could it be that at one moment we were equals and the next so far apart, with myself at the disadvantage? At night when all the lights had been switched off, that wretched globe mesmerized me with its sinister blue glow. In the early morning light it looked just like a skull swinging backwards and forwards above my bed. It symbolized the hopelessness of my own existence....

I smashed it in the end but it didn't help me sleep any better. All I could think of was California and the eyeless sockets of the skull....

He saw it all clearly now: his illness was all due to that bloke, the one who could not wait to be off. But since then ...

They were interrupted by the little nurse bringing up an afternoon cup of tea.

The doctor waited patiently for him to continue. She seemed to be thinking about something, yet all the time her face, with its many tiny wrinkles on the forehead, was an inscrutable mask.

"During the course of my many years of research into nervous disorders I have come to the conclusion

300

that the best way to effect a cure is to let my patients tell me of their innermost suffering, no matter from what frustrated desire that suffering springs." Her voice was cool as she spoke.

He shifted once more and glanced outside. No, there was no one else, only trees. This floor must surely have been built for this very purpose, the divulging of secrets. That unwavering, all-seeing gaze of hers...He wondered if she would fuss about everything that she saw.

At last he felt safe enough to begin.

He wasn't too sure what he was saying, it just came out, the truth, that which she had wanted him to tell in the first place and which he could not now withhold, seeing the trust in her eyes. For the first time he discovered what it felt like to let some one else help you dislodge that fish-bone stuck in your throat. For after the pain and nausea would come an indescribable sense of relief, like being born anew. His memory was working again, just like the watch after it had been fished out of the water. He could talk for ever if he wished, though not a coherent talker, it wouldn't cost anything. Suppose there was someone who would have listened to him, as she did now, beside his pillow ...his wife, that woman had a grasping hand but not a sympathetic ear. As for those who had returned from the countryside with him, if only they had shown something like what was in this pair of eyes and had not laughed behind his back. They had nothing to be proud about themselves.

"I can tell you plenty about ...about suffering," it was an effort to speak. "I'm a Party member, but I don't particularly think like one. I'd still like to go abroad, buy my family a color television, fridge. But how can I, with no influence or connections, no, none at all? Night after night I lie awake, thinking about it. Sometimes I even have weird dreams where the globe is crawling with ants...." His voice trailed off and he took a deep breath. "That's all I have to say at the moment." This catharsis had left him numb, his forehead burned, his hands felt clammy on the armrest.

He looked·up at the vaulted ceiling and likened it to a bay with brightly colored starfish floating on top of the light blue water. The world seemed to be turned upside down as he looked into the water and saw the doctor smiling up at him. It was a sympathetic, all-knowing smile. She had probably known all along that that globe had been the cause of all his anxieties.

She took out some knitting, a child's sweater. The wool was pale green, swaying to and fro as she worked, so that in the green tinted light, one moment it would be visible, the next not. "What does that account for?" she began to speak.

As far as going abroad to study, having overseas connections, having a professor for a father are concerned, of course you can't compare with him. But once he comes back, even with a doctorate, won't he be just the same as everyone else? Haven't you seen what sort of flats university professors usually live in, what sort of benefits they get, if indeed any at all?

He went abroad and you didn't because you didn't have connections. But that's not your fault. You would be the very last person to blame. So you didn't have much of an education and spent ten years instead in the countryside, working in support of a glorious revolutionary cause. But because you now have nothing to show for it, you should be blaming the times, and the people in charge who kept back anyone who was any good.

Why should you be angry that he's gone abroad? Is the capitalist West really so wonderful? It's a place only for the rich. If you were to make some money for yourself it would probably only get stolen anyway. An honest person like you probably wouldn't last five minutes there. But there's really no need to take it to heart, I wouldn't go even given the chance. Here, even if there's not much money, at least life is more easy-going. Don't you think so?

He watched the wool writhing in loops across the floor and then sliding upwards to be woven into rows before a pattern emerged.

Talking to her was like talking to his mother, it was all so relaxed and intimate. Each word seemed to caress his throbbing temples, gently massaging his taut nerves and giving them play once more. An energy which hitherto had met only with obstruction began to flow through his veins. He had never felt so relaxed.

It struck him suddenly that the pink flowers on the curtain were not lotuses after all, but water lilies. When he had been on business once in the south he had called them lotuses then too and people had laughed. To watch them now floating on the water gave him a feeling of utter contentment, tinged with not a little envy.

A ribbon of violet light streamed through the pale green curtains and danced across the woman's lap like a butterfly. He realized it was getting dark.

Murmuring something to herself, she began to gather up her things, "I have a suggestion to make to you. It's also my professional opinion," she said crisply.

Her expression was unfathomable as she told him to explore new areas in his work and gain success that way. "Look," she said, "you've been ten years in the Party, and you held an important post on that farm. If you acquit yourself well in what you are now doing, you'll be in the running for sure for head of the General Affairs Section. Aren't they always talking about reform of the system? At the moment they're grooming the next generation of leaders, promoting young cadres as the "third echelon." You're bound to be one of them. People with ability will always make it and those who haven't won't. Everybody has his or her own particular talents and own path to follow. In a few years time you'll become a bureau head, but if you came back with a doctorate you'd still be a subordinate!"

His eyes shone as it suddenly all dawned on him. If he had known it was that easy, he would have said to hell with the globe and all it represented long ago. This method of treatment was a thousand times better than taking any medicine. As for the doctor, she was really something too. No doubt she could earn a lot of money from this sort of thing, for it was a business which yielded a thousand-fold profit for a minimal investment. "Well, time to leave now. I'll be sure to come back to thank you if I'm completely done with that insomnia." He stepped out of the white house into the twilight of Sun Island.

Now it was August. After a lot of rain the island was more lush and green than ever, tempting even greater numbers of visitors from the town.

But to him the sun looked green too. The sky was black, the island grey. He had to find that white house as quickly as possible. As he hurried along, he happened to glance into a pond and saw a face with the wrinkles of age and hair that was already turning grey.

As was to be expected the little nurse didn't recognize him, for her very first words were to tell him to fill in the form. This time the queue stretched right out of the building onto the steps, men, women, old and young were all there. Obviously more and more people were finding it difficult to sleep; no wonder the clinic was thriving. No doubt she was making a name for herself in the process too.

Outside you couldn't help but notice the large mirrors with red writing hanging against the wall on which people had testified to various miraculous cures. His eyes widened as he read them and at that moment she came down the stairs to see someone out. She saw him and must have remembered who he was, perhaps because his case had been of particular interest to her, for she turned to the nurse and said: "This isn't his first time so he needn't queue, just register!"

Quickly he drew out two *yuan* and twenty-seven *fen* and handed it over saying: "Last time that tin of sardines was only worth one *yuan* seventy-three, so I still owe you something, it's been on my mind all the time. Here's two *yuan* twenty-seven *fen*." The nurse's lips twitched, with amusement or disdain, he could not tell: "You still owe seventy-three *fen*!" "What!" "It's gone up. The registration fee is now three *yuan*." Very well, if it had to be three *yuan* there was nothing he could do about it. He had had a relapse and there was nowhere else to go, so this wasn't the moment to start worrying about money. As he tiptoed his way upstairs he realized the doctor had let him jump the queue.

She took out his file from the cabinet and began to leaf through it, her face kindly as she asked: "Well then, about what I suggested last time, didn't it work?"

He shook his head vigorously until the doctor seemed to be swaying about: "On the contrary, it worked very well." The words came quickly. "After I left you I went home and fell asleep straight away, I didn't wake up until the next afternoon. For two months afterwards as soon as it got dark I would be all too ready to go to bed, I would sleep like a log and I never had any dreams. The wife must have thought I had caught sleeping sickness instead!" She smiled as he spoke, then looked up and scrutinized him, her expression as hard to gauge as ever. "It's appeared again, hasn't it?" she asked. He nodded, but couldn't bring himself to speak.

"Because of the Head of General Affairs?" The tone of her voice told him she knew she was right.

"Yes!' What a relief not to have to pretend with her, there was no point of pretending since she was a doctor and such a good one. Anyway, it wouldn't have done any good.

"He didn't want to step down, not at all. Is that it?" She enquired softly. "No ...not that," he measured his words carefully. "If that had been the case, things would have been much easier. He retired all right and what did they go and do but replace him with someone nine months younger than I am, who went to school five years later than I did and was in the countryside for eight years less. He was never a class monitor, let alone a model worker. After two years of country life he sneaked off to join the army and went back to the city to drive a truck. A driver, bah! There's nothing special about that. And they had to go and choose him. Now is that fair, I ask you? Wasn't it bound to bring on another attack? Is it any wonder I can't sleep?"

Although she smiled the doctor did not reply. Instead she went up to the window to arrange the flowers. He could see chrysanthemums, roses, tulips. Then she put on another record. The music was soft, yet had quite a beat to it, so that he could feel the floor vibrating.

She poured him a cup of tea. Glancing at her face he longed to know what was going on in her mind.

"Didn't you do as I suggested after you got back?" she asked. Her question made him start up and exclaim:

"Of course I did, how couldn't I? These past few months I've been on the go all the time, nobody could say otherwise. Everyone at the college remarked on it. " 'You're overdoing it, Ding.' they would all say. As far as attitude to work went, it should have been me to get the job...." He couldn't carry on for he was too upset. He could feel himself becoming more and more tense, his nerves contracting into a tight little knot which he would never be able to undo.

Who was it, do you think, who made sure the teachers in the school all got their gas cylinders? It's all very well for those at the top to draw up policies on how to do this and that, but do you think the fifty-*jin* sack of rice for each staff member can deliver itself? And what about fruit and vegetables for the summer? They all have to be fresh. Melons, large yet cheap. Do you think it's easy to find all this?

A band of right little ladies and gentlemen, that's what they are. Who do you think it was who saw to their breaktime snacks so that they didn't have to leave the classroom? As for the state of their dormitories, if it hadn't been for me, going on at them until they eventually did give the place a sweep, they would never have got a commendation the way they did. Finally it came to the point of a glass window in the women's dormitory. They weren't allowed to cover it up with paper. It was only to make things easier to manage, but what did they go and do but complain that the "cell window" made the place into a prison, a PRISON, I ask you! Wouldn't you have been angry too? So I just ignored them and tore the paper off, but it was back up the next day. I tell you it's almost impossible to cope with such a bunch of little prima donnas!

Then there was that driver, able to travel all over the place delivering goods, giving rides, doing a little business here and there. You name it, he did it. Somehow or other he had made a pile of money and on the quiet had bought the school a video recorder, saying that that was what the staff needed. After that he couldn't put a foot wrong. The whole school gave him the thumbs up saying how clever he was, what brains he had, how good at his job he was, how he was heading for the top, etc. Upstairs, the Cultural Bureau, buried under a mound of red tape as it is, without so much as looking at the actual circumstances, went and made him Head of General Affairs. It must have been because of his father having had a word in the right ear, it must have been. If he had had some qualifications, fair enough, but he didn't have any; he studied for a year less than I did. But his old man's head of the Education Bureau, so is it any wonder he's always one up on the others? You wouldn't be able to stomach such an insult either, would you? ...

A muscle at the corner of her mouth twitched. An eyebrow was raised ever so slightly as she listened in silence. That hovering smile was back, as elusive as ever. He felt uneasy.

"Any dreams?" she asked.

"Yes. But oddly enough it's always the same one,

millions of ants crawling all over me, biting me, yet it doesn't hurt ..."

At this she got up and began to stroll backwards and forwards across the center of the room. She was wearing a thin irregular print dress, its long, full skirt giving it a trumpet-shaped appearance.

"As there are so many patients today I'll be brief," she said, and her eyes, framed in that beautiful face were cold. Then her expression changed and became very keen, giving her an older and more worldly air.

That driver's father is a bureau head, but yours is only a retired boiler factory worker. They may not be in the same league, but at least you're not to blame. Yesterday a woman came to see me, she couldn't sleep either. As her father is a big-wig in the provincial government, her unit wanted to promote her to department head, but she was so nervous she couldn't sleep. She said to me: "How can I be the department boss? I've asked them to drop the idea, but they won't listen." Now look at you, the average man in the street, you could work yourself to death and not have anyone notice. That video recorder, where did he buy it? He must have still more connections. To be honest about it, what's so wonderful about being made a section chief? Even if you did eventually become one, you would still be under pressure from all sides. It wouldn't be easy. If you're no good you get kicked downstairs, and if you are any good, the money still isn't worth it, nothing to compare with what you can earn on a snack stall at the night markets. That's true, isn't it? So stop worrying about it so much. It's not doing you any good.

He could feel a cool breeze blowing ever so gently

on his forehead. He could see it making the hem of her skirt ripple slightly too. At her words the turbidity that had been clogging his brain had begun to clear, seeping out slowly through every pore on his scalp until he was left feeling perfectly relaxed. No doubt the lines of care criss-crossing his face had been smoothed away too.

She picked up a pen and started to write something on his file. When she had finished she gave it to him to have a look, four words which he seemed to have seen before, but about whose exact meaning he felt embarrassed to ask. He hesitated for a moment then asked in a timid voice. "Would it be at all possible to give me something more specific, like last time? It doesn't matter if it would cost more. I could let you have the money in a few days' time." She sat back down on the sofa, thought for a moment, then did as he asked. This time he understood everthing, including the meaning of those four words, so that for those few minutes he felt inexpressibly happy. This was luck indeed!

"There are those who have gone abroad or obtained high positions, but there are others too who have thought of making a name for themselves. Doesn't fame outstrip everything else? You would be in the newspapers, on the television for all the world to see. Everyone would admire you, and respect you too. An office boss is nothing, but as soon as you become famous the whole country ...

"Look at those small businessmen who have made it, without a degree or people in high places or overseas relatives to help them. You can do the same too. Make people respect you, give them something to be jealous of. If anybody can do it, why not me, Ding Xiaoshen? So what if you're the head of such-and-such? As soon as my name has come out in print ..." The tension had left him by now, all resentment washed completely away. He gave a long, long yawn.

He would have liked to ask the doctor to be even more specific, but she seemed tired and got up and made to see him out. He was more than a little afraid to ask anyway, in case it meant an increase in the fee. He could see that as far as her income went, she was not in the least bit vague. He would just have to leave it at that. So with profuse thanks he went downstairs.

Other patients seemed very impatient and looked at him askance as he went past. All he could think however was how strange, almost ridiculous it was, that they couldn't sleep.

Outside it was just midday. The air had a chill to it and a breeze was rustling through the trees.

Now it was October. The autumn winds had come and the grass turned golden. As leaves fell to form rustling carpets on the forest floors, the forest themselves took on a wide, empty feeling. As day by day the sun lost its heat, visitors began to seep back into the city. By now the fallen leaves were a riot of color, crackling almost painfully under his quick stride. The withered grass, wearing a coat of early morning frost, bore the marks of his footprints as he passed.

One leg felt too short, the other too long; his head was like a stone, yet at the same time as light as a feather. He could have exploded or just as easily fizzled away. As for the brittle nerve fibers supporting the back of his neck, they could have snapped at the slightest provocation. If he didn't see Dr. Tong again he would die. Each attack was worse, more unbearable than the last.

Yet there was the white house, as pristine as ever, with its unhurried, welcoming air. From a distance it looked like a white mushroom.

Strangely, the number of people waiting had in no way been affected by the desolation of the island. Instead they crammed the waiting room and were queuing right to the bottom of the steps, thus able to enjoy the sunshine. Obviously, an ever increasing number of people suffered from insomnia.

"I'm afraid you'll have to wait a while. All those queuing have appointments and some are making a repeat visit. Please sit down over there." The little nurse had greeted him warmly, yet almost straight away stretched out her hand and asked for four *yuan* registration fee. It had gone up again! It was a good thing he had come well prepared. There had been an unexpected bonus for National Day, twenty *yuan*. It didn't matter too much if he was left with sixteen. So he too sat down to sun himself. Leaning against the pillar with his eyes half closed, it felt rather comfortable.

Those who were not here for the first time were whispering conspiratorially among themselves. One old woman was saying. "Don't you think it's odd? There's this doctor, and I tell her I can't get a wink of sleep. She keeps telling me not to worry, that it'll soon be better. Soon? It's been more than half a year and it's worse than ever?" His eyes shot open as he asked, "Why can't you sleep?"

"Because of my son," came the reply. "He gave up a steady, secure job to go and set one of those 'briefcase' enterprises![1] What sort of work is that for an honest man? There's no money in it, that's for sure. And what happens if he loses this job too? He's like a man possessed. I've been so worried, but he gets a decent rest every night...."

Damn, there it was again, somebody else who had

joined the rush to set up his own small business. It seemed as if this craze was set to engulf the whole island. A man broke in furiously, "I agree with you, this doctor's up to no good. My wife came to see her a few days ago and you just have a guess at what she told her? It's more than I can bring myself to say but I'll tell you one thing, she carried on so that my wife now wants a divorce." His voice was rough yet clear and as he spoke he had his face turned up towards the first floor window, as if he wanted the doctor to hear. 'Your wife's got someone else," the elderly woman chipped in. "Exactly. She hasn't been able to sleep for a long time and she's always carrying on because she suspects that I'm being unfaithful. She says we're living in a permissive society, where a wife can't be sure of her own position any more so what does the doctor go and do but tell her to find herself a few boyfriends, so that she won't be driven to suicide. Saying men and women are equal is all very well, but twice in three days she's gone out in the evenings, bold as you like and then come home and slept like a log. Now it's ME who can't sleep, worrying about the state of my own household!"

An authoritative, resonant male voice said:

"In my opinion, this sort of private clinic is a menace to society. Who gave her permission to open it, that's what I'd like to know? She's up to no good for sure." At this Ding couldn't help starting up and was about to refute the man's words strongly. Had he himself not derived a lot of comfort and hope from the treatment here? After every session he had been able to sleep again, and if he did have relapses, it still was not the doctor's fault. Look at the pace of life today, for example. After all she was not some sort of fortune-teller. That man should just go and have a look at that mirror

313

presented by one of her satisfied patients.... Ding suddenly stopped in his tracks. The man was very fat, wearing a serge Zhongshan-suit and leaning on a red walking stick. He recognized him as the one from the first time, the one whom the doctor had told to retire and take up fishing instead. Ding bit back what he had been about to say. The old man was still talking:

"I took her advice and retired, and what do you think the result is? All cadres, from grade thirteen downward, every man jack of them, get a salary rise. I say she's been extremely irresponsible in her actions, as far as both the Party and the people are concerned. What's more, with the salary reform, they're going to get even more. And where am I going to get any compensation for it? It's a fact that since I followed her advice I've been worse, not better. Sooner or later I'm going to have her license taken away," he added in a loud voice, hammering the stick on the floor, "just you wait and see."

Ding had turned deathly pale. What if the man carried out his threat and had the clinic closed down, what would he do? Somebody came out of the waiting room to have a look. Then he saw the doctor's head appear at the upstairs window, underneath a green canopy of leaves. He could feel the scorn in her gaze as it swept over the assembled people. "What do any of you know about it?" Her voice was low yet vehement and in a flash she had turned on her heel and gone, still with that inexplicable smile on her face, kind yet at the same time with a trace of sarcasm in it. It wasn't her but just the flowers on the curtain. Just as he had plucked up enough courage to try to reason with the old man by way of his own experience, another man dressed in jeans and a checked shirt came up to them.

"Ladies and gentlemen," he said, "I can't help but

disagree with you all." He was standing in the center of a ring of people, waving his arm, looking for all the world as if he was about to make a speech. "You are all wrong," he continued. "Because I myself can testify to the success of Dr. Tong's therapy. When I came here for the first time three months ago, I was on the verge of a nervous breakdown. I couldn't sleep, and I couldn't get anything done in the daytime. But after just one session, I was completely cured in a matter of days. One week later I was better physically and mentally than I had ever been. I've been putting on weight ..." People began to exchange whispers as he continued: "Since then I've never looked back. In fact, I can't sleep enough! You all want to sleep but can't, but my problem is that I simply haven't time to sleep!" By now there was uproar, the old woman shouted. "You're mad! She's made you worse, not better."

"That's ridiculous," he retorted, striding around in a circle before explaining himself. It turned out that he was a former student of the Central Drama Academy who had been assigned on graduation to a theater company as a librettist. However, it didn't matter how hard he tried, he couldn't for the life of him produce even one word. While his bosses waited, he suffered one sleepless night after another, all to no avail. He wanted a transfer, but without any works to his name nobody would have him.

The fervor in his voice was evident as he explained that the doctor thought he simply was not cut out for writing librettos, and that his insomnia had been brought on by the stress. So she suggested he take up writing television plays instead, and that was an instant success. He even started to win prizes. Television stations from all over the country came to order scripts;

315

there was a scramble too, as each strove to have him transferred to their unit, so he had the pick of the lot. Now he had more than enough to do, and though he was often tired, he felt happy and relaxed.

"Since it seems you can't sleep enough now, what are you doing here?" the middle-aged man interrupted him.

"I've come with a friend," came the reply, and, realizing that he had let slip something vital, added, "I recommended that he come and try this course of treatment. Since he's got nothing to do all day he hasn't been able to sleep properly for thirty years." Fortunately at that moment the nurse called a number and it was the old man's turn. He was in a furious mood when he went up and it had not altered by the time he came down. It was unlikely he had come for a consultation, but rather to demand his money back. When the old woman and middle-aged man had finished seeing the doctor, however, they seemed more contented than before, even the tiniest bit happy. What he was at a loss to understand now was why on earth, if they were all so dissatisfied with the treatment here, did they still want to come and see her? By now there was only him left.

Upstairs the room was warm, flooded with sunlight. A thin rug covered the floor and in one corner stood a potted vine, its leaves a fiery red, its fruit a rich, gleaming purple. As she handed him some he noticed the powdery bloom frosting its surface. It was cold and so was she, to the point of indifference, even apathy. He could hear it in her voice as she asked if it was the same trouble as before. Indeed it seemed as if she had been expecting him, but this time there was no smile of welcome. He felt he had been done some kind of injury. It was a numbing sensation.

Who would have thought that in the race to get on there would be people who would succeed before he did?

Who would have thought that managers would be allowed to appoint themselves, or that that woman could turn the Academy's costume workshop into a highly profitable fashion company, or that with such a company anyone could make good? Look at the money she was making: a monthly bonus of three hundred dollars, not to mention seasonal, annual, holiday, birthday, and other bonuses. Then there were the factory and academy uniforms, and all that.

And what about the school bathhouse for which she threw in all the money needed with an easy flick of the wrist. Whereas take the time when I tried my hand at fund-raising—I worked even on Sundays, collecting broken bricks from all over the city with nothing more than a handcart; I organized a benefit performance of "Where Three Roads Meet" and "The Jade Bracelet," but on the night they did not even take enough to cover people's overtime or the hire of the props, or the wear and tear of costumes—all of my effort in vain. The whole thing had run at a loss, and as for my hopes of a claim to fame, all I succeeded in doing was making a fool of myself.

As for that female, how had she managed it all? With a wave of a magic wand she had fixed up an old rehearsal room and turned it into a night school of dance, with the full cooperation of the academy's dancing instructors, who naturally had seen something in it for themselves. Not only that, she had also set up a tea salon which put on performances of traditional operas; in fact she had thought of everything.

317

I suspected the woman of some shady dealing, otherwise how could she have made such a pile of money? I reported the matter to the Cultural Bureau and had them send someone to investigate. I also wrote to the newspapers about my suspicions. After a long investigation she had appeared in the papers after all, but to be praised as one of the reforms' young trailblazers!

Who had not been taken with the idea of reform? I had been dreaming of it for years and the increase in salary it would entail, but I had never expected that when it ought to have been my turn, I would end up with nothing. All it had done was to leave me exhausted and thoroughly confused. The day I went to try out the new bathhouse, I almost passed out with indignation. Is it any wonder I haven't been able to sleep? As soon as I closed my eyes all I could see were newspapers, millions and millions filling the streets and not one with my name on the front page....

What sort of society is it where such a small amount can make such a world of difference, where once you fall behind you can never hope to catch up? At this rate the reforms will be just one headache after another, without a moment's peace for anybody, and there am I, unable to sleep night after night....

This time the doctor had a pale yellow shawl draped around her shoulders. Her hair was different too, decorated with a plum-colored curved slide, and setting off her perfect complexion. The eyes contemplating him seemed darker and larger than ever, their depths still unfathomable.

She had listened to him in silence and for a good few minutes after he had finished speaking she still said nothing. Finally she lifted her hand and began to stroke the tassels on her shawl, carefully separating each strand.

"What shall I do with you," she sighed, "You're so ..." Stupid! He could just imagine his wife hurling the word at him. "You're so unlucky," she observed in a logical tone. Then, after a moment's reflection she straightened up slightly and asked. "That girl who set up the fashion company, did she have overseas connections?"

"No, I checked," he replied shaking his head.

"Is her father a professor?" "No."

"A bureau chief?" "No, her parents have been dead for a long time."

"Has she got any qualifications?" "She's studying with the Open University at the moment." "Did she graduate from high school before 1966? "No, when the Cultural Revolution started she was still at elementary school." "Has she been selected by the Party as a model?" "She's not even a Youth League member." "Well, then, she must be very attractive." "You're joking. She has a limp. In fact, there's nothing special about her whatsoever." Suddenly the doctor burst into laughter. It was a loud, shrill laugh which left him totally confused. "I can't see that there is anyone to blame this time," she said matter-of-factly, shaking her head and spreading out her hands to emphasize her words.

Insomniacs are good at forgetting. He was aware of her laughter, and after a long mental struggle he was indeed forced to admit that the girl was in no way to blame. The recognition left him feeling perplexed and in a bad mood. That numbing sensation began to creep over him again; his veins felt as if they were contracting.

Outside a gust of wind, a cold, passionless force of

nature sent leaves swirling, a rustling mass of red and yellow, and would eventually return them to the earth whence they came.

"What shall I do?" he asked pitiably and cautiously. 'You just can't leave the job half done, casting someone aside and not bothering about them anymore. You must have some other suggestion to make, anything that will let me sleep."

The doctor kept her gaze on him as she laughed and said: "After three visits you still don't understand? This is a course of treatment and it's almost finished."

He did not understand. Surely she didn't want more money? As he fingered the dirty, crumpled sixteen one-*yuan* notes in his pocket he suddenly felt that he had been made a fool of.

All of a sudden the doctor stopped laughing and said in a serious tone: "My suggestion is this: after work go and open a snack stall at the night market and sell sweetcorn and preserved vegetables. In winter baked yams and roast potatoes."

"What ...are you saying?" he interrupted her, stumbling over the words. At her words he had had to take a deep breath and stride to the window. His face was livid with rage. "Are you seriously suggesting that I go and become a stallkeeper. I'd rather die first!"

Without the slightest trace of emotion, she continued: "There're millions of ways that you may take to get rich nowadays, but not everyone can do it. Could you have come up with ideas for camping equipment or river cruises? I doubt it. But they're both forms of individual enterprise, and there are many others. Which one are you good for?"

Her icy, scornful stare seemed to envelop him. He gave an involuntary shudder, for the thought that there was worse to come had just streaked across his consciousness. He was now trembling with terror. He wanted to dispute the fact that his sole objective was money. But what was it then, the aim of a conscientious, dependable person like himself, who, moreover, disliked feeling alone? Calling to mind the dissatisfied comments of those other patients, what the old man had said, he felt a sudden uncontrollable hatred for the white house. "You're just out to cheat people, you and this clinic of yours," he screamed hysterically.

With a disdainful shrug the doctor walked slowly away.

"This is going to be a world only for those with talent." He could hear her voice floating up the stairs to him.

In this ancient land of ours, practical ineptitude is no longer going to be regarded as a virtue. For the people of the East, the age of leisure and complacency is now probably at an end. Busy people, constantly on the move, constantly creating; it's a progress that has been very late in coming. Commerce will overcome the power of the tides to slow down the revolution of the earth and will instead become its new high-energy accelerator. This planet will eagerly look forward to becoming part of an intelligent galaxy in our universe, henceforth to cast aside poverty, ignorance and backwardness."

She had quietly come up the stairs and now stood before him without a trace of anger towards him. However, her very calmness, self-possession, conviction of being in the right only served to provoke his temper to a pitch which became intolerable. He took a grip on his cup and his voice shook as he said:

321

"And what about you then? Why are you able to sleep?"

Only you can cure your depression and sleeplessness. Can't you see that?

...Men are always seeking and therefore never content. Some people can sleep well at night and they think clearly by day only at the cost of others' sleeplessness. Why don't you go and learn to do the same? Start from the very beginning, since you're not willing to put up with the coldness of others. You've still time to increase your own worth.

"I don't understand you!" he expostulated, feeling ever more confused.

The doctor opened a cupboard and took out a sheet of white writing paper, then sat down on the sofa smiling, yet with an apologetic air. All he could do was stare at the swaying curtains, at those bright, white flowers.

"While I've been treating you I have made three suggestions, all of which have failed. As for this last one, you still don't understand; it seems your nervous condition doesn't react well to this sort of drug-free treatment. Actually, the success of psychotherapy depends very much on the patient; it's not everyone who experiences a miraculous cure. But even I cannot help those who are past hope. That there are disturbed people who are not coming to me for help is what I regret most. I think I'd better prescribe some sleeping tablets for you. I've got permission from the hospital."

"I don't want any sleeping tablets! No librium, wintermin, or miltown!" As he spoke his whole body convulsed and his hands clasped his head.

"Well, I could prescribe something else, like many-prickle acanthopanax, that might be of some effect," she rapped on the armrest of the sofa as she spoke, a ruthless, unfeeling tone now to her voice. Her pen scratched quickly across the page, leaving a line of writing that he still could not understand. Last of all she signed her name with a flourish.

"Here you are," she said and handed the paper to him. He did not say anything but took the paper and his eye fell on the name with its arrangement of strokes. It looked like a letter of the alphabet, and in that instant he remembered. At that time he had gone to a lot of effort to find out the doctor's name. Was it really her? The woman doctor once with the town's psychiatric hospital who only knew how to prescribe sleeping tablets. He had almost quareled with her then. Although it was a long time ago he had not forgotten. There must be some mistake....

He had come back on home leave and taken his uncle to the doctor. His uncle had been the vice-president of a large factory. "He can't sleep at all. It's so serious, he's begun to imagine he's hearing things. He's afraid of the dark. He starts at every sound...." He had not finished explaining before the prescription had been written out and thrust towards him. Thus he had come home with a huge pile of sleeping tablets. The second time it had been the same, and by the third time his patience had been exhausted.

"Excuse me, but you still don't know all the details of the case," he had pointed out.

"Details?" she had snapped. "It's all one and the same. Everybody's ill and everybody has the same disease. Anxiety, stress. If they don't take this, what else is there? If everybody took sleeping tablets the world would be a more peaceful place. I'm right you know." She had been even more impatient ...

"Have you by any chance worked in the psychiatric hospital in town?" he asked, unable to suppress his curiosity.

"What do you think?" she retorted. "If I remember rightly, I came here only last year."

"Where were you seven, eight years ago?"

"How should I know," came the indifferent reply. 'I can't remember. I hadn't been sleeping at that time either."

The woman was a riddle, he thought to himself, an enchantress from the forests.

"Give it a try," she was saying, her voice was soothing yet also held a slightly malicious note. No doubt she hoped everybody would be an insomniac.

So braving an icy wind he had got home, exhausted. The prescription was still tucked inside his jacket. The signature was one he had known ten years ago. He had not been able to pick up the medicine as the pharmacy was already closed. It did not seem to matter, however; merely having the piece of paper with the prescription written on it had an effect. During dinner his chopsticks fell out of his hand while he was chewing on some cabbage leaves—he fell asleep laying his head on the back of the chair. It was a miracle! Or was it because he had had no other option?

He did not know how long he had slept, but he woke up to a white world.

He found that, having made up all that lost sleep, his mind was clear and he felt full of energy. Yet it was strange that although he had not followed her advice, nor taken any medicine, he had still been able to sleep. Anyway, the fact was that he had slept enough, and if it hadn't been for the wife's prodding, he would still be asleep even now.

He had to tell the doctor as soon as possible about this, his great discovery, and also get back his medical file at some point. From now on he would not have to ask for leave and waste all that time in going to the clinic any more. He could even open his own and make himself director.

Although her manner had been so frosty that last time, he suddenly felt immeasurably grateful towards her. He just had to tell her about last night.

Outside the wind brought the first of the snow now gusting, now drifting down. A frosty powder was falling from the branches. Earth and sky were white, gleaming in the bright sunlight.

As he walked he would look back occasionally, and see no trace of his footprints.

Silvery birches stood in glittering clusters, shrubs dotted the white landscape. The rows of small, wooden dachas, which in summer had red or green, round or pointed roofs, now looked as if they had been carved out of the snow, or yet like white china ornaments under a white, glaring sun.

He could not find the small white house. He remembered it was in a wood, but there were woods everywhere. He remembered it was beside a small road, but now no such road could be found. He remembered it was white, but now all the houses were white. As he wove his way to and fro among the trees, the layer of white on his cap grew and grew. The white house was now beginning to seem like a dream, like a secret that was no longer a secret, an illusion that was quietly slipping away into the white expanse.

"Tong Dazhuang ..." he began to shout, but all he heard was his own voice. Surely her license had not been revoked? But then there was that fat old man. It couldn't be that she had moved her practice up country? He tried to recall what she had said ...or was he mistaken about the location?

He remembered that he had once been unable to sleep, but then his memory was never very accurate. He began to doubt that he had ever come to this place. Perhaps there had never been such a clinic on Sun Island, and Tong Dazhuang had never existed. Everything would then be nothing more than a fantasy of his own creation.

His mind was perfectly clear now, but he did not understand what had been going on. He dropped down into the snow, and for the first time in his life despised himself.

Translated by Katharina Byrne

Note:

[1] A business which operates quite literally out of a briefcase, making money out of empty promises and speculations.

ZHANG XIANLIANG AND HIS FICTION

Li Jun

Zhang Xianliang's works are chiefly autobiographical, based on his twenty years' banishment to the countryside in northeast China, after having been labeled a Rightist.

Zhang is one of the most popular writers in China today, and one of the most controversial. Almost all his novels have created a stir nationwide upon publication, making him an important name on the literary scene. Many of his works have been translated into other languages.

He was born into a capitalist family in 1936 in Nanjing. He received his primary education in Chongqing and Shanghai where he stayed until 1949. He then attended middle school in Nanjing from August 1949 to August 1951, during which period he published his first poems in the *Xinhua Daily*. When the family moved to Beijing, he continued his education at the Beijing No. 39 Middle School, graduating in 1955.

Having failed to enter college, Zhang moved to Ningxia Hui Autonomous Region in Northwest China, where he found employment as a clerk in the Jingxiang Township Administration in Helan County. Soon afterwards he became a teacher at the cadre school in the regional capital, Yinchuan.

In 1957, when he turned twenty-one, he started to write in earnest, publishing some sixty short poems in the

Yanhe, *China Youth Daily*, *Star* and *Poetry*. These poems expressd his excitement at China's vigorous reconstruction in those days, but they also laid bare what the author saw as the weaknesses of the new society. This is what got him into trouble.

Within a month of publishing a lyric poem, entitled, "Ode to the Wind," he was attacked as a Rightist and the poem labeled anti-socialist. This was in the aftermath of the "hundred flowers" campaign when a backlash against artists who had displayed sentiments considered too liberal resulted in many of them being persecuted and banished to the countryside to "remould themselves through labor."

Zhang himself was stripped of his post at the cadre school and sent off to the remote Ningxia countryside to work as a farmer. He was kept at this toil right up until the fall of the Gang of Four in 1976, except for brief periods of penal servitude and "re-education."

During those eighteen years he endured spiritual loneliness and physical hardship; he was deprived of the right to love and be loved. All that was allowed to him was back-breaking labor. But, instead of railing uselessly at his cruel fate, he resolved to "turn misfortune to advantage" and toughen himself both mentally and physically. He took delight in feats of strength—for which farm work offered him no few opportunities—but, more importantly, he managed to squeeze in time for reading, especially the Marxist classics, taking copious notes. With his body and soul in purgatory, he never lost hope for a better life.

Even after the ousting of the Gang of Four and the Communist Party's new policy of rehabilitating wrongly labeled Rightists, he had to fight hard to clear his name. After repeated appeals to the authorities, he was finally given a minor teaching post. But he left this after only one month and returned to the farm for reasons not entirely clear. His objective then was to distinguish himself by writing theses on philosophy and political economics. This venture, too, resulted in failure as publishers turned a deaf ear to all his overtures. Finally, at the instigation of friends, he decided to make a last desperate attempt to draw attention to his plight by writing short stories.

This was when the tide really turned in his favor. Starting in 1979, his stories of the disastrous years of the Cultural Revolution found an eager audience in the pages of the *Ningxia Literature and Art*. Not long afterwards, his case was reviewed and Zhang Xianliang was rehabilitated.

The first thing he did was to go to work for the publication which had been the key to his return to the world of literary creation. As an editor with the *Ningxia Literature and Art*, he joined the Chinese Writers Association and blossomed as a full-time writer. Wasting no time, he published in 1980 two short stories which were recognized as masterpieces—*Old Man Xing and His Dog* and *Body and Soul*.

The story of *Old Man Xing and His Dog* is set in the arid Northwest which Zhang knows so well. It tells of the personal tragedy of Old Man Xing, an aged widower, during the days of the Cultural Revolution, when the ultra-Left line then holding sway, deprives him of the companionship not only of a beggar woman who comes to live with him for a time, but also of his dog.

It was *Body and Soul* that really established the author's reputation as an important contemporary writer, winning him a national best short story prize in the year of its publication. It relates the hardships of a young intellectual with a capitalist father living overseas. The

329

biographical touches lend an obvious realism to the story and it was an instant success. *Body and Soul* was also hailed for its patriotic message and later made into a film that won an honorary award at the Manila International Film Festival in 1982.

He published the third major work of his initial phase —*Love in the Dungeon*—in the literary bimonthly *October* in 1981. This is a tragic love story about a young intellectual who betrays a naive country girl who has befriended him in prison.

Beginning in late 1981, he embarked upon a series of novels dealing with the problems of China's current reform efforts. *Longzhong* has as its protagonist the new Party secretary of a state farm who struggles to transform the farm's production methods. The second, *The Gentleman Style*, similarly centers around the experiences of a new municipal Party secretary. Critics have not been as enthusiastic about these two works, which they accuse of sacrificing realism and pace to abstract theorizing, perhaps because the author has been unable to resist the temptation to assert his earlier ambition in the direction of philosophy and political economics.

The third work in the series, *Descendants of the River*, shows deep concern with the fate of China's peasants, and the fourth, *Bitter Springs—A Truck Driver's Story*, originally bore the title, *Xiao'erbulake* or "caustic" because Zhang maintains that only those who have drunk a bitter cup, i.e., who have born hardships, are real men.

In 1984 he started work on a series of novels, nine in all, with the overall title, *The Making of a Materialist*. Again drawing heavily on his own experiences, the author struck a chord of realism which brought him instant acclaim. The series is the saga of a young poet banished to the countryside, who struggles to remake himself ideologically from the bourgeois humanism of his capitalist family background to Marxism (Zhang himself joined the Party in 1986). Five of the nine novelettes were to be devoted to the protagonist's experiences prior to 1979 —a turning point, it will be remembered, in the author's own life—and the other four to the years since then.

According to Zhang, he got the inspiration for the *The Making of a Materialist* series from Soviet writer Alexei Tolstoy's *Ordeal*. In this work Tolstoy describes the ordeal of intellectuals brought up in Tsarist Russia as "thrice soaked in water, thrice bathed in blood, thrice boiled in caustic soda."

The first of the series to be published, *Mimosa*, won an award for the best novelette in 1984. It tells of the protagonist's experiences over a two-month period in 1961. The hero, Zhang Yonglin, is released from a prison camp and sent to a state farm, where he suffers from, among other things, starvation as the nation nears the end of a three-year famine. The depiction of the characters is sturdy and a triangular love affair adds spice to the tale.

In the same year Zhang Xianliang produced another major work, *The Romantic Black Cannon*. Humor and satire abound in this story of an intellectual's encounters with bureaucracy, suspicion and red tape. Under the title *The Black Cannon Incident*, the book was made into a movie by Huang Jianxin at the Xi'an Film Studio.

Halfman, the second in the Materialist series, was the first serious novel since the founding of the People's Republic in 1949 to deal with the subject of sex as a major theme. First published in the literary bimonthly *Harvest* in late 1985, *Halfman* later was produced in book form and sold thousands of copies. In this episode of his life, Zhang Yonglin marries, and finally divorces, the passionate Huang Xiangjiu. The loss and restoration of the hero's virility is the vehicle for a cry of indignation from the author at the cruel trampling down of human nature.

Zhang Xianliang holds the following positions: member of the Chinese People's Political Consultative Conference, director of the Chinese Writers Association, chairman of the Ningxia Provincial Writers Association, and vice-chairman of the Ningxia Federation of Literature and Art Circles.

July 13, 1988

Bitter Springs
—A Truck Driver's Story

Zhang Xianliang

HEY, don't doze off. The thing I fear most on the road is people next to me falling asleep. Dozing's contagious.

Have a cigarette. You don't smoke? How can a good writer not smoke? Anyway, I do. City drivers aren't supposed to smoke on the job, but here it doesn't matter. At any rate, sitting in a cab by yourself all the time gets to be depressing. It's not like back east. Here you can go for hundreds of miles without seeing a village or any sign of life, on and on, until you just can't keep your eyes open any longer.

Take a look, either side of us is desert. That's the Gobi. You probably used to think the Gobi was flat and yellow, but it's not. It's just these fist-sized rocks as far as you can see. After the Gobi you start getting up into the mountains. They're not like the ones you see in movies either—they've all got flat tops like iron nails. We have to go along a place called Dry Gully to get into the mountains. What a name! It's so dry, if you cry your tears are gone before they have a chance to fall; there's no grass, no trees, not even any birds or ants, it's just like being on the moon. You'll see it in a bit. After driving in that for a while, how could anyone not fall asleep? Anyway, I'm lucky to have a journalist along with me this time—we can have a chat.

Have you traveled a lot? Until you got to Xinjiang you probably didn't realize the country was so big. The Uygurs always say that in Xinjiang even beggars have to go round on a donkey because if they don't, they'll starve to death before they get to the next village. Of course, that was in the old days, but it gives you a good idea.

I like having company when I'm driving. Whenever I see people walking along the road, I always slow down a bit and see if they want a lift. Out here, in this empty desert with those mountains looming up ahead and this heavy sky, when I see people puffing along all alone I feel sorry for them. I sort of admire them too. In a truck you don't realize it, but if you're walking you know what it feels like to shuffle along step by step on a road like this.

If I've got someone with me, then we're company for one another. We long distance drivers spend more time with machines than we do with people. If you pass someone you know on the road, you don't even have time to smile before you've both whizzed by one another. It's better working with animals. When I was a kid I used to drive a donkey cart—though they're cranky animals, they're still living creatures and if you're feeling in low spirits you can always talk to them. They always seem as though they can understand you, twitching those floppy ears. But a truck isn't an animal—if it was alive, you'd have a lot of trouble. When you've been driving for a while, you get to feeling an odd kind of loneliness. That's why when they get to a station and stop drivers like to have a good laugh and a swear. Why do they swear? They just don't want to get out of practice talking. People have a need to be together.

A few years back we used to have a company chief

who absolutely forbade us to give people lifts, said it was dangerous. But then he used to take cigarettes and liquor for carrying people's goods on the side, and he ended up being given the boot.

Giving people lifts is not such a small thing. Somebody signals you, you stop, he gets on and just in that tiny moment he thinks to himself that there are still a lot of good people about. And when you see his smiling face, it makes you feel better; you drive with a bit more energy and don't get sleepy. I'm not much of a talker, just so long as I've got somebody along with me then I don't get to feeling too lonely. I'm talking more than usual with you today. I like talking with educated people.

How did I get to Xinjiang? That's a long story. Actually, you could say I was a returned educated youth. You can tell from my accent that I'm from Henan. I got as far as junior middle school back in my home county. Had a lot of hopes in those days. When I saw soldiers in films I wanted to be one, or if I saw doctors I'd want to be a doctor, or if I read a book I'd think about being a writer. Anyway, whatever I thought, I never expected I'd be a long distance driver. When I was in my third year at middle school, I wrote a poem on our blackboard bulletin which had a couple of lines which went something like, "My hopes are like a ribbon of stars, glittering across my forehead." Not bad, you say? Now, don't make fun of me, I was only seventeen then. My teacher said that a village youngster with ambitions like that ought to go far.

Who would ever have thought that in 1960 things would have been so tough at home that my mum and dad wouldn't have enough to eat, so this promising "village youngster" had to give up school and get back to look after them. But three people at home was too many. I was an only son, and the two of them sat down and cried and said to me, "Child, you'd better leave and try and make a go of it somewhere else. You've got nine years' schooling, you'll definitely be able to earn a living." We Henanese are survivors you know, since right way back, we've moved where we had to to make a living. If there's been some kind of natural disaster at home then we take off to another province. Well anyway, just then we got a letter from someone in our village who'd gone to Xinjiang, saying it was a good place to live. You could get work and enough to eat. I was reminded of a song we learned at school called "Our Xinjiang Is a Fine Place," so I decided to come here.

Those days they were strict about vagrants. We waited for a moonless night for me to leave home. My dad went with me for a couple of miles to the end of the commune land, but then he couldn't go on any longer and squatted by the side of the road, wheezing. I took out a couple of cornmeal pancakes my mum had stuck in my bundle and slipped them inside his jacket. "You go on back," I told him. "I know the way, I've got a map. When I get there and get a job I'll send you back some money."

Young people don't feel so attached to home—even if they go without food they're still strong and want to flap their wings and fly away. So I didn't even shed a tear, nor did I really have the least idea what my parents must have been feeling then. That's the sort of thing you come to understand more as you get older. Now, whenever I try and think of the last few words my dad and mother said to me, or even what they looked like the last time I saw them, all I can see is that image of my father squatting by the roadside. It used to be that when

I drove alone at night that image would always appear in front of me, always in my headlights just by the side of the road. It seemed to be stuck to my windscreen like a traffic permit—it went with me everywhere, nothing would make it go away.

Now and again I forgive myself and think if it'd been my mum who came with me that night then the two of us would've said more to one another. My dad was a tight-lipped old farmer and I wasn't much of one for talking either. Sons are never as close to their fathers anyway, I guess, but they'd brought me up for eighteen years and when we had to say goodbye I didn't even have a grateful word to say to them ...

Well anyway, on with my story ...

That's how I got to Xinjiang. In those days that railway line only came as far as Weiya. It's not a bad-looking town now, but then it was just a bunch of broken down old mud houses stuck on the desert. People just pitched tents all round the houses one after the other, several rows deep. Since Weiya was the terminus, everybody coming to Xinjiang piled off there. The buses kept on going west and the trains kept bringing people from out east. They were all shapes and sizes and ages. There'd often be a few thousand of them living in those tents, trampling the snow down until it was just messy slush.

What kind of people were they? Well, some of them were transferred here officially, university graduates assigned to work here, people who came with factories which moved here, but most of them were "illegal vagrants," what they later called "drifters." Now they give us a pretty fancy name—"voluntary pioneers." I guess you could say that that was a kind of rehabilitation in itself. To be frank, those vagrants or voluntary pioneers have a lot to do with Xinjiang's being so much better off today. I know a lot of them who've become outstanding workers and professionals, engineers, and production and construction corps leaders.

We drifters got on pretty well; in fact when we got together you'd think we'd known one another all our lives. Just a sentence or two, and you'd have a good picture of somebody's background. The tents were originally just for production corps and factory recruiters, and the recruiters were looking for unemployed drifters like me. Weiya was really like a big market in those days; noisy and crowded, as busy as Nanjing Road in Shanghai. You'd get recruiters shouting, "Hey, come on over here! We'll give you good salaries, plenty of grain, you can't afford to pass it up!" or "Hey, this way, we've got all the milk you can drink, apples as big as your head. Miss this one and you won't be able to do anything about it later!" or they'd shout things like "Hey, we don't want any of you corn-eating yokels over here. Bumpkins brought up in barns and suckers who can't stand the feel of money had better not head this way!" They all made it sound as though if you signed up with them, you'd eat the best, live in a big house and have your pockets bulging with money.

On the train, I was worried that without papers I wouldn't be able to get work. But when I got to Weiya, one of the old hands told me that if you didn't have a commune change-of-residence certificate, a voter registration card would do; if you didn't have that, then a letter from a friend or relative in Xinjiang would be all right. The places that needed people most, the ones with the noisiest recruiters, were the poorest places with the toughest labor. As long as you weren't missing an arm or a leg and had eyes, ears and a nose, they didn't need to see anything else!

The guy who told me this was in his forties and always used to wear a greasy worn-out padded jacket. He said he knew a little about medicine and wanted to find the right sort of job, so he hadn't signed up with just any of the recruiters. Since he seemed to have a little education, I took out my lower middle school diploma and gave it to him. I remember how his eyes lit up and he said to me, "Hey, you're a real treasure. With this, the very least they ought to give you is an office job. Don't go to any of those loud-mouthed recruiters." Then he pointed over at one of the tents and told me to look for work there.

Not surprisingly it was a little quieter round that one. It had a sign on the front flap which said "Xinjiang Education Department, Weiya Office." The people inside were a lot better mannered, not like those fast-talking barkers. Inside the tent they had a petrol drum stove and a bare wooden bench with a row of job applicants sitting there. The man in charge of registering people was fat, I remember. Those days fat people were a rarity so he made quite an impression on me. Not all of the applicants there had papers either. If you didn't have any certificates, then the fat man would give you an oral exam. The questions were to find out what level of education the applicant had, and he asked things like "How many continents and oceans are there" and "What type of country is the People's Republic of China" or "Who discovered the periodic table of elements" and "What is meant by 'Confucius said: Is it not a pleasure having learnt something to try it out at due intervals'?" I listened to him and found that I could answer all of them. The fat man was from Shaanxi and seemed well educated and friendly. When he got to me, I handed over my diploma. He looked really pleased and just asked me when I'd arrived, how many there were in my family and whether or not I'd come alone. Then he quickly wrote my name in a registration book and told me to turn up early the next morinng to go to Urumqi.

When I came out of that tent, I was beside myself with excitement. I just spread my wings and soared across that site. Being an administrator would have been even better, but being a teacher wasn't bad. I remembered a Soviet film called *The Village Schoolmistress* which I'd seen twice as a kid and which had made a strong impression on me. Since the main character in the film was a woman, I can't say I'd completely identified with her, but now, with that kind of prospect opening up before me, I remembered how I used to want to be a teacher. I thought of how when I got old I'd be just like that schoolmistress—white hair, glasses, surrounded by scientists, writers, army officers, all former students of mine....

Just as I was letting myself get all carried away I suddenly ran into two young girls. They were about the same age as me and were dressed a bit like students. Both of them had braids. They'd noticed me while I was talking to that other drifter and came over to have a word. I could tell from their accents that they were from Henan and it turned out to be a place less than fifty kilometers from my commune. They asked me if I'd found a job. I told them I had, and a good one too, and just spouted out everything that had happened, bragging about how the fat man had been so impressed with me that he hadn't even bothered to give me an exam. They looked miserable and told me they hadn't found anything and couldn't really do manual labor. I believed them too. They were thin and sallow, not like these healthy teenagers you get today. Anyway, without thinking twice about it, I just blurted out that they should go to the same place I had been to and see if they could get jobs as teachers.

That night I put up at one of the local inns. I don't know whether it was a state place or one privately run by a Uygur. It had two long brick *kang*s with a hollow brick wall for heating running in between, but the wall was icy cold when I touched it. I remember the place was three *yuan* a night and there wasn't any bedding at all. It was so crowded you had to wedge yourself in as best you could.

I discovered there that some of the others had changed jobs a lot—wherever the going was good, that's where they went. These old hands would squat on the *kang*, backs against that wall and talk about their experiences, rolling cigarettes and smoking all the while. Listening to them, it seemed there wasn't a place in Xinjiang they hadn't been to. You know, reporter, in those days Xinjiang was really wide open, not like back east where you've got to have a pile of permits every time you take a step. Xinjiang really used to be the most backward place in the country, and the changes here over the last thirty years have a lot to do with their more open labor policy.

Anyway, to get back to what I was saying, when I got up next morning I thought to myself that since I was going to be a teacher from then on, I'd better try and make a good impression on my first day, so I spent thirty *fen* on a small basin of fresh water and had a wash. When I got to that tent, the other new employees were already getting on the truck one by one. The fat man was standing next to it counting them. But as soon as he saw me, he scowled and said, "Get out of here. You seemed an honest sort, but you were up to no good. We don't want you here, find yourself some other place!"

I was really shocked. "What do you mean?" I said.

"What do you mean?" he mimicked my accent. "What sort of young man drags two girls all over the place with him? What's going on? When I asked you yesterday, you told me you came here alone. What a liar!"

I tried to stick up for myself. "I didn't come with those two girls. If you don't believe me, give me a test."

"Test what?" He just threw up his hands. "They all say they've had middle school educations, but if you ask them the simplest arithmetic they can't answer, or they think Gorky was a Chinese. Absolute nonsense!"

Intellectuals are always stubborn and this fat man more than most. Maybe those two girls had used my name, lied to him, made him angry. Anyway I could see he wasn't going to back down, whatever I said.

The truck started up and I just stood there alone. The fat man swiveled around in the cab, pushed the door open and shouted to me, "Young man, if you want to be a teacher, decent behavior is the first requirement. If you don't have that, it doesn't matter how much education you've got."

So I'd got all excited for nothing, my dreams of becoming a teacher were shattered and all of those scientists, writers and army officers vanished. The fat man vanished too and the tyres of their truck spattered me with slush. I was totally down in the dumps and turned to go, but just then I saw those two girls standing timidly beside a tent watching me.

"What did you do! It's all your ..." I remember I started to give them a real tongue-lashing.

They stood huddled together, looking down and

said, "We had to ...we didn't even get through primary school and when the fat man wanted to test us we told him not to bother since we'd been at school with you. We told him we all graduated at the same time and that you brought us here. But we didn't expect ..."

I could see they were on the verge of tears and that they knew they were in the wrong. When people are drowning they grasp at straws; they hadn't deliberately meant to harm me. So I didn't say anything more and just started off to the recruiters' tents.

"Hey," one of the girls shouted. "Quick, take us with you. We come from the same place and we trust you. We'll go wherever you go."

"Forget it," I told them. "Whether you trust me or not, if people see me hanging around with two young girls they'll get the wrong idea. Didn't you see the way that fat man shouted at me? Isn't that enough?"

Then the two of them started to cry, "Well, what can we do? We're out of money, we don't know a soul here. We can't even get back ..."

As soon as I saw the tears falling, I couldn't hold out. Anyway, we did come from the same part of the world so I told them, "OK, don't cry. While we're all out of work we can stick together, I've still got a few clothes I can sell."

Like I said, I was an only child and so, although my family were poor peasants, I was never short of clothes. During that couple of years when the peasants did so well, my parents bought me a lot—they really wanted me to look good—and sent me off to school.

When I think about it, if the country had gone on the way it was in 1956 I'd probably have been a university teacher by now.

I was saying that then Weiya was just like one great

big market place. The recruiters would be standing in front of those tents shouting, and then all round you'd get people selling things. They'd sell whatever they'd brought with them, some of them even sold black market grain coupons. Of course, they were all drifters like me, because who'd need to be doing that if they already had a job? You didn't have to set up a stall or hawk your wares, you just stood holding whatever it was and people would come over to see what you had. I took out my warmer weather clothes, a pair of blue twill trousers and a new white cotton shirt, and sold those for ten *yuan*. Money wasn't worth that much in the 1960s—a bowl of tea was thirty *fen*. Three people eating for a day managed to eat their way through that trousers and shirt of mine.

That night I went back to the inn but the two girls didn't have any idea where they'd sleep. The next day the two of them came to me with their eyes all red and puffy and said, "We're really sorry, we mucked up your job and now we're using up your money and we feel even worse. We've talked it over, and we've decided to go and sign up at the manual labor place. It's about all we can do."

Well, I could hardly even look after myself, never mind anyone else, so if they'd decided to go off and do that all I could say was, "All right, go on the two of you. But try and get the lighter work and conserve your strength.... At any rate, it's got to be better than back home. At least you'll have something to eat."

They went off to sign up, and that afternoon they got on a truck to leave. I sold another shirt and went over and gave them each a couple of *yuan*. The barkers were still standing there shouting, "Hey, come on with us, all the milk you can drink ..." and the two of them just sat up there on the truck sobbing their hearts out. I couldn't help feeling totally miserable as I stood there —it was as if they really were my classmates and we really had come together to this strange new life in Xinjiang.

We drivers get all over the region. A few years later I happened to be in Korla and there was a truck ahead of me unloading pears. I realized that I knew the woman carrying baskets but it took me a while to finally work out that it was one of those two girls. She was a lot stronger and fatter and I would guess that she had married and had a kid. I watched her for a while but I didn't have the nerve to talk to her.

After the two girls left, I stayed on in Weiya and evenings I'd get together with the other drifters. You know, those people were a goodhearted lot. Despite all the hard times they'd been through, they were always pretty kind about anyone else's problems. When everyone heard what had happened to me and they'd all handed round that middle school diploma, they came up with all sorts of advice and finally pushed me into going to Hami, where they said I could get a job in accounting.

Being an accountant would be all right too, I thought to myself. I'd learned how to use an abacus at middle school. I decided to head for Hami.

In those days the Weiya buses were always packed to the gills, and there was no way you could get yourself a westbound ticket in less than a week. I only had a few *yuan* left and no more clothes to sell and couldn't wait that long. So I did what the drifters advised me to do, and went to try and hitch a ride on one of the goods trucks.

The parking lot was to the west of the tent city. It

was all crisscrossed with tyre marks and the snow was spattered with oil; there were vehicles parked all over the place—I reckon there must have been a good hundred of them. Some of the drivers looked all right but others looked pretty fierce. I hung around for ages that morning, too shy to talk to any of them. I remember the sun climbing high up in the sky. I just stood there timidly as the trucks moved out one by one. But then I suddenly heard someone who drove a fuel truck speaking my local dialect, so I moved over in his direction as though I was interested in watching him fix his engine.

After a bit, somebody he'd been talking to left and the driver finished his repairs. He closed the hood, turned round and suddenly saw me. "Hey, young fellow, get me that bucket of water over there, would you?" he said.

I took him the water and said, "Master, where are you going?"

This driver had a ruddy, kind face and smiled as soon as he heard my accent, "Hm, seems like we're from the same neck of the woods. Where're you headed?"

I told him I wanted to go to Hami. He said he was going to :Urumqi and could take me along.

After putting water in the tank, he jumped down from the bumper and told me to hurry up and get my suitcase. I just held up my bundle and said everything I owned in the world was in that. I remember the way he laughed and patted my head. "Come on," he said. "Let's go!"

I guess you could say that this driver was sort of my "master." As we went along, I told him all about the situation back home. He asked me what I was doing going to Hami and what relatives I had there, so I told him exactly what I had in mind and even gave him my diploma to look at. He said to me that I shouldn't look down on manual labor, that the world had been built by human labor and that it was really the most noble sort of work. He'd started driving back at home in 1947 after joining the army and had come to Xinjiang in 1949. They'd wanted him to take an office job, but he wasn't interested and went back to driving after leaving the service. The two of us seemed to see eye to eye on everything and before we even got to Hami, he'd decided to take me on as an apprentice.

So in the end I didn't get out at Hami and the two of us just went straight on to Urumqi together.

Now he's retired and spends all his time gardening. I go over to his place a lot. He told me not to bother bringing him any presents unless I ran across good plants. You see that orchid behind you? I bought it yesterday from a trader in from the Northeast. Cost me fifty *yuan*. I'm taking it to him tomorrow, he's really going to be pleased.

Are you fed up with listening to all this? I know you reporters write about VIPs and heroes and the like. I've never done anything important in my life, it's all been pretty ordinary. I've been commended and won awards and that kind of thing but that was all just in the company; they didn't even put it in the *Xinjiang Daily*. I know you don't write about the sorts of things I've been talking about: no newspaper would publish it. Just thought I'd try and keep you amused for a while.

Sit tight, we start heading up into the mountains after that next bend.

Anyway, from then on I started driving. I think life is sort of like moving tyres, spinning round fast; good times are like when you step on the gas, bad times like being stuck in the mud—you spin round and round but you can't get out. Well, all the same, twenty years has gone by in a flash. Of course, I've changed my actual vehicle a lot during that time. The very first one I had was a Soviet truck. After that I drove one of our Liberations, then a Czech Skoda and even a Romanian truck. This Japanese Hino, I just started driving recently.

The age of a car has nothing to do with time but with how much mileage it's put in. I think it's the same with people. Some people live fifty or sixty years without running into bad times or trouble and you could say that they stay pretty young. Others have a rough time right from the start; by the time they're thirty or forty they've been through so much they're already old. You know, Mr Reporter, it's the people who've known bad times who can give you something to write about. Take me for example: I've been to the Soviet Union, Afghanistan, even to Pakistan. I nearly lost my life in accidents a few times when we were building roads in Pakistan. I can tell you, piloting a spaceship would be easier than driving in foreign mountains with no proper roads. In Xinjiang too in those days, who'd ever heard of a good road? It was always either like driving on a washboard or just straight desert. Crying wouldn't help you much if you got caught in a storm and stuck somewhere out on the road. In winter, when the snows came, the roads just turned into rivers of ice, so hard nothing could crack it. When you got up to three or four thousand meters, you were taking your life in your hands every inch of the way and if you made a mistake then you and the truck would just go plunging straight down the mountainside.

The second spring I was here my mum and dad died, working at an irrigation site. I got a letter from my uncle saying that just before my mother went she kept calling out my pet name. Afterwards they found two money orders I'd sent her in her pocket. She'd never even gone to the post office to cash them—there wasn't any grain in the shops or the market anyway, so I'd sent her the money for nothing. My uncle used it to buy her a flimsy coffin and fix up my father's grave. In 1964 I scraped together enough to go back, and their graves were already covered with grass. The willow trees planted that year were as thick as your arm.

While I was there, I went out to have a look at the road I took the night I left home and the place my father had sat, but it had all changed; now it's a wide road, all graveled, and the place where my father sat would be in the center with tractors going up and down it. The old master driver put it nicely—he said that vehicles always had to move forward, that you always had to keep your eyes on the road; it's okay to check the rearview mirror now and again, but if you do it all the time then you'll turn the car over. So I decided to come back here and go on driving.

All the same, I didn't have anyone left in the world and I felt sort of lonely all the time. We drivers don't actually get a chance to see that much of one another; you're always pulling out when someone else is checking in. I hardly ever got time to spend even the odd day or two with the old driver. Then the Cultural Revolution started, and even old friends wouldn't tell one another what they really thought—nobody trusted anyone else. If you met a stranger, you had to give them a good once-over and work out first of all whether they were class enemies and what their class background was. You couldn't say what you thought to somebody you'd just met, like now. But people still aren't as close as they were during those tough times in the 1960s. What do you think makes people most miserable? For me, the worst thing is when you can't say what you really feel. When people get up in the morning, they put on their underwear, then their clothes, then a padded coat and finally they encase themselves in an invisible suit of armor before going out. Everybody's huddled inside their own suit of armor, so even though there might be a lot of people working in a company, they never really get to know one another.

In those days, I always kept things pretty much to myself. One day my old master said to me, "You ought to think about getting married, you know. You're already in your late twenties. If you had a home and someone to look after you, then maybe your spirits would pick up a bit." I thought about it and realized he was right, so I decided to fix up a wedding.

Finding a girlfriend in Xinjiang isn't easy. There are a lot more men than women and the chances to meet a girl are few and far between. But, luckily, we go all over the place; and not long after that, a lot of our company drivers met up in a Dabancheng canteen. They got to talking, and one of them suddenly shouted out, "I've got it! Right under our very noses too. There's a girl right here in Dabancheng who's just come in from northern Shaanxi—I'll go and see about her for you." The others all started ribbing me about it and one of them started singing a Kazak song:

> You Dabancheng girls have long, long braids
> And lovely sparkling eyes
> If you want to marry, then please don't get married
> To anyone else but me....

The singing got me all worked up. All right, I thought, let's give it a try.

The girl they had in mind was from Mizhi County. They'd had really bad harvests in that region, so she was like me in the 1960s and had left home because there wasn't enough food to go round. They say in Shaanxi "a Mizhi girl makes a happy man," like the Uygurs say, "Dabancheng girls are as pretty as flowers." She'd just turned twenty and had a primary school education. She wasn't bad-looking, and although her braids weren't that long, she did have large, pretty eyes. Her aunt used to sell tea at a roadside stall and they had a tough life. The aunt didn't ask for much, just that the girl got a residence permit and grain coupons. I could tell from the way the woman spoke that she and the girl didn't get along, and that all she wanted was to see the back of her as quickly as possible.

It was all fairly easy to arrange. A few of us talked it over and then went and settled the matter with the aunt.

When I got back, my old master was very much opposed to the whole business. He shook his head and said to me, "How can you be so casual about this? You hardly know anything about her. You're talking about something that's for the rest of your life. Don't be in such a rush; I'll come up with someone for you." I said to him that I'd been around a lot in the last few years and met a lot of people and wasn't that inexperienced. The girl was serious, not the flighty type, and I'd made up my mind. To tell you the truth, I'd never even thought of getting married all those years, I'd just sort of pushed on day by day. So when the old driver brought it up, it triggered something off, and suddenly it seemed the most important thing in the world. I wanted to go through with it as soon as I could, so I didn't listen to him and went ahead and married her.

You're still pretty young—are you married? No?

Well, I'll tell you a thing or two about marriage. I've been married twice, so I guess you could say I know a little about it.

When two people live an uneventful life together day after day, without any difficulties to really test the strength of their feelings, then you have to look at the ordinary things, at the housework, the cooking, that sort of thing, and at their facial expressions, to get some idea of what they're really feeling. It's nothing to do with education—you have to rely entirely on feelings, or as you intellectuals would say, on a kind of "intuition." If a woman really cares for you, then you can feel the warmth of her hand even if she gives you a slap across the face: if she doesn't, then she can hold you in her arms all day long and you can still feel the iciness in her heart. You know, in the outside world, people can put on false faces and win honors for themselves; but it's at home, living together, day in and day out, sharing the same bed, that the real feelings can't be hidden. With some couples, it doesn't matter if they're always squabbling. If you just carefully watch the looks they exchange, you can see that they could still be a loving couple. Other couples treat one another with every possible courtesy, but they never share the same dreams.

This Shaanxi girl was good, very hard working and a good housewife, and she never spent time gossiping with the neighbors, never caused any trouble. She kept a very careful record of how the housekeeping money was spent every month. Whenever I got home from work, there would always be a hot meal waiting for me on the table, and my clothes were always washed and mended without my saying a word. As for affection, however, there wasn't an ounce of that.

Here in Xinjiang, we tend to get married first and fall

in love later. We think affection is something that can develop after you get married.

I'm sure I don't have to remind you how chaotic everything was in those days. It was pointless thinking of trying to do anything for the country—all you could do was throw yourself into fixing up your house. I made a lot of furniture; Czech-style, Polish-style—varnished and polished it till it gleamed—a sofa, a standard lamp too. I'd saved a bit of money while I was working in Pakistan, and my monthly salary was enough for the two of us.

But her attitude towards me was like a servant to a master, perhaps not even that. Even servants used to have a joke with their masters now and again, but she never cracked a smile. Nor did she take any pride in the furniture I made, never even sat on that sofa. She wouldn't wear any of the clothes I bought for her either. I came to realize that this wasn't to economize, but to deliberately keep her distance from me. If I had time off, or when I'd come home from work and the two of us would be together, she'd either fuss about doing things she didn't have to do or just sit there like a martyr, away in a corner by herself on a little stool. She'd just stare off into space and keep on heaving great big sighs. If I tried to drag her out to see a film, she wouldn't even turn round, she'd just say, "What's there to see? They're always showing the same old films!" That was more or less true, so we'd just chat. But she only talked about things to do with the housekeeping, and never said anything affectionate, or anything that didn't concern domestic matters. I don't care whether you laugh at me, reporter, but I think a husband and wife should be affectionate to one another. But she was absolutely blank. I got more and more depressed and upset.

353

Even when she slept next to me, she never took off that invisible suit of armor. Can you imagine how that gets to you? Was I blind, pockmarked, disabled or something? I was twenty-eight years old and thought I wasn't *that* bad-looking nor that cranky, nor had I done anything really bad in my life. So what was the reason? It didn't seem to be in keeping with her natural sort of character either. I used to sit and brood about it all day long; actually I couldn't get it off my mind. You know, trouble in a marriage is a lot more unbearable than political or financial trouble. If you get knocked about politically, but have a happy marriage, then there's still some consolation when you get back home; you can be poor, but if you've got a good woman you can still be happy. But with this kind of wife, it was even worse than being a bachelor. To tell you the truth, that's when I started smoking—drinking too—not past the three *liang*[1] limit, mind you, I still had my driving to do.

So we went on like that for half a year. After a bit, I noticed that whenever the neighborhood women saw me coming, they always looked as though they felt sorry for me, as though there was something on their minds. Just after we got married, they'd always stop me or my way home from work and have a few jokes. Those old biddies liked to rattle on about whatever scandal they could find. But I noticed when they talked to me, they were always kind of hesitant and never mentioned my wife at all. I began to wonder why. Although the two of us weren't exactly affectionate, we didn't squabble either!

Then one day our company had to make deliveries to Yili, and we stayed overnight at the Oasis Hotel. A few of us got together and bought some kebabs and a couple of bottles of the local liquor and sat around talking and

354

drinking. We'd got through half the drink and everyone was feeling merry when the driver who'd sung that Kazak song started up again, this time singing a Shaanxi ballad:

> *I come from a family, quite well known,*
> *In Thirty-li Village, Mizhi County.*
> *This Fourth Sister's found herself a Third Brother,*
> *Who's become her dear, dear one.*
> *Third Brother's in the army, down in the valley,*
> *Fourth Sister's blue, working in the fields.*
> *How I long to go down and see him,*
> *But I'm afraid that people will laugh.*

Then everyone started saying how Shaanxi girls were the prettiest and most loyal in the country and how once they'd got themselves tied up with someone it was for life. A few of them started teasing me because my wife was a Mizhi girl. Then in the middle of everything a young guy who'd had a bit too much said to me, "You'd better be careful. Your woman's Third Brother isn't you, it's someone else...."

The whole place went silent as soon as he'd said it, and the other drivers shot him filthy looks. He knew he'd spoken out of turn and just leaned over and ate his kebabs without saying another word.

There was obviously something in what he'd said. I was distracted and couldn't pay much attention to the other's fooling about. After a while, the young guy got up to go to the bathroom, and I followed him out.

Out in the corridor I grabbed him by the arm and said, "What did you mean by that? Don't be afraid, I won't hold it against you."

He went red and just sort of mumbled, "I didn't mean anything, I was only joking...."

Just then one of the older drivers appeared and said, "Since it's come out, we'd better all talk about it and not leave him in the dark. Come on, let's go back inside."

So those drivers told me what everybody else already knew. Three months back a guy from northern Shaanxi had arrived looking for her. The neighbors didn't know who he was, but they used to hear them crying and whispering together in the house. Our company's living quarters are set out in rows, about a hundred families or so, not set off from one another, and you can't hide anything much from anybody else. A lot of the drivers' family members didn't work and the women would spend their time visiting one another, catching up on all the gossip. They did a good job too—police detectives were no match for them—so before long they'd put together a fair amount of information: this young guy was from the same village as my wife, had just finished doing his military service and had made the trip specially to find her. They obviously meant something to each other. He'd got himself taken on as a temporary stoker in the animal products company across from our compound. He used to go to my place a lot when I wasn't home, and apparently the two of them would close the door and sit whispering to one another.

"Now don't get too worked up and jump to conclusions," the drivers said. "We didn't mention it before because the two of you seemed to be doing okay, and if we'd made a mistake we would've messed things up between you. You're a broody sort too, and we were afraid if we were mistaken, we'd stir up big trouble."

I listened to them with a lump in my throat and fighting back tears. "I'm grateful for your concern—actually you should've told me earlier. Things haven't been what they seemed between us anyway; I've had a pretty miserable half year ..." I said.

When I told them what it had been like, they all got really annoyed. Some of them said we ought to catch the guy and beat him up and then pack him off home. Some of the others thought that was letting him off too lightly, and that we ought to turn him in to the police. The older ones said we should just keep it to ourselves, and once we'd got rid of him, everything would all be all right; she could have a baby and perhaps she'd settle down a bit.

My head started to spin like a kaleidoscope—all sorts of ideas of a way out took shape in my head—evil, kind, treacherous, generous—in the end, I couldn't make up my mind.

So when I got home, I kept an even closer eye on her. But she was the same as always; careful about money, neat and tidy. I wanted to get at her but I couldn't find a reason; I wanted to get the thing out into the open, but I couldn't somehow find a way of bringing it up.

Then we had to have an overhaul and I stayed home for a few days. After it was finished, I was just about to set off when I discovered there was something wrong with the gear box: it was making a grinding noise. The mechanics were pretty sloppy then; they never fixed anything properly and they often messed up perfectly good vehicles, so we drivers had to do a lot ourselves. So that day I didn't go out and instead spent the morning working on the truck.

At lunchtime I headed home, carrying one of the mechanics' wrenches with me. When I walked in the door, I found her together with that young guy.

She was sitting on the bed, and he was sitting next to her on a stool. They were hanging their heads and had long faces as though they were trying to think of a way out of something. When they saw me, they jumped up. He looked absolutely panic-stricken, but she seemed quite calm and quickly moved in between the two of us, not so much to shield the guy as to give me a look which said, "Well, what are you going to do about it? If you lay a hand on him you'll have to deal with me too!"

To be quite honest, despite the fact that when my head'd been spinning I'd wanted to grab the pair of them and beat them up, when it came to the crunch all I could do was shake all over. He took advantage of my hesitation, slipped out from behind her and made off. She went over to the bed and sat down, grim determination written all over her face.

I asked her again and again, "Who was that guy?"

At first she didn't say a thing, then slowly tears started falling from those big eyes, splashing down onto her clothes. She didn't lower her head, turn her face, or say a word, she just sat there weeping.

I'm a softie and I can't stand to see people cry. As soon as she started, my anger cooled down. I tossed the wrench into a corner and threw myself down on the sofa. I just wanted her to lie to me, say he was her brother, or someone from her village and leave it at that. The older drivers had been right; we'd get rid of him, and then we could have a child and be like everybody else.

But she didn't lie to me, she just kept on crying and didn't say a word. I put my head in my hands and just sat there. I looked round at the new furniture, at that fashionable sofa and standard lamp, and slowly it dawned on me that there was nothing between the two of us. All that highly varnished furniture was just like ice and it seemed to send out a chilling kind of light. What was it all worth? So we'd have a child, then what? I'd seen plenty of drivers who had a whole pack of kids at home but who drank themselves silly because husband and wife were unhappy and looked elsewhere. Driving's a good job; the money's good, you don't get political worries and all that, so why do some of them drink like fish? If you look into it, you'll almost always discover it's because of problems at home.

Since she wouldn't talk, I went out to look for him. Whatever, I had to get to the bottom of it. I didn't have anything to eat—who could eat at a time like that—and left.

The guy lived in a little place next to the animal products factory. It consisted of two adobe walls fitted against the chimney, and managed to be sort of triangular and crescent shaped at the same time. Since it got steam from the chimney, it was quite warm. It was certainly a new kind of building.

The guy was no coward. As soon as he saw me pushing open the cardboard door, as though he'd known I'd go looking for him, he very politely indicated I should sit down and then poured some tea. You can't hit a man with a smiling face, so what was I supposed to do? Nor can you start knocking someone about the moment you walk in, so in the end all I could do was sit and listen to what he had to say.

He told me that the two of them had grown up in the same village, collected firewood in the mountains together, gone to school together; and that when they were in their teens they'd decided to marry. Both their families had given their consent. He'd then gone into the army and they were going to marry when he came out. But during that time, there was a famine, her father died of illness, and the family couldn't cope, so she had to come to Xinjiang to live with her aunt. That aunt knew all about this, but since I had a good job, earned good money, and could arrange a residence permit, she'd pushed the girl into marrying me. The girl, seeing her aunt wouldn't budge and with her boyfriend so far away, didn't know what to do. She finally gave in and married me. But, she told him, she'd never for one second stopped longing for him.

"We're both young and I'll tell you straight," he said to me. "I came to get her to divorce you, to take her with me, whether here working in Xinjiang or back home —but in the three months I've been here, I've been able to see that Xinjiang is a good place to live. Although she doesn't love you, she says you're a good person and she doesn't want to hurt you, but she's caught in the middle. Lately I've come round to thinking that since the three of us are in this fix, I'll stand aside. But I do want to say this—first, we haven't been up to anything behind your back; second, I was engaged to her first even though you married her, and we were together for eighteen years or so, while you've only lived with her half a year. You didn't love one another when you got married and even now how much do you care for each other? We got engaged because we were in love; I thought of her every single day those three years I was in the army, so if you want me just to take off and forget about her, I can't. If you can understand this, then you'll forgive me. If you can't, then hit me, but I'll have to fight back, because I haven't done anything wrong, and I still feel I haven't acted unreasonably!"

Well, he more or less rambled on in that vein and, while he was talking, he took out all the things she'd made specially for him—a sash, embroidered slippers, a little pouch, to prove her affection for him. I guess they were the sorts of keepsakes Shaanxi girls give. As I listened to him and looked at all those colorful things, my heart ached—she'd never made anything for me. But I remembered she'd said I was a good person and I felt a bit better—she'd said what she really felt about me to someone else. I hadn't been wrong about her; she was no flighty girl all right, but a serious young woman who had deep feelings. The trouble was, her feelings weren't for me.

But I still hadn't cooled down completely and said to him, "You told me you didn't get up to anything behind my back, so why did you run off like that when you saw me?"

He went red and replied, "Because you had a big wrench in your hand, and I thought that in your state you might bash me with it!"

"So you ran, but weren't you afraid I'd hit her? And you still say you love her!"

He looked down and mumbled, "I was standing just outside the door ..."

As we were talking, she suddenly burst in, probably thinking the two of us were having a fight. Seeing us calmly sitting there, she relaxed a little, but then leaned against the chimney and started crying again. This time she did make a noise, a heart-breaking sob.

The two of us didn't speak and all you could hear in that little hut was the sound of her sobbing. As I listened, I suddenly thought of those two girls in Weiya. What would have happened if they'd found themselves in the same situation? I guess like her they wouldn't have resisted that much either, and just married anyone to get by, to keep body and soul together. What had she done wrong? Nothing really. I don't know why, but just then, while my brain was spinning round, all I could think of was that scene in Weiya.

After a long, long pause I finally said, "Come on, it's no use crying over spilt milk. It's all clear now. you can only be with one of us. You'd better make up your mind now, which one is it going to be?"

She kept crying and didn't say anything. It seemed that she was using up a lifetime's tears. After a bit, the other guy, choking on his words, mumbled her pet name and said to her, "You should stay with him. Now that I'm here and I can see you've got a good life, I can relax a bit. The two of us weren't meant to be, it was all for nothing, let's just leave past things alone."

As he said this she started crying even louder, sobbing uncontrollably. Don't you think that just about said it all? How could I torment her any longer. My heart went out to her and I just felt bad that the good fortune wasn't to be mine.

"Well, I can understand her attitude," I said. "If she stays with me, she'll be unhappy, I'll be unhappy and you'll be unhappy. I'm the same as the two of you, drifted here from back east. I've seen a lot of this kind of thing come about, all because of troubles back at home. But China's a big place, if you put your mind to it, you can do anything, and the two of you can live a good life here. The two of you should be together."

After I'd finished talking, she stopped crying and seemed a little calmer. Although just at that moment I felt as though a great burden had been lifted, when I thought of how I'd never have her love, thought of being alone, I felt wronged again and wretched and couldn't help crying. So the three of us sat in that little hut and cried.

She and I very quickly got a divorce. There was all kinds of talk, but I turned a deaf ear. This thing was happening to me; I was the one who had to make the decision. On the last afternoon after she'd packed up her things and was about to leave, she suddenly seemed reluctant to go, made supper for me one last time and then said quietly, "I could stay one more night here."

That was the only time she ever said anything affectionate to me. I knew what she meant. Only a country girl would express her gratitude that way. But it was only gratitude and nothing more. "No, you go," I told her. "I'm more interested in affection. You two be happy, don't lose one another again. Although we won't be man and wife, we'll still be friends. If you need anything, just let me know...."

They were a capable pair. Since private businesses have been allowed, the two of them have set up a stall selling snacks, mostly Shaanxi style. Seems to me they do a better business than the Uygur kebab stalls, and now they've saved several thousand. Of course I've eaten plenty of their food. They know when I've checked back in and send something over. Now, we two couples see a fair amount of one another. Whenever my wife comes to Urumqi, she wants to have their buckwheat dumplings. You ought to go and try some—they're pretty good! Their stall is just by Hundred Flowers Village.

Right, I've wandered a bit from the subject, I'll go on with my story.

When my master got back from a meeting back east and found out what had happened, he got his wife to make a special meal and invited me over. "I wasn't wrong about you," he said to me, "picking you up on the road and making you my apprentice. You did the right thing, you did what you should have done!"

I drank a couple of glasses of alcohol and started getting miserable. I don't know, I just felt as if I'd been wronged. My old master said, "Don't feel so bad about it. She was someone else's to begin with, she was never yours—you just gave her back to somebody, that's all. If you think she was yours to begin with and you let someone else have her, then you're wrong."

I said, "That's not what I was thinking. I just feel that I had good intentions and that I didn't get anything in return."

"Then you're even more wrong," he replied. "If you have good intentions just so you can get something back, then your intentions aren't good to begin with. Being a human being isn't like doing business."

He was right. When he took on this aimless "drifter" as his apprentice, did he think I would give him anything in return? A driver isn't like somebody who works in a factory; you finish your apprenticeship and then you're gone. My master has a lot of apprentices, they're spread all over Xinjiang; some of them still come to see him when they come through Urumqi; some of them finish their apprenticeship, spread their wings and fly away, and you never see them again. He doesn't mind whether they visit or not, it's up to them. Thinking about what he said, I felt calmer.

But, my reporter friend, I tell you, once you've been married it's not the same. Before, no matter how she treated me, when I'd come back from a run, there'd always be hot food on the table and clean clothes to change into. I felt good and I looked good. After she left, I didn't know what to do with myself and felt all empty inside, sort of apathetic, out of it. Do you know what the life of a long distance trucker is like? All year round, rain or shine, you're always out on the road. You spend more nights in inns than you do at home. Today you share a room with this bunch of people, tomorrow with another bunch. The blankets are filthy, it doesn't matter which end you put over your head, it'll still stink of smelly feet. Drivers with families have something to look forward to; it doesn't matter what you go through out on the road, because after you check back in you can go home. But me, I went home, the pot was cold, the stove was cold, if I wanted a hot meal I had to go out to a restaurant. On the road I'd often see drivers stop and buy things like garlic and peppers and eggs from the peasants by the roadside. I felt sort of envious: look at him, he's a man with a family. If I bought something good, fresh vegetables or whatever, I hadn't got anyone to give them to.

Did I feel regrets then? It wasn't a question of regret. Sometimes I'd check in, come back and see the two of them outside in the yard in front of the boiler house making adobe bricks. They'd be dripping with sweat and smiling, and look over and wave at me. It made me feel a kind of warmth and a certain sadness; can't really say what it was, but it wasn't regret.

As time went by, as the days passed, it all faded away, I got used to the idea. We drivers, we have something; we get to see a lot of the world and at the same time, being in Xinjiang is good. When spring comes and you drive along the banks of the Sayram Lake, and you look at the blue, blue water, and the swans which have just flown back; or the slopes all covered with kirghiz grass and irises, and the straight pagoda pines in the valleys, it takes the pain away. In summer, when you drive with your windows rolled down for the first time to let the mountain air in, you get filled with a kind of hope and energy....

Oh, we've come to the top of the mountain, it's time to go down. Going uphill is easy, it's going down that's hard.... But don't worry, I know this road....

Do you want to hear more? How did I get married a second time? Okay, just so long as you don't nod off. It's sort of interesting, it was a time when I wasn't thinking about marriage at all....

Two years later, I was driving along this route. That day, the wind was blowing hard, the dust and gravel were kicking up against the glass, you couldn't see a thing for five meters around you. I'd just passed Kumux and was heading into Yushugou; the sun was already down behind the mountains. On either side of Yushugou are cliffs, with a stream running down the middle. There are elm trees along the banks of the stream. Don't know how long they've been there, but they're huge, with crooked branches and knots all over them. Every single one of them is a weird shape. The tops of the trees were swaying back and forth like they were drunk. But the wind wasn't blowing so badly there; there was water and some trees and the visibility was much better.

I was gliding along with the wind. In the distance, I saw a woman wearing a grey scarf, holding a child, sitting by the side of the road. She seemed to be wearing a cotton-padded overcoat, the child wrapped inside it, looking too fat to move. You couldn't tell how old she was. She had two bags next to her. I thought she wanted a ride, so I slowed down a little. But when I drove up to her she didn't wave at me, she just glanced inside the cab.

I drove on past. But that look was like a blinding flash, which had flickered across my face and imprinted an image of her expression. What was in that glance? Suspicion, fear, hope, expectation? I'd already gone past a little way, but I just didn't feel right about it. It was like she was a load that had fallen off my truck—if I didn't give her a ride, I couldn't drive on.

I stopped the truck and opened the door. What a wind there was! It almost blew the door off. I held on to my hat and ran over to her. "Where do you want to go?" I asked her.

She said she was headed for Bitter Springs. "Then what are you waiting for?" I said. "Get in."

She shrank back from me, looking me over. It was only then I noticed she was a Shanghai "educated youth." She wasn't wearing an ordinary cotton-padded overcoat, but a dark grey parka, and her face was half covered by a brushed wool scarf. The child she was holding was about four. His soft, white face was frozen blue and he was nestled in his mother's parka, staring at me with big, frightened eyes.

A gust of wind blew into the valley and whistled through the trees. I didn't have my overcoat on and was shivering with cold, and I urged her to get in the truck. She was still hesitant and clutched the child even closer, like I wanted to grab her.

I knew why she wouldn't get in the truck. My reporter friend, I'll be frank about it; there are bad drivers, they take lone women hitchhikers along for a while and then look for a place in the mountains or desert, saying the engine has broken down and they can't go on any further. A woman is helpless, there's nothing she can do except let him take advantage of her, satisfy his lust. Then there's the kind of driver who likes to pick up young girls or married women. They really don't have anything as bad as that in mind, they just want to tease or flirt. Shanghai educated youth are pretty sharp. When they come back to southern Xinjiang after visiting home they usually get off the train at Daheyan to save money and then hitch a ride the rest of the way.

If it's a couple or a group, they always get the women to stand at the side of the road to flag down a truck. Once it stops, the men climb out of their hiding place in the ditch. That will tell you what Shanghai educated youth think of us drivers. She must have been waiting for a bus or a truck driven by an older guy. Or one with other women in it. She didn't trust a lone young driver like me.

The wind started to blow even harder and the sun had completely disappeared behind the mountains. I remember the swaying trees were a screen of pitch black. If she let my truck go by, she would be hard put to find another. I pulled my driver's license out of my uniform pocket, waved it in front of her and said, "If you don't trust me, take my driver's license as security. The last bus has gone past already and even if you wait for another truck, they won't necessarily give you a ride. Anyway, there aren't any behind me, I know. Even if you don't care about yourself, you ought to care about the child. Look how frozen he is, come on, get in the truck."

She didn't take my license. She threw a worried glance at the child, looked me over again and finally stood up with a sort of helpless expression. I helped her carry her bags and quickly put them into the cab.

I've given rides to plenty of people and lots of three, four and five year olds. They never sit still at that age. If they're not touching the gears, then they're playing with the dashboard or shouting at the top of their lungs out of the window. It was strange though, because this child didn't make a sound. He lay in his mother's arms, and didn't move a muscle. After a while, the sky got dark. Xinjiang is like that, it gets dark all of a sudden. The child began to cough badly. She got upset and started stroking him. She kept turning him over and over, wrapping him up more and more tightly. I took my foot off the accelerator and listened: the child was wheezing badly. I reached over and touched him. His forehead was burning.

"God, that's bad," I said. "That child is sick!"

The mother didn't answer, she just suddenly started to cry quietly.

The child wheezing and the mother crying, I hurried up and stepped on the gas. Ahead of us, the lights of Uxxaktal winked from the mountain pass. Uxxaktal is a tiny place, just a few houses. We usually stop there on overnight runs. But I didn't stop, I just kept right on through.

"Stop! Stop!" she yelled and shouted, banging on the door.

"Don't worry," I told her. "We've got to find a hospital right away. I know Uxxaktal better than you do, there isn't even a barefoot doctor here."

She was crying and shouting and pulling on my arm. "It doesn't matter! It doesn't matter! I want you to stop, I want you to stop!"

My arm was caught in her grip and I had to drive with one hand. There was a curve up ahead of us. I said nervously, "Don't worry, I'm telling you don't worry. I'm not a bad person, really, I'm not ..."

"No! No!" she shouted, frightened. "Where are you taking me? I beg you, stop! Please, stop! ..."

We were almost at the curve. One side of it was mountain and on the other was a drop. It was no laughing matter. I struggled to pull my arm away from her, but she just wouldn't let go, as if by pulling my arm she could make the vehicle stop. Finally I roared at her, "You think I don't want to stop at Uxxaktal? If you're

369

not tired I am! I want to take you to Yanqi to find a hospital ... Please, let go of me, let go of me.... Look, I'll show you something!"

The woman probably saw the danger ahead of us in the headlights, and loosened her grip. I made the turn smoothly and pulled out a white porcelain mug from underneath my seat. Trembling I said, "See, this is my prize ...I told you I wasn't a bad person. Don't worry, you hold on tight to your child ...but I beg you, please don't make so much trouble."

My action must have been pretty funny. What could a white porcelain mug prove? It only had the word "Award" painted on it in red letters. Almost everybody has one; it doesn't prove anything at all. I don't know whether the porcelain mug actually did anything or whether this educated youth just gave up, but she finally calmed down and hugged the coughing child and let me drive on to Yanqi without any further trouble.

I don't have to tell you what hospitals were like in those days. It would have been easier to fish a needle out of the ocean than to get a doctor in the middle of the night. I drove back and forth through the empty streets of Yanqi, trying at one hospital and two clinics. The lights were on in all of them but there was nobody on duty. We shouted till we were hoarse but no one answered and we ended up wasting a good hour.

"Damn it! Let's go!" I got back into the cab angrily. "To Korla! I know a doctor there."

Just then the child's breathing weakened and his forehead got boiling hot. He was shivering, already in a coma. Tears rolled down the woman's face, I remember how the blue light of the roadside lamps was reflected in them. She was at her wit's end and all she could do was listen to my directions.

I stepped on the gas and raced on to Korla. Along the way, all I could hear was the wind shrieking through the cracks and the road seemed to stand up and fall into our faces. Black shadows flashed by on either side of us. There was no other traffic, and no one stopped me from driving at top speed. I'd never driven so fast, all I could feel was the front wheels bouncing as if they would fly off any minute. I couldn't think about smoking, my hands were wet from gripping the wheel. All I was afraid of was that it would slip out of my hands.

We passed Bosten Lake and came to the banks of the Konqi River, the water in the truck's radiator was boiling and the truck hissed like a tuckered out horse. I jumped out and said, "Don't be afraid, don't be afraid, we're almost at Korla," took out a hammer and smashed a piece of ice and put the pieces on top of the radiator.

I'd stopped the truck in the middle of the night in this deserted place and the woman seemed scared again. She sat in the cab hugging the child to her. I didn't turn off the headlights and did all my work as far away from her as I could. When I got back in the truck, she seemed to let out a sigh of relief and asked me in a trusting tone of voice for the first time, "Can we find a doctor in Korla?"

I told her we could.

My friend, once you've got someone's trust, it gives you a certain kind of strength to push on and get something done. I thought to myself that even if that doctor was hiding under his bed, I'd drag him out.

It was dawn when we got to Korla. I didn't drive to the hospital but went straight to the doctor's house and knocked on the door.

"Who's there? Who's there?" he asked grumpily after we'd knocked for a while.

"It's me!" I shouted. "Have you forgotten? ..."

This doctor was from Sichuan. Last year, when he got back from a home visit loaded down with trunks and baskets and furniture, he was stuck in the middle of Daheyan and couldn't find transport. The weather was turning and he was in a complete flap, all worried. I was the one who helped him get everything home. He was very, very grateful and insisted on giving me something, but I didn't accept anything. He said if I ever ran into any trouble, he would help without question. So this time I took him up on it.

He opened the door and asked in a sleepy voice, "Whose child is this? Is it yours?"

I looked back at the woman sitting in the truck and said, "Yes, it's mine. Hurry up."

He woke up, pulled himself together and started looking for the duty doctor at the hospital, a nurse and the pharmacist, and put mother and son into a hospital room.

There was nothing else for me to do. I drove the truck over to "Hostel two," drained out the water, found a room and took a nap. As soon as it was light outside I was on the road to Aksu.

A week later, on my way back from Kashi, I thought to myself, even if it's none of my business, I should at least go back and thank the doctor. I went to his house with fifty *jin* of that famous Aksu rice.

The minute that short little doctor saw me he shook his finger at me and laughed. "What on earth were you doing? That woman from Shanghai said she doesn't know you and yet you claimed to be the kid's father. You didn't tell me the truth. I couldn't even get a decent night's sleep."

I kept saying sorry and asked how the child was.

The doctor laughed, "Your kid is fine, he can leave the hospital tomorrow."

I unloaded the truck and in the evening didn't have anything to do. I listened to the people in the hostel playing the *buqin* violin and singing from the "revolutionary model operas." My thoughts were like the notes from that *buqin*, constantly changing key, never settling down. All right, I thought, go and see the child.

I took two tins of food and walked into the hospital room. I saw at a glance that she was sitting next to the child's bed. The child was lying there gesticulating and babbling away happily. Now I could see her properly. She was at most twenty-six or twenty-seven, with big eyes and a pale complexion, and had a sort of sadness about her. When she bent over to tend to the child, I noticed she was a gentle and kind woman, completely different from that night when she seemed almost crazy, grabbing my arm.

She looked up and saw me standing by the bed and her eyes suddenly shone. She said with some embarrassment, "I can never apologize enough for that night. I ...I've been through the worst and it got to me."

"Forget it," I said. "How's the child?"

"He had acute pneumonia. The doctor said if we'd come any later, it would have been too late. That night, thanks to you ..."

Her expression was filled with gratitude, her eyes moist. I felt embarrassed and lowered my head to play with the child.

The little boy had obviously grown up in Shanghai. He spoke with a Shanghai accent and had fine, light skin just like his mother. After we'd played for a while, I asked him, "What do you want to be when you grow up?"

The child said, slowly and clearly, "My — mama — wants — me — to — be — a — Driver — like — uncle — when — I — grow — up!"

My nose felt as though I'd just sniffed vinegar, my eyes were suddenly blinded by tears. I turned my head to stop them from falling and pretended to laugh out loud. The child's words meant more to me than any award or praise. It seemed like there was a soft tender little hand stroking my heart, forcing all of the words into my throat, stuck there so I couldn't say anything.

The child hooked his little finger round mine and asked this and that. I just answered whatever came to mind, feeling a growing sense of responsibility towards him as I did so, as though he were my own son. What would happen to him in the future? Coming from a big city on the Huangpu River, could he ever get used to this Gobi Desert where water is more treasured than oil? I know what life is like for Shanghai educated youth. The first group of them who came to southern Xinjiang came here in our truck convoy. They were all about seventeen or eighteen. They raised a red flag on top on the truck, singing and laughing, and when they saw the alkaline patches on the ground, they said it even snowed in summer here. The following year, some of them went home for a visit and sat in my truck crying. After seven or eight years, "educated youth" weren't young anymore, like this woman, they'd become "old bags" in everyone's eyes. But they still had to live in huts dug into the earth, eat salted vegetables, and drink water from cisterns....

Then, well, it's the sort of stuff I don't really have to say, you reporters should know it better than I do. At that time, I never thought there could even be a "gang of four," much less that there could be a fall of the Gang of Four. I thought things would just go on the way they had, and you could more or less predict what the child's life would be like.

"Weren't you going to Bitter Springs?" I said to her. "I'll take you there tomorrow."

She blushed and looked down, "Is it on your way?" she said. "How could we trouble you any further? ..."

"Don't worry about whether it's on my way or not," I told her. "Tomorrow you just get everything ready and wait for me."

The truth of the matter was that that small fellow had hooked his little finger round my heart. I wanted to go with him to see his father, make friends with his father, so that if some day they ran into trouble I could help out a little.

The next day I switched loads with another driver, so he would take the Bosten Lake reed mats back to Urumqi and I would take a load of fertilizer south to Yuli.

By the time I got to the hospital, they'd got their things together. She was wrapped in that thick brushed wool scarf, smiling, her eyes sparkling. The child held out his hands, wanting me to carry him. I picked him up, and he turned and said to the nurse, "Goodbye auntie." What a bright sunny day that was! It was the happiest day of my life, like I'd just come to fetch my wife and my newborn son to take them home.

On the road, the child was even more lively. He was just like other children, touching the gearshift, feeling the dashboard; he'd never ridden in a big truck before and everything was new to him. He never stopped asking questions. It was the first time my small cab had ever been so full of life, and I was like the child; it was the first time I discovered that these things I touched every day were actually so interesting. That day, the engine ran on happily as if it was singing! The hard seat felt especially springy; one little bump and my head could touch the roof.

Some time after ten o'clock we reached Qunke. After unloading the fertilizer, I bought a few buns, got back in the cab, and said:

"Come on, let's get going to Bitter Springs!"

I don't know if you've ever been on that road. It drops down gradually into the Tarim Basin and then to the edge of the Taklimakan Desert. A lot of it's often covered with sand. In fact, you can only tell it's a road from the tracks left by other trucks. A lot of the place names in the area have this "Springs" ending, but don't think there's a lot of water in these parts though. Quite the opposite. They choose those names because water is so precious.

So you can imagine, the further you go along on this road, the more barren it gets. At the start you can still see scattered poplars and willows, then after a while, when the winds start to blow, all you can see outside the window is yellow sand, and it's like the truck is in a cloud, and you can't see a thing.

We went slower and slower, and the child got bored and fell asleep in his mother's arms. The smile on her face disappeared.

"Come on, let's make him comfortable," I said.

I stopped the truck and made a bed for him in the space behind the seats. Sleeping in there would be just like sleeping in a cradle. He snored away quietly behind me, his little puffs of breath tickling the back of my neck. I can't tell you how nice that was.

There was only our little truck crawling along like a tiny insect in the middle of that endless yellow sand.

Outside, there seemed to be some sort of invisible force, making everyone inside feel closer to one another. As we were going along, she gave a quiet sigh, and said:

"Look, this is where I've got to go."

True enough, it wasn't much of a place to look at. I asked her, "What about his father? Is he coming to Tikanlik to fetch you?"

It was a long time before she answered, and then finally she said, "He doesn't have a father."

"Oh!" I was a little surprised, unexpectedly a little happy. "Then ...what happened?"

She gave me a wan sort of smile, frowned and said, "My family doesn't know anything about this ... but I've always wanted to tell somebody. Not saying anything, it feels like it's suffocating me...."

She was from a capitalist family. In 1964 when she graduated from middle school, everyone at the school came beating drums and gongs in a parade to send the students off at the train station. She'd come to Xinjiang resolved to remould herself and build up the border region. She was a teacher when she first arrived. But in 1967 a group of "rebels" took over their set-up, and she was sent down to the company to do manual work. Afterwards of course, she got discriminated against more and more. One day, one of these "rebels" who'd become the company commander suddenly decided she was all right. He told her to take a gun and come up with him to the grassland to hunt gazelle, which improved the company's diet. The company had people out hunting every week and only the militiamen with a good family background were qualified to carry guns. At the time she was overjoyed, since she thought she'd been "re-educated" by the poor peasants. She went with this "little commander" away from the company and ended

377

up being raped by him under a grove of willow trees. Not long afterwards, she realized she was pregnant, but she couldn't report it to anyone and couldn't get an abortion. All she could do was go back to Shanghai and have the baby. So her parents wouldn't get too upset, she lied and told them she'd gotten married in Xinjiang. She had left the child with her family until recently. Her parents were not having an easy time. When the campaign to criticize Lin Biao and Confucius and the Red Typhoon hit Shanghai, they were evicted from their home and sent to the countryside to do manual labor. She didn't want to add to their burden, and went and brought the child back to Xinjiang.

"I want to bring him up," she said. "He hasn't committed any crime.... My scoolmates all advised me not to bring him back, but I had to. I've already suffered all kinds of hardships and as far as I'm concerned there isn't anything worse that can happen."

"Where's that villain now?" I asked angrily, only just realizing why she'd been so timid that night.

She gave a bitter laugh. "He got himself transferred to another regiment as head of the security section."

Life is like that; you can tell your secrets to someone you don't know, to a stranger, just like I have today. She told me matter-of-factly, without any emotion, as if she was talking about someone else. She was telling me all of this, but more than that she was telling herself, she wasn't trying to get my sympathy or to beg me for even more help, she was just going over her past in order to deal with even bigger, more difficult problems. Her tone of voice said as much.

I looked over at her. She was deep in thought. Not like that night when her eyes were filled with tears. I believed she could do what she said she would. In her eyes, there wasn't anything else now that could prove more difficult.

Precisely because of this, because I couldn't help feeling a certain admiration and sympathy for her, I asked with concern, "Why don't you genuinely get married?"

She told me there were no more young single men from Shanghai in her area and that she didn't want to marry someone from anywhere else, although other Shanghai girls had done so. She said if she married anyone else, she'd never be able to get back to Shanghai.

So I told her boldly, "I'm from back east too. In my experience, how you get along in life doesn't depend on where you are but on who you're with."

She chuckled a little and said, "That's a cliche."

"There's a saying in Pakistan," I replied. " 'Run at the sight of a cat is a rat's cliche, but as far as the rat goes, it's a truism.' There are a lot of cliches that are truisms for people too." She looked at me and gave a little sigh, "What you said may be true, but there's a gap between truisms and reality."

Fortunately, we had an empty truck, so by the time the sun set over the desert, we'd reached Bitter Springs. It's an oasis: the scenery is nice and the soil is fertile, but it's been ruined by the kind of people who treated her so badly. The group of Shanghai educated youth who came to meet her all had a bellyful of complaints. One particularly scruffy fellow whom they called "American GI" patted me on the shoulder and said, "Thank you, sir! If we were in Shanghai we'd invite you to the 'Lao-zhengxing' or if you like Western food, the 'Maison Rouge.' But here ..." He threw up his hands to show that there was nothing he could do.

I knew if I stayed, I'd only make them feel uncomfortable—there was nothing much to eat and nowhere to stay; she'd just got back and needed to put everything in order. "I'm going back to Tikanlik," I said. "I have something to do there. I won't trouble you."

The child ran over to me, took my hand and shouted, "You stay here too, I won't let you go!"

I squatted down, patted him on the head and said, "Uncle has to go off and take another load. There's a lot of stuff waiting for me to carry. You be a good boy and stay here with mama."

He tilted his head to one side and thought and then asked, "Are you coming back?" "I'll be back," I said. "Is Uncle going to drive his truck back?" "Yes, I'll drive my truck back." "Promise?" "Promise."

She was standing next to the child. I stood up, saying to the child and repeating to her, "I'll be back."

Back in Urumqi, that image of her and the child was always in my mind, no matter what, I couldn't get rid of it. I was lost, as if I'd left my heart in Bitter Springs. After my old driving teacher came back, I went to his house and told him the whole story and how I felt. "All right!" He banged the table. "If you don't go after her, who are you going to go after? She's a real treasure for she's been soaked in bitter water."

I went out and bought a load of special holiday food and a number of toy cars, then hitched a ride on a friend's truck and on New Year's Eve reached Tikanlik. Against the wind and snow, I walked to Bitter Springs and pushed open the door of her "home," just as all those Shanghai people were eating their New Year's Eve dinner....

Later on she'd ask me, "Why did you fall in love with me?"

"I always think love is something you can't explain,"

I'd reply. "I like *pingju* opera, but there's one line in Liu Qiao'er that I've never liked. It goes something like, 'I love him: he can write, he can add, he can work, when he comes home he can be my teacher.' How can you analyse love so objectively, how can you weigh it up like that? To tell you the truth, I've been married before...." I'd told her everything about my relationship with that Shaanxi girl. I said, "Objectively speaking, no matter how you look at it, I was a better bet than that Shaanxi fellow in every way. But that girl just didn't love me. She'd rather suffer hardships with him, living in a hut that wasn't even a hut, a cave that wasn't a cave; making adobe bricks in the summer sun till the skin burnt off their faces and making matchboxes in the winter till their fingers cracked. Why? It puzzled me, I couldn't understand it. Now I do—it's love! I feel about you the way that Shaanxi girl felt about her lad. And you're asking me to tell you why ..."

She listened, her eyes red and then nodded and said, "I guess I understand."

Okay, ahead there is the place you wanted to go. Where do you want to get off? ... It doesn't matter, I'll take you to the door.

Now? Oh now, everything's fine. She's the vice-principal of the Bitter Springs Middle School. Me? They show me a little consideration and let me just drive this one route. Every winter and summer vacation they come to Urumqi.

I get home once a week. The child is already at middle school, but he doesn't want to be a driver any more. He wants to be a writer, says he wants to write about me and his mother. I told him, "Your mother and I aren't heroes, and anyway there are lots of things that just can't be written about. If you write about them, people will criticize you and say you've written about the darker side of life." He said, "But dad, you don't understand, the essence of literature is truth. And you and mama are real people!" Well, my reporter friend, I don't know whether that little fellow's right or not!

The year before last, her father got rehabilitated and got his back salary. If she hadn't married me, she could've moved back to Shanghai. Once I drank too much and got a little tipsy and said to her, "See, you regret it all now, don't you? If you hadn't married me, you could have gone back to Shanghai, couldn't you?"

She didn't say anything at the time, but that night she lay next to me in bed and sobbed and said, "What did you mean? Weren't you the one who said 'How you get along in life doesn't depend on where you are but who you're with?' Why should I want to go back to Shanghai? You're underestimating me." I knew I'd been a little too heavy with the joke and cajoled her for a long time before I could get her to smile. Since then, I've never drunk more than I should....

Ah, Bitter Springs. When I think of all the people I've met in my life, my friend, I'd say it's not only her who's drunk bitter water who's a treasure—all those who've tasted bitterness, drunk bitterness, are our country's treasures, all of them have hearts of gold. Don't you agree, reporter?

Translated by Rui An

Note:

[1] One *liang* equals fifty grams. Both *jin* and *liang* are Chinese weighing standards. One *jin* equals ten *liang*.

图书在版编目(CIP)数据

中国当代作家及其小说:英文/殷边著.—北京:
外文出版社,1991(1995 重印)
ISBN 7 - 119 - 00742 - 4

Ⅰ.中… Ⅱ.殷… Ⅲ.小说—作品集—中国—当代
—英文 Ⅳ.I247

中国版本图书馆 CIP 数据核字(95)第 13856 号

中国当代作家及其小说

殷 边

*

©外文出版社

外文出版社出版
(中国北京百万庄路 24 号)
邮政编码 100037
北京外文印刷厂印刷
中国国际图书贸易总公司发行
(中国北京车公庄西路 35 号)
北京邮政信箱第 399 号 邮政编码 100044
1991 年(36 开)第一版
1995 年第二次印刷
(英)
ISBN 7 - 119 - 00742 - 4 /I·109(外)
01580
10 - E - 2344P